ENDORSEMENTS

Memoir? A James Herriot tale of adventure after adventure with large animals and rural Virginia country life? An account of a heartbreak-childhood intercepted by the goodness of God? Mary McDonald's new book can't be pigeonholed. Where would it be displayed in an honest to goodness old fashion bookstore? I'm not sure, but my suggestion is "Right at the Front" so no one will miss it. Thank you Mary for a book of substance and a lively read. Well done!

Sally Breedlove, author, spiritual director,
cofounder of JourneyMates

Grab your cowboy hat, step into your boots, climb into the saddle and be ready for an insightful and absorbing trail ride led by your guide, Mary McDonald. In her book, The Magnet, Mary thoughtfully and honestly shares her spiritual journey from her troubled childhood to the fulfillment of her dream of becoming a large-animal veterinarian. With candor, humor, and relevant quotations, you will be challenged in your faith and encouraged to see the Lord at work in a woman who is drawn to serve the God she loves.

Cynthia Heald, author of the
Becoming a Woman of ...Bible study series.

THE MAGNET

Also by Mary Ashby McDonald
Starting and Running Your Own Horse Business

THE MAGNET

A LARGE-ANIMAL VETERINARIAN'S JOURNEY

MARY ASHBY MCDONALD, DVM

About the author

Mary Ashby McDonald is a veterinarian, aid worker, mentor, spiritual director, deacon, author, speaker, wife, and mother of two grown children. She managed a horse farm in Texas before moving to Kenya, where she assisted orphaned elephants and rhinos. As a missionary and a vet, she has practiced her faith and her calling to bring the improved care of large animals to Bolivia and Uganda. On her farm in Catawba, Virginia, she holds animal health-care workshops so that others can do the kind of work she does. Her bestselling *Starting and Running your Own Horse Business* has been in print for twenty years (and royalties paid for the wooden fences on her historic farm that she is renovating with her husband Jack, an international development banker). She went to vet school at Virginia-Maryland Regional College of Veterinary Medicine in Blacksburg, Virginia.

About the Illustrator

Pam Talley Stoneburner's artwork is displayed in houses across America and abroad. Since graduating from Virginia Tech with a degree in Animal Science (where she met Mary McDonald), she specialized in creating life-like portraits of animals. Breyer Animal Creations and Red Mill Manufacture Company commission Pam to do their sculptures. Her artwork has been published in *Western Horseman Magazine* and Tom Moate's books, as well as in Dr. McDonald's *Starting and Running Your Own Horse Business.* She lives in Waynesboro, Virginia, with her husband, Rob, and has three grown children, who all enjoy horseback riding.

Xulon Press Elite
2301 Lucien Way #415
Maitland, FL 32751
407.339.4217
www.xulonpress.com

Printed in the United States of America.

ISBN-13: 978-1-54561-438-9

This book is lovingly dedicated to Jack McDonald III, Ashby McDonald, and Jack McDonald IV.

CONTENTS

PREFACE

The stories that appear in this book come from my life experiences. Many of the names of individuals, companies, and other identifying facts have been changed to protect the identities of individuals or their families. Therefore, any identifying resemblance to actual individuals is merely coincidental.

ACKNOWLEDGMENTS

I would like to begin by thanking my husband, Jack, who journeyed with me through many of these adventures because without him, most would not have happened. Thanks also to my dear children, Ashby and Jack, who we dragged on many of these outings before they were old enough to know better, and they still come home for the holidays. I love you beyond measure.

Thanks to my dear siblings, Pete, Cat, and Jean, for letting me tell my version of our youth. You helped me greatly along this path of life. Also thanks to John Ittner, my step-brother for his helpful advice about writing.

Writing a story and publishing it are two different things. Thanks to my friends who helped me understand and grow through this journey. They trekked deeply with me and encouraged me to pray and press on through the healing and writing. Jane, Sarah, Melissa, Veronika, Sheri, Margaret, Marcia, Darla, Judy, Helen, Mary, Beth, Lucy, Debbie, and Gayla—you are the best. Also thanks to my spiritual mentors Julie, Cindy, Theresa, Bari, Merry, and Ellen—without you, this book would have no soul.

I have been privileged to mentor many wonderful women over the years. In the process, they have shaped me as well. You have been a joy and encouragement to me and my writing. One went to be with Jesus before she could be a missionary vet to Mongolia. Rest in peace, Dr. Erica Geary.

Thanks Charlene Fu, Jeannie Light and Karen Smirmaul with the early writing and providing useful ideas on the book's approach and structure.

My admiration and appreciation go to my veterinarian friends who have encouraged me along the way. Your diligence in assisting His creation, two- and four-legged, will not go unrewarded. Blessings on you and to all animal owners who provide veterinary care to those in their charge.

To Pam Stoneburner, whose illustrations bring this book to life, thank you for your constant encouragement and prayers throughout the process. Without you, this book would still be a manuscript, gathering dust on my cabin shelf.

Sknaht ffuN gnag, evol uoy.

The greatest thanks, praise, and honor go to the Lover of my soul—may You be forever worshipped and glorified.

INTRODUCTION

The Magnet is the story of my journey from childhood to my early career as a large-animal veterinarian. The chapters you will read are based on my actual experiences as a vet and I hope you find them meaningful and humorous. Many large-animal vet stories mimic life, in that there is humor in them, once the bleeding stops.

Animals have always brought me succor, and if you picked up this book, that may be true for you as well. No one escapes this world unscathed, and we all need courage to stay the course.

My life, perhaps like yours, has been like a game of checkers, filled with joyful red pieces and sad black pieces, constantly jumping one another. Providentially, the red ones are winning the game. I hope this chronicle will encourage you as much as I have been encouraged through the years to work through the most difficult times.

As I share this journey with you, my desire is that these stories will bring you some laughs, tears, and courage. My prayer is that something may resonate enough from my heart's progress to bring you a measure of hope and perhaps healing in your own heart as well.

Please know you have inestimable value apart from anything you do or don't do, and know that you always have options.

Press on, dear one, press on.

Mary Ashby McDonald, DVM

PART I
VETERINARY TALES

CHAPTER 1

THE FLOYD ZONE

You can't drown your troubles in a bottle, cuz they's can swim.

—Anonymous

As the high-powered rifle blast split the silence of the swiftly falling snow on that dark night, I waited for her to die. This wasn't how I expected the answer to my lifelong prayer to become a veterinarian to be played out. Those childhood dreams of being a vet only included perfect cases: warm, sunny weather, fluffy calico kittens, and fat speckle-bellied pups bubbling over with good health—not midnight cases on the side of a mountain in the middle of a blizzard, trying to save a hopeless case of a mean cow with a prolapsed uterus, and a bourbon-filled assistant.

The drunken neighbor staggered back a few steps, his gun butt recoiling hard into his decrepit shoulder. At my request, he pulled the trigger. Tonight, I had no options. The acrid smell of gunpowder wafted behind my truck where I herded the old farmer out of harm's way. Looking down my headlight beams, I saw the cow's legs flailing against the frozen ground. With another blast, it would be finished, even with the neighbor's unsteady whiskey aim.

Normally, I would humanely end her life with an injection of intravenous euthanasia solution, but using the sodium pentobarbital requires burying the body deep or it becomes a toxic waste dump for hungry interlopers. Tonight, the ground was frozen, and there was no way to bury the body, so she had to be shot, or scavenging carnivores in the cold night would have found her warm body and gorged on it, thereby euthanizing themselves.

3

Immediately, a second shot shattered my regretful musings. This time all was still, except for the vapors from her last breath rising heavenward—the old cow was dead.

Dazed, exhausted, and half frozen, I stepped into my vet truck, calling out, "Lord, how did it come to this? Me, on the side of this snow-clad mountain with a drunken man and a dead cow? I'm going to need therapy after this case." I wondered if there are therapists who specialize in forty-five-year-old female large-animal veterinarians. Note the word order: not large female but large animal. We are vets who treat cattle, horses, sheep, and goats, not cats, dogs, hamsters, or snakes, especially not snakes.

I grew up in Virginia, which is south of the Mason-Dixon line. In the South, words like "prolapsed uterus" are not spoken aloud by ladies. It's just not done. My grandmother wore white gloves to church every Sunday. She was a debutante and a general's daughter. *Prolapsed uterus* never crossed her lips. Although I inherited a great many of my grandmother's attributes, I did not inherit her proclivity for domesticity. A good Southern lady does not go to vet school and become a cow doctor. This frigid night, though, I had grave doubts about the merits of the woman's movement. What was wrong with staying home and sipping mint juleps in the warm parlor? I just had to be a doctor! Whiskey sounded pretty good about now.

But here I was in my fourth month, working in a large-animal practice in rural southwest Virginia just after graduating from vet school. I was thirty-nine years old when I started the rigors of vet school, mother to a second-grader and a kindergartener, with an international banker husband who traveled bi-monthly to Washington, DC, five hours away. Trust me: vet school is best done when you are young, childless, and single!

At the Amboseli Veterinary Clinic, I worked Monday through Thursday and was on call every Thursday night and every other weekend. The night of this prolapse call was a Thursday, and the call came in at 6:15 p.m. Our secretary, Beulah, said to me, "Dr. McDonald, a farmer in Floyd has a cow with the calf bed out."

"What?" I asked, thinking if she repeated the phrase "calf bed," it would jog some vet school lecture hidden in the recesses of my mind.

"The farmer needs help, his cow calved and the calf bed is out."

Nope. That term must have mentally jogged out a long time ago. In fact, I was certain I never heard it before. Just as she repeated it, a cold blast blew Dr. Healer into the office. Dusting the snowflakes off her head and seeing my blank expression, she said, "Calf bed—that's what the old-timers call the uterus," and she marched back out to her truck.

Sometimes when a cow calves, not only the calf but her entire one-hundred-pound uterus everts and is delivered as well—in technical terms: a prolapsed uterus. Okay, it's the bed where the calf lies until it is born. Gotcha, but why not just say prolapsed uterus, instead of using colloquial terms that reduce me to idiocy?

Since I was on emergency call that night and since the office was closing in fifteen minutes, the call was mine. Dr. Healer stepped back into the office with that selfless look that told me she was lending me one of her special pieces of veterinary equipment. With a smile on her face, she thrust a dirty plastic feed bag into my hands and said, "Here, you'll need this!"

Thanking her half-heartedly for her prized equipment, I took the sack and stared at the dusty frayed bag still speckled with dried blood. The same dumb expression that the "calf bed" term elicited trotted across my face. Again, Dr. Healer stepped in, "It's my special tool. Have you ever reduced a uterus before?"

"No," I said with a mix of excitement and dread.

"Well," she said, "you need three people to help—one to hold the cow and two to hold the uterus up off the ground while you massage it back into the cow. You have the helpers put the uterus on this bag and hold it up high. You can't get it in by yourself. It's my favorite tool, so bring it back," she added, as she headed out the door for her nice warm home.

Great, I have a blood-stained plastic bag. That was it. No experience, no clue. I will be pulling out my textbook on the way to the call.

Stepping out of the office, my face fell as I looked at the sky. This wasn't going to be a dusting. My windshield was already white. I thought of my kids and wished I was home, falling on my back in the snow, creating snow angels with them.

Backing inside, I asked Beulah, "Please call the farmer and make sure the cow isn't loose in the Back 40, but caught, and ask him to get two helpers." I did a mental check: *umbilical tape and Buhner needle on the truck.* I grabbed a cup of day-old coffee and strode out into the storm.

Driving down the hill from the office to the main road, I tested my brakes and felt a mild skid. I wondered how I would make it home. Pulling onto the windy mountain road, I thought back to my only other prolapse experience. It was in vet school on a call with one of the large-animal medicine vets, Dr. Washington. The main thing I remembered was being frightened as he drew the procedure while driving down a winding mountain road. I made a quick pit stop to gas up my truck and reviewed Buhner stitch in my *Techniques in Large Animal Surgery* book. I was excited to do my first uterine prolapse.

As I drove to Floyd County, I wondered how my kids were doing. They were probably sitting in front of our fireplace, watching *Barney.* I thought of my husband cooking, or should I say, defrosting. When I was in vet school, I used the *Once a Month* cooking method, following the book that teaches you to chop, combine, and cook ingredients for two entire days. Then you freeze these main courses for a month's worth of dinners. When I phoned my husband to tell him I was headed to Floyd on an emergency case, he reached into the freezer and pulled out another UFO (Unidentified Frozen Object).

My heart longed to be with my children. Yes, today's women can, "bring home the bacon and fry it up in the pan," but there is a cost, and the sacrifices along the way pull on one's heart, leaving a fragmented feeling. It is part of the package. Superwoman only lives in Hollywood.

Following the typical farmer's imprecise directions, I missed his house. Applying the brakes on the newly covered road, I slid past the driveway. Backing up, I pulled into the circular gravel driveway, which was lined with ancient boxwoods. Two mountain laurel bushes, their leaves curled in defense against the cold, crowded the front door. The white porch light shone bravely out into the dark, snowy night. Out stepped an old man, somewhere between eighty and death.

"Are you Mr. Jones?"

"Yep."

The farmer's regular vet was Dr. Davis, an old, salt-of-the-earth vet who doctored his cows for a hundred years. Dr. Davis probably screened his calls that night and decided not to go out in a blizzard. That is why he lived to practice as long as he did.

"You Dr. McDonald?"

"Yes, sir."

I could tell he was surprised to see a woman vet step out of the vet truck, but he was enough of a gentleman not to register it. I was equally surprised to see a feeble old man with no one around to help.

"Where's the cow?"

"She's in the back field. You got four-wheel drive?"

"Yes, sir." My enthusiasm was waning. She was supposed to be caught, and there was supposed to be help. "Lord, you are really going to have to pull this one off tonight," I murmured.

"Follow me," he said as he got into his old Bronco and headed out past the farmhouse, across the cattle guard, down over a hill, across a pasture, and then went sledding up and down the side of a mountain. As I engaged my truck into four-wheel drive, I thought, *I have four-wheel drive, but I don't have a snowmobile. If this snow keeps coming down the way it is, there is no way I'm getting out of here tonight.*

It was dark, so we both left our headlights on as we stepped out of our trucks. The light chocolate Charolais cow was lying down with about two feet of uterus trailing out behind her in the snow, leaves, and frozen muck.

Her adorable oatmeal-colored calf was lying about 100 feet away, close to the creek, blinking the snowflakes off her long, brown lashes. No doubt she wondered what kind of cold and crazy place she was born into. As I pulled on my quilted coveralls, I wondered the same thing. I asked the farmer if he had any help coming.

"It's hard to get folks out on a night like this, Doc."

No joke, Jose, I thought to myself.

"I called my neighbor. He is my oldest friend. I think he will be here shortly."

Mercy, if his oldest friend was coming, surely his name was Methuselah.

Pondering this special friendship, he added, "I ain't got but one friend'll come out in this stuff." He dusted off his jacket with a gnarly old paw, "but my buddy Jimmy and me grew up together in these here mountains. Been friends since we was kids. We been helping each other with our cattle fow 'bout sixty years. He hits the sauce every now and then, but nobody's perfect. His granddaddy taught him there's more money in selling corn by the quart than the bushel, and he's been making moonshine ever since."

I figured most of his friends that night were in the local rest home, with a couple of blankets over their knees, sipping a warm cup of Ensure.

"Glad your friend's coming," I said doubtfully.

Thinking he was better at lassoing a cow than I was, I said, "You go ahead and catch her while I get my instruments ready," and handed him my rope, which I had never used. As I was getting out the Betadine scrub and my surgery pack, I heard a scream.

"Help, Doc!"

I looked up just in time to see the old man scrambling backward in the snow right in front of the charging mama cow. *Lord, have mercy! I am going to have to bury the farmer and the cow before this night is over. It doesn't matter because I'm going to freeze to death out here anyway. They'll find the three of us in the spring thaw, all huddled together like volcanic victims in Pompeii. Shaking their heads, "The Floyd Zone" is all they will say and look knowingly at one another.* I heard that Floyd County's two main cash crops were moonshine and marijuana and that so many unusual vet cases occurred here that vets called the place "The Floyd Zone."

As the cow stopped short of trampling him to smithereens, I yelled out, "Careful there, sir! Why don't you let me get her?" Thinking to myself, *Great, I get to try my first lassoing on an angry momma cow who likes to charge.* "A little help here, Lord," I breathed into the frosty night.

If the farmer had just dropped the rope over her head while she was down, he could have wrenched her head around to the side, and she wouldn't have been able to get up. Now that she was up and angry, I was going to have to lasso her and snub her to a tree. But, there were no trees close by, and there was no way I or anyone could hold this 1,000-pound angry Charolais who thought we might hurt her calf. I feared the trailing uterus was straining the fragile uterine artery, which, if ruptured, would cause her to bleed out.

She walked toward the creek and into the trees. I thought I could use the creek as a barrier as well as what looked to be a new barbed-wire fence. As I was getting close enough to throw the rope, the cow started walking oddly instead of running, and then she just stopped. I saw a few bundles of old barb wire on the ground that the farmer must have pulled off the posts, rolled up, and left there in the woods. The cow had walked through about three of these bundles. Now the old wire was wrapped around her legs and her uterus. The barbed wire had essentially shackled her, and she couldn't move. I walked up to her side and dropped the rope over her head. She couldn't charge me or bolt away or do anything evil even if she wanted to, which she did. *A funny answer to prayer,* I thought, *but hey, I'll take it, Lord.* She glared at me, showing the whites of her eyes, and bellowed for her calf. I knew she wanted badly to hurt me. I pulled my truck around, tied her to my trailer hitch, got out my wire clippers, and started cutting her free.

The old farmer seemed tuckered out. I hoped he wasn't going to have a stroke or just flat-out die on me. As I cleaned up the uterus, she started kicking big, long powerful strokes with her hind leg, reaching all the way up to her chin and then sweeping through the air as far back as she could reach.

"She's gonna take somebody's head off, Doc."

"Yeah," I said, "and since I'm at the business end of things here, that would be my head."

Enough of this craziness; it's time for sedation. At this point, I wasn't sure which of us needed it the most. I went back to the truck and pulled up one milliliter of xylazine, jacked her tail up, hit the tail vein, and squeezed the plunger, sending in the clear liquid of tranquility. We all relaxed after that, and the leg stopped its deadly swings. I resumed cleaning off the uterus; which was covered with frozen leaves and twigs. A half hour had already passed since my arrival, and I hadn't even started pushing the uterus back in yet. Snow was still falling, and the snowflakes swirling against the side of the mountain produced an effect that made it seem as though we were inside a snow globe. I grabbed Dr. Healer's bag to put the uterus on and saw headlights coming over the hill.

"Well, looks like your help be here, Doc," the farmer said with a satisfied grin.

"Thanks be to God," I said out loud, already chilled to the bone and exhausted.

"Yeah, good friends always be true to their word, no matter the weather," the old farmer said.

I realized the origin of "fair weather friends" and wondered if it started on the side of a mountain in a snowstorm.

As the neighbor staggered out of his truck and came close, I could smell the whiskey. I didn't care. I needed his help. I handed him a pair of exam gloves, explaining to him that we were replacing the uterus and that he needed to hold it up and gently massage it back into the cow. I told him he also needed to be sure he didn't push his fingers through the uterus. We pushed until we were just about cheek to cheek. He hadn't shaved for a few days, and his brewery breath fogged my glasses, but no matter, I was happy for the help. If the Abominable

Snowman had come over the mountain, I would have given him a pair of gloves.

We reduced the uterus three-quarters of the way, and I felt a joy and pride in my chest. This was working! I got a burst of new energy. That's when I saw them, strewn out along the ground. I turned white. How could that have happened? Somehow her intestines spilled out and were stuck to the frozen ground. Had the barbed wire torn holes in her uterus, or had the drunken neighbor shoved his hand through it? As a horse doctor, I knew this would mean a sure death for a horse, but I wasn't sure about a cow. I pulled off my gloves and tried to call my backup associate vet for a quick consultation. Should I put the intestines back in or should I put her down? Cell phone—no signal. CB radio—no signal. What kind of a Floyd Zone was I in?

I walked back to the cow and looked at the frozen intestines in the muck. I thought if I shoved them back in, the cow could get a raging peritonitis, go septic, suffer, and die in a few days. Maybe she would live; maybe not. But I would have to pull her uterus back out, find where the intestines came through, stuff them back in, suture up the hole, and put the uterus back in again. She would probably get adhesions and therefore not be able to calve again since she was a pretty old cow. Looking at my drunken help and the old farmer, I knew they would not make it much longer. We were all half frozen to death, and the cow was looking pale. She was probably bleeding out. I told the farmer what the options were. He told me to put her down. The only problem was the frozen ground. I asked the farmer if he had a gun. The drunken neighbor perked up.

"I got a high-powered rifle in my truck, Doc."

Great, what's wrong with this picture? An inebriated old man standing next to us and shooting a high-powered rifle in a blizzard? But with no other options, I herded the old farmer behind my truck. It was ugly, but with two shots, it was over. And now I had an orphaned calf to save.

A light blanket of snow covered the top of the hungry calf's back as she lay shivering alone in the cold. "Some entrance into this world," I mumbled to her. To the friends now huddled together for warmth, I said, "Let's get her back to the barn."

They struggled to pick up the calf but managed to throw her on the back of the neighbor's flatbed truck and just leaned against the bumper like they were done for the night.

"That won't do," I said. Surely the calf would slide off the back of the truck when the drunk driver hit the first partially submerged boulder in the pasture. "Why don't you put her in the back of your Bronco and turn the heat up high to thaw her out."

They just stared at me. They were spent. Well, I'm no Wonder Woman, but I had a little more reserve energy left in me than these old guys at this point. I yanked off my gloves and tossed everything in my stainless-steel bucket. I'd clean up later and hope I didn't get called out again tonight and need any of this. I pulled the precious calf off the truck and put her in the back of the warm Bronco. Then the three of us fishtailed it out of the pasture.

I put the calf in the barn and dried the little one off with some straw. Next, I whisked together a packet of colostrum with some warm water and pressed the rubber nipple on the bottle to her cold lips. She protested at first. This wasn't her warm mother's udder. But she was hungry, and after I poured some on my finger and let her suck on that for a second before quickly substituting the rubber nipple, she had no further objection and sucked the warm, nourishing mixture down.

I told the farmer I would bill him and thanked the neighbor for his help. He said, "No problem, Doc. We are neighborly in these here parts, just like Jesus taught about the Good Samaritan. Who is your neighbor? Anybody who needs help; that is who. I shares, too," he said pulling out a flask of moonshine and holding it out for me. "Care for a little nip to thaw you out? I knows you can't drown your troubles in a bottle, 'cause theys can swim, but it'll warm you up!"

"No, thanks," I said still pondering his words about who my neighbor was, and thinking I just saw the parable lived out by this old man with a high-power rifle and white lightning.

"I hope one of you has a granddaughter who would think it great fun to bottle-feed this little girl twice a day," I said, handing the farmer another packet of colostrum. "Don't forget to dip that navel cord so she doesn't get an infection," I yelled back over my shoulder as I headed for my truck.

Driving back, I checked my pager as soon as I had reception. All was quiet. I thanked the Lord for that and for getting me through the prolapse call. As I passed the county line from Floyd into Montgomery County, the roads were clear and the snow had stopped. That's weird, I thought to myself. Then I thought about what a strange night it was and realized I just left the "Floyd Zone." No, this was not how I expected my lifelong dream of being a veterinarian to be fleshed out, but at least I was able to save the calf. They would both have died if I had not been there, so even though I was frozen and tired, I was living out the tattered old bumper sticker that had motivated me to go to vet school: "Do Your Dream!"

CHAPTER 2

MARLA AND BUDDY

God is the Lord of angels and of men—and of elves.

—J. R. R. Tolkien

It was a court-ordered castration. Marla was fourteen years old and loved her sheep, Buddy. But the neighbors complained about the smell and told her mother that the law stated that no livestock could live within the Roanoke city limits. Intact male sheep, known as rams, can be aggressive. They sometimes butt their owners with their heads and cause injury. Buddy's future seemed uncertain, but the ram had proved so valuable to the family's well-being that they went to court to keep him. Marla's erratic and sometimes violent behavior improved dramatically when her mother bought Buddy for her. Despite various treatments for Marla's mental illness, her mother had endured years of her embarrassing tantrums, and she wasn't going to let the law take Buddy away from her daughter without a fight. She hired a lawyer and went to court. Hearing the special circumstances, the judge allowed Buddy to continue living within the city limits; however, he would have to be castrated. I was the vet called upon to citify the boy. Even though I had taught a therapeutic riding program and worked with children with various emotional swings in Texas, I was unprepared for Marla's onslaught. It's one thing to get disabled children on a horse; it is another thing to do surgery on their beloved sheep.

"Ba doc-tor, bad doctor! You are going to kill Buddy," Marla hissed as I walked into the house. I was taken aback by the agitated girl in front of me. Her strawberry blond hair was cropped close to her skull, but tufts still jutted out in different directions and from the look in her eye, I doubted a comb dared to get too close. I did not know her history or what situation I had gotten myself into. But the reason the other vets in the office preferred me, a newbie, to castrate this celebrity sheep was beginning to become clear as she stood blocking my way, all four feet, two inches of her, looking thick, strong, and menacing.

"I'm sorry, Dr. McDonald. Marla was with the other doctor when he put her dog Bess to sleep, and now she doesn't like vets. She pitched such a fit in that vet office, I had to carry her out kicking and screaming," her mother Gayla informed me.

"He lie! He said he was going to put Bess to sleep, but she never woke up. He killed her," Marla said, grinding her clenched, crooked, yellow teeth together.

"Marla, your bus will be here soon. You go right now and get yourself ready," her mother said firmly.

"Where is your ram?" I asked.

"He is in the backyard, but I think you should fix him right here on this here table. It's hot as blue blazes out there in the sun," Gayla said, walking out to catch him and bring him in.

I was fresh out of vet school with precious little practical experience. I had castrated a bull, dog, horse, and half a cat—my lab partner did the other half. All species react differently to anesthesia, and the castration procedure varies depending on the size and placement of the testicles. Dogs require general anesthesia and sutures. Young bulls and boars: no anesthesia—just cut and pull. Horses can be done under standing procedures with heavy sedation or dropped on the ground. They need no sutures but require a big incision to drain.

This ram was older than the usual castration age, so the surgery was more complicated. My boss gave me the recipe for a special sheep cocktail to knock Buddy out, but I had never used it before, so I didn't know how he would react. I was only thinking how expensive the famous sheep had now become and that I had better not screw this up.

Driving to the call, I reviewed the normal heart rate for sheep before I got to the house. I was now listening to his heart before I gave him any anesthesia. This is something that must always be done first to make sure the heart is beating normally so the anesthesia doesn't kill them. Comparing the heartbeat to the one other sheep I listened to in vet school, it sounded good to me. Then I took his temperature, sticking the thermometer into his rectum. Buddy didn't like where I placed it and let out a bleat of indignation. I jumped out of my skin when the daughter yelled at me, "Bad doctor, bad doctor; you gonna kill Buddy."

Her mother told her to go out and wait for her bus. But she was soon back, pleading with me now, "Don't kill Bud. Is he gonna die?"

I proceeded to give her the standard memorized spiel taught in vet school: "All anesthesia and surgeries have the risk of complications. Death is the most serious complication."

As soon as the words left my mouth, I regretted it. I had knowledge, but not wisdom. Now she was really upset. She paced around the room, agitated. While keeping one eye on her, I got out my surgical pack and started to scrub Buddy's scrotum with some Betadine to prep it for surgery.

Mortified, Marla yelled, "She is touching his private parts, bad doctor!"

When is that bus coming? I thought to myself. I wanted to do the surgery outside, but they insisted I do him inside, right in front of the bay window for all the neighbors to see. So here we were on the dining room table, towels spread across it, making a mock surgery suite. The air in the room was tense. As I drew up the anesthesia cocktail into the syringe, Marla started again, "She's going to kill Buddy. I don't like doctor!"

The mother said, "Oh dear, I'm sure Dr. McDonald has successfully done this surgery many times before."

I remembered the joking suggestion in vet school that when a client asks how many times you have done a new procedure, you just say, "a number of times" because zero is a number. I pondered this response as I started looking for Buddy's jugular. With Marla's eyes scrutinizing my every movement, I started to shake a bit. What if he does die? What if this cocktail is too strong? My boss isn't a sheep expert. Buddy's owner will have me in court next.

I decided to wait for Marla to get on the bus. Judging from her reaction to me doing the surgical scrub on Bud's scrotum, I could only imagine her shock to see me cutting off his testicles. Out she went, giving me a final glare and spitting in the air in my direction.

Now that it was safe to proceed with the surgery, I wondered how much time this anesthesia would give me. I had asked my boss, "How much time once the ram is down will I have to castrate before he wakes up?"

"Enough," was all he said.

It was enough for a seasoned vet who has been doing surgeries for years, but maybe not enough for a new grad who has never done this surgery before. I wondered, more than enough or not enough? I thought about calling my husband and saying, "Start worrying, details to follow."

Trying to find the vein I thought, *Could Gayla possibly hold this sheep still? Where is that stupid jugular? I know when I stick him, he is going to move, and she will let him go halfway through my injecting. Then I won't know how much went in the vein and how much in the muscle. If it goes into the muscle, it will take longer to drop him and be absorbed differently. Then he will jump off the table when I pull the first testicle out.*

"Could you hold him nice and tight while I am injecting, please?" I asked calmly, trying to beam both patience and confidence.

"I'll try, but I can't stand the sight of blood. I may just pass out right here on the floor," she said blanching white.

Thankfully, I hit the vein the first time, drew back blood, and injected the liquid quietude. Bud's head slumped over to the side, and I laid him gently on the table.

"My knees are getting right curious-acting," Gayla said as I sat her in the closest dining room chair.

"You just sit there and watch your soap opera, and I'll be done soon," I said donning my sterile gloves and unwrapping the surgery pack. Normally castrating a sheep is not a sterile procedure, but Bud was a "special ram," and I didn't want any complications from infection. I loaded my scalpel blade onto the handle and started to incise the skin . . . and heard screaming behind me.

"*He's dead!*" He's dead! Buddy's dead! You killed him! You killed my Buddy!" Swinging at me with both fists, Marla continued yelling, "You killed him! Liar! I hate you!" Marla had decided to take one last peek inside before she caught the bus. Seeing Buddy laid out on the dining room table like the Christmas turkey sent her into a tailspin. "He's dead; look at his sides. He isn't breathing. Bad Doctor, bad! I hate you @#$%^**," she said as she continued to swing at me. I quickly jerked the sharp blade up in the air out of harm's way, just missing her arm.

Her embarrassed mother yelled, "That is enough, Marla! Say you are sorry and get your heinie on the bus before I get a switch!"

I looked at Buddy's chest, mortified. It looked still to me, too. Maybe she was right—I had killed him. Surely he wasn't dead. What a nightmare! So this is why I suffered through four years of vet school to go out and kill the dear pets of emotionally disturbed children! I broke my sterile field, grabbed my stethoscope, and with all the poise of a polished professional, put in the earpieces backward. My own heart stopped when I didn't hear a heartbeat. Realizing I put them in backward, I righted them and—to my relief—heard a heartbeat. "Thank you, Jesus!"

"He is fine. He is not dead. He is just asleep—I mean resting. Would you like to listen to his heartbeat, Marla?" I said, still rattled.

She didn't say anything, just frowned, and shook her head hard in both directions, crossing her arms over her chest and puffing out her red cheeks. I had no idea how much time was left before the sheep would wake up. I would have had one testicle out by now if not for Marla's interruption.

"Could you maybe help Marla get on the bus?" I suggested to her mother.

"Yes," she said, dragging a sobbing Marla out the door.

 In my mind, I saw Buddy, bleating and bleeding, scrambling off the dining room table, running out the now wide-open front door in full view of all the kids on the bus, dragging one testicle behind him. I decided to not take the time to reglove with a new set of sterile gloves, but just go ahead and castrate. He was an older ram and

particularly well endowed, so I used the emasculators, which crush the spermatic cord and blood vessels before cutting, thus reducing bleeding. Just as I was removing the first testicle, I heard the bus pull off—much to my relief. I put a few sutures in, so there would be no possibility of this old boy bleeding out. Off with the other one, and I was done.

The surgery was finished, but the anesthesia was not. Buddy was still and hadn't even flinched when I crushed and cut the last cord and vessels. I grabbed my stethoscope and listened for his heartbeat again. It was still beating. I waited and waited. How long would this stuff last? I packed up all my instruments, sprayed the incision with some antiseptic and fly spray, and explained the aftercare to the mother.

After fifteen minutes, Buddy was still groggy but standing and showed no signs of bleeding. I reminded Gayla again not to give him anything to eat or drink for a few hours and to keep him calm for twenty-four hours. Just as I congratulated her for winning the court case and now fully complying with the law, I heard the bus pull up in front of the house. The bus driver opened the door, and Marla raced out, "Sorry, she was sobbing like a baby over some sheep, so I thought I'd just bring her on home."

A clearly distraught, tear-streaked Marla, afraid to come into the house, whispered through the screen door, "He's dead, ain't he?"

"No, Marla, come on in. He is doing fine," her mother beamed.

Buddy perked up at the sight of his friend. Marla nearly ripped the door off its hinges and bolted to his side. She wrapped her arms around his neck and sobbed tears of joyful relief, blowing her nose on his neck before turning her bloodshot eyes on me. She beamed a crooked smile and, to my surprise, came over and hugged me with the same love she gave Buddy, "Good doctor, good doctor," was all she could say.

Hugging her back, I told her, "Buddy will be just fine. Marla, you are a good owner. I wish half of my clients cared about their pets as much as you do."

"Yep, yep, yep, I love him," she repeated three times, rocking from side to side hugging herself as if to contain her joy.

Waving my goodbyes, I stepped slowly into my truck. I was tired. I breathed a prayer of thanksgiving, "Today I realized that life and death are from you, Lord. Thanks for keeping old Buddy alive for Marla and me. Let him have an uncomplicated recovery."

"We are going to the fair to see the sheep, we are going to the fair to see the sheep, we are going to the fair to see the sheep," Marla yelled after me as I pulled out of their driveway.

It was September, and the State Fair had just opened in Richmond. Driving back to the office, I reflected about the lesson Marla taught me, a lesson about who was in control. It made me think about the first time I went to the fair when I was six years old. All of us kids bolted out to the little cars. I jumped in the pink car and started honking the horn, spinning the steering wheel all the way around, and stepping on the gas pedal. The cars started to move in unison. I was having the time of my life, driving my first car. The cars moved in and out from the center, and I waved confidently to my parents, even took my hands off the wheel. I was in control! When the ride was over, the operator pushed down the lever and slowed to a stop. I hopped out, beaming. The old man nodded at me as I skipped through the gate confidently. I had driven my first car. God is like the old fair ride attendant, smiling and nodding at my foolish confidence as I skip through life, thinking I am driving my own car.

That night we read J. R. R. Tolkien's, *The Hobbit,* to the kids. Kissing them goodnight, I quoted Tolkien, *God is the Lord of angels and of men—and of elves.* Then, I told them about Buddy and added, "Yes kids, God is the Lord of angels and of men—and of elves—and sheep."

CHAPTER 3

BOS DOMESTICUS

When we try to see a damaged person as one of God's regular customers, instead of a lost cause, it takes the pressure off everybody. We can loosen our death grip on the person, which usually results in progress for everyone, also known in certain circles as grace.

—Anne Lamott

*B*os *Domesticus* is the main subspecies of beef cattle raised in the United States. The Latin word *Bos* means bovine and *Domesticus* means domesticated. This suggests that beef cattle are domesticated. I beg to differ. Latin is a dead language, and I realized that something was lost in the translation when I was on my first *Bos Domesticus* emergency call. Whoever coined the name never took a calf from an angry Angus cow with mastitis.

Beulah took a brief history from Mr. Smeg before handing me directions to his farm.

"The cow done calved prit' near three days ago and nursed just fine. Now her udder's big and hot-looking. She kicks the calf whenever he tries to nurse," the farmer said.

This was a classic case of mastitis. When the teat gets sore and damaged from the calf's zealous sucking, bacteria ascends the milk canal and an infection ensues. Nursing mothers of all species wince at the thought of mastitis. It feels like sizzling needles being jabbed in and out of your inflamed breast. It makes your toes curl, and you don't want to nurse. This cow had mastitis, and the calf wasn't getting enough milk to survive.

"Good morning, sir. I'm Dr. McDonald," I called out the window to Mr. Smeg as I pulled into his driveway, "How are you?"

23

"I'm happier than a puppy with two peters," he said. Sizing me up, he asked, "Where's Doc Amboseli? Is that vet school not putting out any men these days?"

"Not many," I deadpanned. "Where is the cow?"

"Over the hill. Get in," he said, miffed that Dr. Amboseli had not come and that a female vet was on his property.

I grabbed a bag of fluids and an IV line from my vet box and hopped into the farmer's truck. It was an old Dodge Ram, a dually with a flat bed. Judging from the layer of red dust on the dash and caked mud on the sides, its mileage was acquired on dirt roads.

"Just push that stuff out of the way," he said in a huff, tossing a worn leather halter behind the seat as I slid over some ear tags and an empty Red Man tobacco bag and sat down. We drove silently through the field in search of the cow-and-calf pair. I was a woman vet and instinctively he disliked me. In his book, a vet without testicles was as useless as his old bull would be: weak and impotent. I decided not to try to make conversation as I suspected he would say something sexist, and I didn't want him to get my dander up. My boss once said if you have a difficult client, charge until you like it. I couldn't think of an adequate additional "Gender Jerk fee" to charge him. I would do good vet medicine and hope that was enough to begin to change his bias.

Hitting a large rock in the pasture bounced an old Southern States feed receipt off the dash, revealing a well-worn *Playboy* magazine. They say that smells and visual images can instantly bring back child-hood memories, and the cover flashed me back to the last time I saw a *Playboy.* It was in high school. My horse trainer made me look at his *Playboy* before molesting me. He thought that a frontal view of a nude woman would arouse me, but it only disgusted me, knowing what was coming next. I would disassociate by staring at a picture on the wall to endure the ordeal. During the tense silence in the cab before we found the calf, I wondered, *how many girls were victimized*

from Hugh Hefner's profiting from his promotion of the feminine form.
How much had abuse increased because of Internet porn and men seeing
women as objects to satisfy their lust, instead of people of great worth in
God's eyes? Was sex trafficking flamed by the easy porn?

Fighting my desire to hate this farmer, I asked, *Lord, help me for-*
give his chauvinism and porn. Help me to be gracious.

"When I was growing up, there was an older man who forced me
to look at *Playboy* centerfolds before he molested me." My words were
out before I could stop them and they froze suspended in the air like
awkward ice cubes in the hot, silent truck. I couldn't believe I said
them. Neither could the farmer. The unpleasantness ended moments
later as we crested the last hill in the pasture and spotted a little black
bull calf lying dull and listless in the tall fescue grass. Thankful to be
jumping out of the truck, I trotted over to him. He was too weak
to resist my physical exam. As I pinched up the skin on his scrawny
neck, it stood like a black tent before smoothing back into place, a
sure sign of dehydration. While I squatted over the calf, touching his
tacky gums, the farmer yelled, "Here comes the cow, Doc, and she's
a good momma."

I learned from the last time I was flattened by a charging cow that
farmers are masters of understatement. "She is a good momma" is a
code. It really means, "She will kill you if she catches you messing
with her baby." I bolted into the truck and slammed the door as she
thundered over the knoll after me.

"The calf needs fluids, and his mother needs her mastitis treated
with antibiotics," I said, catching my breath, and waiting for my heart
rate to slow down.

"You're pretty quick," he said with a mix of admiration for my
speed and disappointment that he didn't get to see the cow nail me.
"I'll try to get my truck between you and the cow, and you can throw

the calf on the truck bed. I got a pen at the top of the hill. The momma cow'll follow; she ain't leaving her baby for nothin'."

The farmer drove around the calf using his old Dodge as a cutting horse to keep the cow away. I jumped out, scooped the limp calf onto the rusty flatbed and vaulted on after him. Poking the needle around for a dehydrated vein, I finally hit one and started the life-giving fluids. I kept a wary eye on the cow as I ran the fluids full bore. Fearful the calf would bounce off the flatbed, I sat straddling him and held the fluid bag high above my head to increase the drip rate as we bounced back through the fields. The saline solution streamed life into his flaccid body. The cow galloped, bellowing frantically behind the truck, attempting to rescue her calf. She wanted to kill the perpetrators of the calf-napping.

Once in the pen, we didn't have to lock the cow in. She wasn't going to leave her calf. Enraged and in pain, she paced back and forth on both sides of us, digging a moat in the mud around the truck. She worked herself up into an angry lather, flecks of sweat dripping from behind her ears and down her heaving flank. A creamy lather had whipped up between her hind legs and on her black neck. The whites of her eyes glared at me as she spun back and forth beside the truck bed. That is when it hit me: she was wild, extremely wild. She would kill me if given half the chance. Beef cows aren't any more domesticated than Cape buffalo. *Bos Domesticus* is a completely inaccurate language breech, no truth of disclosure here. As the fluid bag emptied, I sat with a leg on each side of the calf, wondering how I was going to catch, treat, and milk his murderous mother's mastitis.

That is when it happened. The languid calf I had been strad-dling resurrected. He sprang to his feet in an instant. I was no longer holding the calf down; he was holding me up. I was astride, mounted, in the air. I have ridden horses, camels, even an elephant, but never an Angus bull calf. This wasn't exactly what I pictured rodeo bull riding to be like, but it was just as terrifying. The farmer looked up at me speechless, his bottom jaw dropped open, and his eyes bugged out of their old, sagging sockets. The calf was equally shocked and terrified. He was certain the predator on his back was going to eat him alive. With his renewed vigor, he leaped toward the edge of the flatbed, trying to get back to his half-crazed mother. She was incensed, ready for battle. She didn't care that I gave her son life. No, now she was going take mine! My one hundred and thirty pounds versus her one thousand and thirty—well, the physics were against me.

I remembered my brother asking me, "Why are you going into large-animal practice and not small animals? They are large; you are not. It is simple physics. Mass versus force—the odds are against you."

Why had I not listened to my brother? I looked down into the irate cow's odious, red-rimmed eyes. Seeing me on the back of her beloved son, she attempted to scale a tire and mount the flatbed. The calf took another jump closer to the edge. My brother was right; the odds were against me. Soon I would be under her pummeling hooves. Her head would maul me like a battering ram, fracturing my ribs, and puncturing a lung. Dust and gravel flying, she would trample me with four hammering hooves until I was still and no longer a threat to her legacy. From dust I came, and to dust I was about to return. We were at the edge now, one leap more, and I would be eating dirt with his mother.

I threw all my weight to the right side and knocked the calf off balance. Together we tumbled down, horizontal on the flatbed, smashing my thigh between the calf and a metal pipe. The calf scrambled to his feet and leaped into the pen with his mother.

"Nice bull riding, Doc," the farmer said, giving me his first smile of the day, tobacco juice dribbling from his toothless grin. With a nod of respect, he offered me a pinch of his Redman.

"Yeah, I'm a better bull rider than Doc Amboseli," I said, springing up from my adrenaline rush and declining the chewing tobacco. I had enough stimulants on board and didn't need any nicotine.

"I believe you are, Dr. McDonald, I believe you are. Looks like you fixed the calf, too. Good job."

I nodded, inwardly glowing. It's hard to win over these old timers, but I guess the fancy bull riding did the trick.

Now we had to catch the cow to treat her mastitis, so she would let the little guy nurse again. I slipped the rope over her head from the flatbed and tied her up tight to a post, but her hind end was still a lethal weapon, and she was swinging back and forth, worried about her calf. I herded him to her side. I did not grow up on a dairy farm, and they don't teach milking in vet school, so the momma cow and I were both learning hand-milking for the first time. Since her udder was so painful, she had not let the calf nurse in a few days, and her bag was huge with milk and swollen with infection. Ungrateful that

I was trying to bring relief, she swung a back leg around and kicked me hard in the thigh.

The farmer came over to offer a hand. He grew up milking cows. I pushed her hind end against the fence to keep her still, and he milked her out. Long strokes with his fingers expertly coaxed the fluid down the milk canal and out of her infected udder and teat. I had him squirt some into my hand and showed him the clumps in the milk from the mastitis infection. Pus, bacteria, and milk fell in clotted spurts onto the ground with each of his strokes until finally her teats were stripped out. She didn't like us any better, but at least her attempts at murder slowed down as the pain began to lessen. I injected her with antibiotics and pain killers. I motioned to the farmer that I was removing the lasso. He bolted into his truck, knowing she would not thank us for our help once she was free. I stood on the fence above her head as I loosened the lasso and pulled it over her ears. No longer restrained, she bashed her head into the fence to nail me, but I was well over the top board by the time skull and oak board connected. To anyone who still thinks that *Bos Domesticus* is a suitable name for beef cattle, here's a bucket. You get to milk the next cow with mastitis! I'll be busy dialing 911.

I opened the gate for the farmer to drive his muddy truck out of the pen. Putting my lasso, catheter, and empty fluid bag into my vet box, I sat in the cab and wrote up his bill. Milking out the painful teats and giving the drugs reduced the pain enough, so momma cow would let the calf nurse. I looked up as the calf suckled and the crusty old cattleman pursed his lips together. He rubbed his swarthy chin and grunted approval, leaning back against the fence and shaking his head up and down in acknowledgment. He knew I saved both cow and calf. Stiffly, he climbed in his old Dodge and fished for his checkbook through the morass on the dash and grabbed the *Playboy*, too. I felt uncomfortable as he started walking toward me with the magazine in his hand, but he turned and tossed it in the brown dumpster by the road. Walking up to my truck, he reached out his liver-spotted old paw and handed me the check respectfully, saying, "Thanks, Doc, you done good."

"Thank you," was all I could muster as I took the check. I wanted to thank him for throwing away the pornography, thank him for helping milk out the cow, and thank him for acknowledging a women vet could get the job done. But I felt that if I spoke I would get emotional. After the bull riding and successful treatments, I didn't want to appear weak. I tried to make my escape quickly while still in control, but something made me pause. God gives us tears to prime the pump of our pain and drain the well of our wounds. A tear trickled down my cheek. Seeing this, something in the old man softened, and he brushed his crusty knuckles across his tear-brimmed eyes. There was a shift within both of us, and we nodded our heads in acknowledgment as I pulled out of the driveway.

Heading to my next case, I smiled as I thought of Anne Lamott's words, "When we try to see a damaged person as one of God's regular customers instead of a lost cause, it takes the pressure off everybody. We can loosen our death grip on the person, which usually results in progress for everyone, also known in certain circles as grace."

CHAPTER 4

MRS. KRAVITZ AND THE GO-KART RACE

Gossip is a sort of smoke that comes from the dirty tobacco-pipes of those who diffuse it: it proves nothing but the bad taste of the smoker.

—George Eliot

F our months prior to the cold night in the Floyd Zone, I was still in the getting-to-know-you phase as an associate veterinarian at Amboseli Veterinary Clinic and assigned to ride with Dr. Healer. The first week, she introduced me to clients, taught me practice protocol, and showed me the roads, saying, "It doesn't matter if you are a board-certified equine surgeon if you don't know how to get to the farm!"

This was before GPS, and I would recall her words many times in the middle of the night, wandering around the countryside with no street lights or address numbers, trying to find the sick animal! Often, the farmer's directions included a big oak that had long since fallen or a farmhouse where the farmer passed away a generation ago. Of course, all the locals knew exactly where that was, but not the new vet in town.

Dr. Healer and I were on a call together and were finishing giving vaccines to a couple of backyard pleasure horses. I checked their heart rates, took their temperatures, and drew up the vaccines. Some vets get bored with doing the routine shots, but we never tired of the chance to see healthy horses.

Suddenly, both our pagers beeped. During the day, if an emergency or unscheduled call came into the office, the secretary paged all the vets in the practice. Whoever was available or closest took the call.

My eyes widened as I read: "Bill Wyatt's horse hit by go-kart—bleeding bad. Dr. call ASAP."

Immediately, Dr. Healer radioed into the office, "I know Bill; I'll call him. Can you push back my next appointment?"

"10–4," Beulah responded. "They are pretty panicked," she added.

Dr. Healer called the number on the page, and Mrs. Snodgrass, the neighbor whose house was the closest to the accident answered, "Doc, you gotta come right now! The horse is bleeding to death, and it is all Sid's fault. That boy's been making time with that Shelly girl and darn near got 'em all killed. Teenagers today ain't got no sense. I called to tell his momma, but she won't there, so I called her neighbors and told thems all about it, and then I told thems to get up with her and have her call me. This's the most excitement we've had in these here parts in a while, not since the Feds raided ol' Skeeter's still and he done hanged hisself. That made for some good talk in . . ."

"May I speak to Bill Wyatt?" Dr. Healer asked calmly, interrupting Mrs. Snodgrass's harangue.

"It's his boy, Sid, here. His papa's at work, and we ain't been able to get ahold of him no way, neither," the neighbor answered as she yelled for Sid.

Talking to the teenager, Dr. Healer tried to allay his fears, "We are on the way. Can you tell me what happened?"

Sid relayed the story, "My friend Shelly said her go-kart is faster than my horse, Red. I said it ain't; let's race, and you'll see. So, me and her took off down the gravel road. Just as I was passing her, a truck come round the curve on our side of the road. Shelly slammed on her brakes and the tail end of the cart spun in the gravel right in front of me. Old Red's front leg came down hard on the back of her go-kart and went right through the aluminum plate. When he pulled his leg out of the hole, the shredded metal sliced his leg up something fierce, and he's bleeding like crazy."

Dr. Healer replied, "Is the blood just flowing down his leg or is it spurting out?"

"It is spurting out, and he is trembling."

"That means he probably cut an artery, and the blood will come out faster than if he cut a vein. Lift up his upper lip, are his gums white or pink?"

"Pink, Doc. Is that good or bad?"

"Pink is good. White means he is losing too much blood. You need to stop the bleeding, or he might bleed out."

"Bleed out and die!" the boy cried. I could hear the love for his horse in his voice. "What do I do?"

"You need to put pressure on it. Wrap a towel around it tight and don't take it off until we get there in fifteen minutes."

I asked Dr. Healer, "Do you think he can stop the bleeding?"

"We'll see soon," she responded, grim-faced. "Remember what they taught us in vet school, 'All bleeding stops eventually . . .'"

When we pulled into the driveway, we saw Red standing quietly with his head down. A white towel, now blood-soaked, was duct-taped tightly around his leg. The ground was saturated with blood, and the green grass had turned a red-brown, attracting a swarm of flies. The mangled go-kart lay by the road with its torn aluminum sticking up like a jagged tailfin.

Leaning against the kart was Shelly, a cute redhead, whose womanly form had recently pushed through puberty. She had a sunburnt nose and a flustered, guilty look. Her green eyes were teary. It was easy to see how a fourteen-year-old boy would think she was worth racing.

Sid ran to our truck, his face fear-drained, "I got the bleeding to stop a few minutes ago and he is . . ."

Mrs. Snodgrass, the village gossipmonger, cut him off and started talking nonstop as soon as we stepped from the truck. She was more excited about being able to tell others about what happened than she was about the outcome of the horse. Her face was puffy, big pored, and pink with excitement. She had a high, whiney, end-of-the-world voice and could really dish out the dirt. Dr. Healer asked her if the parents were notified, and she replied that they might have tried to call, but she had been on the phone. Dr. Healer asked her to go call again and stay by the phone. Excited as a child to be the first one to tell the parents the bad news, it was plain she never outgrew her propensity to be a tattletale. She raced back to the house. Smart move, I thought. I was about to get some medication off the truck to treat her for diarrhea of the mouth.

A quick physical exam of the horse revealed that his gums were now a pale pink, and his heart rate slightly elevated from the pain. Other than the leg, he had no more injuries. We gingerly took off the towel, not wanting to jar the clot and start the gusher again. It was a clean laceration through the skin to the bone. Thankfully, no tendons were involved, so after numbing the wound area, this would be an easy suture.

Red was quiet, and we didn't know how much blood he lost, so we decided not to tranquilize him. Instead, we put the twitch—a ten-inch loop of rope at the end of a long wooden stick—on his nose to take his mind off the needle going through his flesh. Grabbing his upper lip, I stuck it through the loop and then twisted the handle, quickly turning it until the horse was more concerned about his nose than the area we were sewing up. They say it doesn't hurt and that it releases endorphins. I'm not so sure about that. I don't see any humans jumping in line to get twitched.

In any case, the 10 cc of Lidocaine where the sutures went made the procedure fairly pain-free. I picked up the opposite foot as Dr. Healer injected the Lidocaine to ensure that he kept his injured foot on the ground. I cleaned up and clipped the hair while the Lidocaine was taking effect. She pulled out her surgery box and put a sterile pack on top of it. Dr. Healer then put on a pair of gloves, picked up the needle with the long-handled needle drivers, and using Maxon suture material, jabbed the needle through the numb skin and up through the skin on the other side. Deftly she wrapped the suture around the forceps and tied a square knot, making sure it didn't slip into a Granny knot, which can easily come untied. The two sides of skin were now together. I cut the ends of the suture, leaving them long enough so they could be removed in about ten days. Fifteen sutures later, and Red was stitched up. Dr. Healer wrapped the leg with Telfa pads, which are like big Band-Aids that won't stick to the wound, then a layer of gauze wrap, and finally, a layer of bright-blue vet wrap.

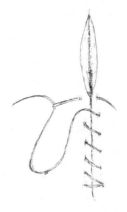

She reassured Sid that his horse was out of mortal danger, and the boy's color and smile returned to his tanned face. I packed up the truck, putting the needles in the sharps container and rinsing off the bloody needle drivers, forceps, and scissors so they would be easier to clean and sterilize when we got back to the office. Pulling out bandage material, I handed it to Dr. Healer as she explained to Sid how to remove and rewrap the bandage in a few days.

I was explaining how to administer the antibiotics when the busy-body neighbor came running out of the house. She finally got hold of Sid's mother between making calls to her friends to give them the latest scuttlebutt. She relished the drama and putting a bad spin on the situation.

"Your Momma's on the phone. I told her all about the two of you racing in the middle of the road, how ya'all almost got killed, and how it was going to be a big vet bill. She is hopping mad and wants to talk to you. She said you were supposed to be at home cutting the grass, not hanging out with that Shelley girl. She's mad as a hornet! You are gonna be grounded from now until the cows come home," she said speaking high-browed as if she were the final judge and arbitrator. Sid tried to cut in and say he had finished cutting all the grass, but as was her habit, she wouldn't let him get a word in edgewise. All eyes were on Sid, pale as his horse.

Smacking her lips together with excitement, the mischief-maker preened, "Lord, this is gonna be gooder than grits!"

Handing Sid the phone, she stood relishing the friction she caused between mother and son. Mrs. Snodgrass reminded me of Gladys Kravitz on the *Bewitched* TV show and had earned the reputation of being the valley blabbermouth. If she didn't outright make up the story, she fueled the fire by embellishing any local gossip. She never let the facts dim her stories. This mishap involving speed, romance, blood, and an emergency vet call gave her all the grist she needed for the gossip mill. By lowering the teen, she elevated herself. Her puffed-out chest and victorious expression showed her self-satisfaction. She was in her element until Dr. Healer stepped in and took the phone. She reassured the mother, saying what a good job Sid did taking care of Red and that his horse was going to be just fine. She added that we were in the neighborhood, so the farm call was half the price, and then she hung up. We all stood smiling around the horse, except for the neighbor who huffed off, unable to make a fracas out of the situation. She spun on her heels so fast, her last pink plastic curler flew out of her hair, and with a quickening pace, like a woman on a mission, she sprinted inside and called her friend Matilda, who had the itchiest ears in the valley, and relayed the embellished story.

I remembered that the donuts I bought on the way to the office that morning were still in the truck. If anyone needed some Krispy Kremes, these kids did. Thankful for them, Sid wolfed down two Bavarian Crèmes before giving a sugar-coated one to Red. Then remembering Shelly, he offered her one.

At least he has his priorities straight, I thought as we pulled out of the driveway. Having had no breakfast, I ate one—OK, so maybe it was two, as Dr. Healer sped around the winding mountain roads, trying to make up lost time in the schedule from the emergency call. As the road continued to wind, what started as delicious chocolate-filled donuts ended up tasting like a lard and sugar stew, churning in the caldron of my stomach. I rolled down my window to catch some fresh air, but it was too little, too late and brew spewed out. Wiping my mouth and mopping the perspiration off my forehead, I thought of the warning from Proverbs 26:11 I read that morning: "As a dog returns to its vomit, so fools repeat their folly." I recognized how I can be a Mrs. Kravitz; while my critical talk tastes like a donut in my mouth, it proves to be like lard in my stomach, and as a dog returns to its vomit, so I repeat my thoughtlessness. Every vet call teaches a lesson, and on this one, I was learning not to build myself up with the sarcastic chips I took from cutting others down. However, change requires a long mindfulness in the same direction, and I needed to go around many more bends before I saw how my own identity issues affected my speech.

CHAPTER 5

THE MAGNET

The truth does not change according to our ability to stomach it.

—Flannery O'Connor

It wasn't an emergency farm call, but my boss always told the new veterinarians, "Look busy, even if it's your only appointment; when you get to the client's driveway, you speed down it like a bat out of hell."

Fresh out of vet school, I followed his instructions, and I flew down the driveway. Unfortunately, I had yet to learn the proper braking distance to slow down and allow the dust to settle before reaching Mr. Parker's barn and accidentally powdered him with the rooster tail of red dust that rose behind my blue veterinary truck.

"Howdy," he coughed, knocking the drift off his worn overalls with the back of his hand. Blinking the russet dust off his lashes, he stepped forward to greet me, "You must be Doc McDonald, the new one at the vet office. Your boss man just keeps hiring them girls; it must be like *Charlie's Angels* over there now, ain't it?"

"It is nice to meet you, sir. Yes, I am Dr. McDonald," I said, casting aside the disparaging *Charlie's Angels* comment and extending my hand in greeting. He reached out his huge paw and fused the bones in my hand with his enthusiastic handshake. "How's the cow you called the office about?" I asked trying not to grimace as I freed my hand from his grip.

"ADR," he said, concern in his old blue eyes.

"ADR?" I repeated, mimicking his expression, and throwing in a raised eyebrow to boot. I knew it was one of the locals' terms they neglected to teach us in vet school, but I couldn't deduce what the initials stood for. All I could recall, which only added to the pressure of failing this vocabulary test, was a professor saying, "Farmers don't care how much you know, but, they expect you to know as much as they do."

"How long has she been ADR?" I asked hoping to get a clue as to its definition.

"She ain't been doing right since she had her young'un," he said.

ADR—I made a mental note. "When did she calve?"

"She freshened prit near a week ago, but she done look sorry for a few months. Ain't nothing between her horns and hooves but hide. She's as thin as Depression soup," he said—old enough to know.

"Did she pass the afterbirth?" I asked, worrying about a retained placenta.

"Yeah, she cleaned up pretty good, Doc."

"What's her vaccination and de-worming history?" I asked.

"Me and my buddy done it all in the fall," he said pleased with himself, despite the fact he had no idea what they gave her.

I surveyed the area to see if there was a place to restrain the cow so I could do a physical exam. I saw that behind the deteriorated remains of a discarded Ford pickup was a splintery wooden chute and rusty steel head catch. He had already coaxed her from the pasture into the smaller pen with some sweet feed. I watched now as he ran her into the head catch at the far end, pulled the levers slamming the metal gates around her neck, and, abracadabra, domestication in a box.

Now that she was captured, I examined her. She was thin. I listened to her heart. It had an odd sound—muffled, like it was wrapped in a cotton ball. I put in the "thinking stick" and contemplated possible etiologies. In vet school, the thermometer is called a thinking stick because, for some reason, clients remain silent while waiting for a reading, as if talk could hinder the mercury's progression. This gives the vet an uninterrupted two minutes to analyze the situation and come up with a diagnosis. I ran through a list of possible differentials in my head: parasites, lymphoma, leptospirosis, traumatic reticulo-peritonitis. I pulled out the ten-inch glass thermometer and wiped the manure off with the cow's tail so it was readable—103 degrees. It was only slightly elevated from the normal for cattle of 102. As if on cue, Mr. Parker started talking again.

"What do you reckon her problem be?" he asked. Before letting me respond, he said, "She ain't been eating much, Doc. My neighbor, Greg, grew up in this here valley and done raised cattle all his life. He reckons she done swallered something."

"She may well have. Hardware disease is pretty likely," I said. He nodded approval, appreciating that I was bringing their experience into the diagnosis. I began to recite my notes from my large-animal medicine class to him, "Cattle are indiscriminate eaters. Without upper front teeth, they use their long tongues to graze and unapologetically scoop up everything in their paths. They can swallow their food whole and accidentally ingest foreign objects, like wire or nails. Any piece of hardware left in the field becomes their dangerous buffet. Therefore, the condition is called Hardware Disease or medically speaking, traumatic reticuloperitonitis.

Mr. Parker leaned against a locust post and his eyes started to glaze over, but I pressed bravely on, speaking louder and faster. The foreign object goes down into the reticulum, which is one section of the cow's stomach. The grinding motion of digestion causes the metal to stab through the wall of the reticulum—ingesta and bacteria leak out into space around the heart called the pericardial sac. An infection ensues. The body tries to protect itself from the intruder by laying down a scar-tissue-like substance called fibrin or by creating an abscess or adhesion. Fibrin, abscesses, and adhesions are restrictive sentinels to have milling around one's heart. It is painful as well. Upon auscultation, the heart sounds muffled and far away. When the heart is not free to function as it was designed, the cow becomes unthrifty. Weight loss, depression, hemorrhage, and sudden death can be the end result.

Seeing that his eyes were now completely shut, and there was a slight rumble that a less confident vet might call a snore, I stopped and cleared my throat loudly. I thought of Will Rogers quote, "When you find yourself in a hole, stop digging."

Scratching his head, Mr. Parker said, "You done said a lot of big words in there, Doc. I'm just a plain farmer and part-time preacher, so's I needs some explain'n."

"Have you heard of putting magnets in cows?" I asked, knowing that if he hadn't, I was about to really lose him.

"Yep, my buddy does, puts in 'em in his cows hisself, but I ain't never done it," he replied. "What's a magnet do, anyways, Doc?"

"Prophylactic or preventive administration of the magnets is done in calves, and the magnet stays in the stomach or reticulum for the lifetime of the calf. When any metal object is ingested, it sticks to the magnet and the metal isn't free to float around to puncture through the stomach to the heart. The block magnet, about four inches long and an inch thick, is put in a bolus gun, a device designed to encourage cows to swallow big pills or boluses. This is usually done when the calves are six months to a year old. Research shows these save lives by binding up most of the hardware onto the magnet, thus preventing the puncture," I said, concluding my lecture with pride.

"Well, me buddy sticks magnets in his herd, so I reckon I will, too." After a pensive moment, he asked, "So you means to tells me that all these cows I see grazing in the fields of Virginia have magnets in their stomachs?"

"Yes, if they are well-managed," I said.

"So," he continued smiling, "you means to tells me, if I found a really big piece of metal and drove down the side of the road I could suck out all the cows out of a field?"

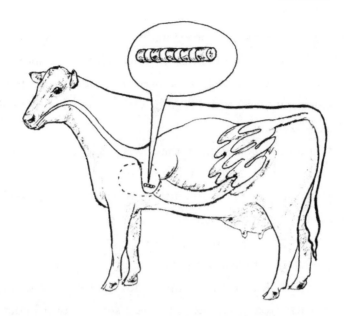

"Doubtful, but it would make a great *Far Side* cartoon!" I laughed.

"One way to diagnose if your cow has Hardware Disease is to do a grunt test, by putting pressure where it hurts. I am going to stand on one side of the cow, and you stand on the other. We will slip a board under her belly and lift it up under her heart girth, behind her front legs. If the cow feels pain from the scar tissue or metal, the pressure of us pulling the board up will hurt, and she will let out a grunt. That is a positive response to the test. Do you have a long two-by-four board around here?" I asked confidently as if I had been performing the test all my life, even though I had never seen Hardware Disease before or performed a test.

"I don't throw nothin' away. I'll fetch ya one," he yelled over his shoulder as he passed a discarded clothes dryer and broken toilet seat on his way to a disheveled lumber pile. He returned in short order with a two-by-four.

"I think this 'un will just 'bout reach from side to side under this here skinny cow," he said, pleased with his find.

He stuck his part of the board under the cow leaving me to walk around to the other side and fish under her belly for the short end, as she shifted her feet nervously and moved from side to side. I grabbed it and pulled it up level with his end, "On the count of three, lift up pretty hard—one, two, three."

As the pressure elicited pain, the cow let out a distinct grunt and shot out her hind leg. Her hoof, like a cannonball, slammed into my shin. My face blanched pale, and little white stars were dancing before my eyes as I dropped the board and staggered back. "Dang it!" I said, straightening up and swallowing the other four-letter words the pain brought to my lips. I pushed my index finger hard under the bottom of my nose, a trick I learned in my tumultuous childhood, to keep back any tears of pain. Gingerly, I took a step to see if I could put weight on it. After a few steps, I surmised that it wasn't broken.

Seeing that I was okay, Mr. Parker said, with a fried-chicken-eating grin, "That's a double positive result, huh, Doc?"

"Yeah, that is what I call the black-and-blue response! It is actually more accurate than just a grunt!" I said, catching my breath and regaining my composure.

"I reckon there ain't much to do for her now, is there Doc?"

"Not short of open-heart surgery, I'm afraid, but we can stick a magnet in and give her some antibiotics and see how she does. It would be good to put magnets in your cattle and clean up your field," I said, limping back to my truck. Resisting the urge to look at my injury in front of Mr. Parker, I grabbed my bolus gun and a magnet and walked back to the cow. "Let me show you how to put this in, so you can prevent the rest of your herd from getting Hardware Disease," I said, putting some lubrication on the magnet and gently thrusting it down the old wench's throat. "Don't jam the end down too hard because you can cause damage. Just slide it in and push the plunger so the magnet goes back far enough that she swallows it."

"The magnet. That'll preach," he said.

"Excuse me?" I responded puzzled.

"Well, Doc, I'm a lay preacher in the valley. I was just thinking that my flock is like this here cow. They swallows up a hardware store full of life's hurts, divorce, job loss, and kids on drugs. It scrapes up their hearts, making 'em tough and scarred over, so they ain't too thrifty. But, God's love is so powerful. He's like a healing magnet, pulling out the nails and drawing us to Him."

Somehow irritated at the mention of his faith and wounds in the same sentence, I laughed at him and slipped another magnet into his big hand. "Right," I said sarcastically. "Here is a visual aid for you; hold that one up in your sermon and call it a Jesus magnet."

I started to head back to my truck, but he looked at me with such a sincere appreciation that I suddenly regretted the remark. Something in his old blue eyes lingered in mine. Something transcendent, powerful, deep, and compassionate that cut to my spine and saw my own scarred heart.

"Doc, maybe you needs a Jesus magnet," he said, as if he saw stray nails embedded in me from my abusive past and my mother's alcoholic death. Caught off guard by his perception and the tenderness in his voice, my acerbic wit failed me. I walked away from him to my truck, tallied up the bill, gave it to him and waited while he went to his house and wrote me a check. I knew he was right, and it made me think of Flannery O'Connor's quote engraved upon the wall at the *Chicago Tribune,* "The truth does not change according to our ability to stomach it."

Pulling up my pants leg, I was amazed at the palette of blues and reds that were already being painted on the swelling goose egg on my shin. Our body's reaction to injury is quite colorful. I wondered what would become of the old cow that inflicted this kaleidoscopic knot. She certainly had enough energy to give me a wallop, but her prognosis was poor, and she would probably be slaughtered soon. Her body's effort to protect itself and lay down scar tissue initially protected her heart. But in the end, it was this protective scar tissue, with its stringy fibrin and adhesions that muffled and constricted the old girl's heart and caused her to waste away, eventually killing her. I harbored no malice toward her. I hurt her with the two-by-four, and she responded in her own defense. Wouldn't I do the same thing if someone put pressure on a nail that was scraping my pericardium? Even my reaction to the old preacher getting too close to my pain elicited a sarcastic response. From an early age, I learned to fortify myself against the pain in my own life. I was casehardened, a survivor. Growing up, my sister called me "brat," and, putting a finer point on my defensiveness, my horse trainer said I was as mean as cat sh-t. Coming to Christ certainly softened much anger, but I still had a long way to go.

I pondered my leathery persona more deeply. I was reading John Eldredge's book, *Waking the Dead.* In it is a quote by Saint Irenaeus: "The Glory of God is a man fully alive," that stirred my somnolent heart. What did it mean to live fully from my heart? I was so far removed, I honestly had no idea. I knew I erected walls of fear and protection. Perhaps I had Hardware Disease.

The barnyard of my childhood was littered with rusty barbed wire, stray nails, and sharp objects: my father's narcissistic abuse, the powerlessness of molestation, and my mother's alcoholic neglect and death. I was force-fed hardware. There was no safe pasture for my child's heart, no magnet to prevent the wounds. My only source of comfort was my pets. But, hadn't the protective layer of toughness with which I coated my heart enabled me to survive?

The week before class, I went to a book discussion on *Breaking Free* by Beth Moore. Her words about how we have empty places in our lives from "a love lost or a love withheld," haunted me. Between the kids and work, however, I could stay busy enough to avoid thinking about this—until now. Recalling her words, I felt their verity rattle something deep within me. Certainly, in the past, I met these holy desires for love in inappropriate ways, but had I ever really allowed God Himself to love me fully? Trying to control the strangeness of my rising emotions, I exhaled, took a deep swig of my old coffee, and realized I was gripping my steering wheel with white knuckles. I laughed at myself and remembered the funny thing that Moore said in the study, "Denial is not a river in Egypt." Well, maybe not for her, but avoiding dealing deeply with my past issues worked well for me so far, I sniggered.

Humor always helped me scuttle away from feelings too painful for me to hold at the moment. The reverberating emotions that rose in my heart made me feel uncomfortable and out of control. *Surely too much soul-searching cannot be good for the soul,* I thought, deflecting further, pondering why the old man's words about God's love caused me to become so introspective.

Still waiting in the truck, my self-condemning voice rose up, *What on earth could take one man so long to write a check! What is wrong with me? Here I am going be a missionary vet in Bolivia, and I can't even absorb some country preacher's words about Jesus taking the pain from my past.* It would take me years to let Him heal those wounds and learn that true Christ followers are, as Henry Nouwen's book is named, *Wounded Healers.*

A spark of dissatisfaction pierced through the scar tissue that was protecting my heart and numbing my emotions. That day I diagnosed

Hardware Disease in the cow and myself, starting me on a journey to live with my heart more fully alive. As Dan Allender says in his book, *Wounded Heart:*

> What is the point in pursuing firm hope and lively joy? The answer is simple: to live out the gospel. The reason for entering the struggle is a desire for more, a taste of what life and love could be if freed from the dark memories and deep shame. No one leaves the lethargy of denial unless there is a spark of discontent that pierces the darkness of daily numbness. To live significantly less than what one was made to be is as severe a betrayal of the soul as the original abuse.

I looked up at the sound of the screen door slamming and the old preacher ambling toward my truck. "Couldn't find my checkbook at first," he said apologizing for the delay. He handed me the check, paused by my door, and said, "Remember the Jesus magnet, Doc. He is the Lover of your soul."

His words fired a synapse in my soul, and I stroked my arms patting down the goose bumps. His compassionate gaze calmed my ricocheting emotions. I felt the embrace of the Lover of my soul. God's deep love, like a magnet's attraction, was drawing out my pain.

It was time to go to my next appointment. I nodded my thanks, and I drove back down the driveway. I watched him grow small in my rearview mirror, still holding the magnet as my dust settled around him—and His peace settled around me.

CHAPTER 6
A CASE OF MISTAKEN IDENTITY

Be an organ donor; give your heart to Jesus.

—Anonymous

As I pulled out of the driveway, my pager went off: "Cow dystocia, Mr. Russell." A cow was having trouble delivering her calf. Since I was driving down a mountain, I waited a minute until I could talk on the CB radio without wrecking and prayed that one of the better cow vets would take the call.

The pager went off again: "Horse colic."

Thank you, Lord, I will take that one. I radioed back, "503 to 500."

"Stand by," was the reply. "Go ahead 503," Beulah replied from the office radio.

"I'll take the colic," I said, glad not to go to a calving disaster.

"Dr. Healer just walked in, and she said she will do the colic, but no one has picked up the dystocia."

In our heart of hearts, Dr. Healer and I were both horse vets, not cow vets. She once told me that the sum total of her cow vet theology, "If it is hanging out, push it in. If it is in and supposed to be out, pull it out. If the cow is down, get it up."

In fact, that takes care of 90 percent of all bovine emergencies: prolapse, dystocia, and down cows. I know she was glad she was going to the horse colic. Helping with calving is physically grueling and usually ends badly, as half the farmers have tried everything, including pulling the calf with a John Deere tractor, before calling the vet.

"Are there directions in the log for Mr. Russell's?" I asked.

"No, but you are pretty close," Beulah replied.

"I'll call the farmer and get directions then," I said.

"10–4," she said.

I called him, but he sounded muddled. He gave a jumbled set of directions and then finally said, "Doc, you better ask somebody else. I'm not much on giving directions."

"No problem, sir. I can call the office."

Calling in, I asked, "Is Mr. Russell crazy or just old?"

"Just old," Beulah said, "Dr. A is right here; he'll give 'em to you."

It turns out I was only ten minutes away, so once I wrote the directions down, I headed off to pull the calf.

We don't ever buy a cup of coffee; we only rent it. My rent was now due from my 7 a.m. cup, and I needed a place to make a payment. I whipped into a country store, but there was a sign that read, "No Public Restrooms," so I drove to Mr. Russell's. As I pulled up in the gravel driveway, I saw through the screen door an older couple seated at the kitchen table. I got out, rapped on the door, and asked, "Mr. Russell?"

"Yep, come on in," he said, with a lovely, southwestern Virginia drawl.

"Hello, I'm Dr. McDonald."

"Nice to meet ya," he said extending his weather-beaten hand. "This here's my wife, Lurinda."

"It is nice to meet you," I said as I shook her flour-dusted hand.

The farmer took another bite of his sandwich unhurriedly. I saw he was in no rush, and I needed to make my bladder gladder. "Maybe I could use your restroom while you finish your lunch?" I asked.

"Sure thing, honey," Lurinda said, leading me down the hall. A copy of the *Daily Bread* devotional sat on the back of the pink toilet, and I skimmed that day's Bible verse to find strength for the job ahead.

"It sure smells good in here," I said as I walked back to the kitchen. The savory aroma of chicken boiling with spices on the stove filled the room.

The husband said, "Yep, Lurinda makes a mean chicken and dumplings from scratch."

"It will be ready by dinnertime if you want some," she said.

He took another slow bite from his sandwich. I crossed my arms and shifted my left foot over my right, anxious to get the calf out before it died, if it wasn't dead already.

"Guess we better go pull that calf," I said.

His wife looked at me quizzically, "Calf? What calf? We don't have any cows."

I looked to the husband, hoping that perhaps he was hiding the fact that he had cows from his wife.

"Nope, sold 'em all a few years ago. Just too old to mess with 'em," he said.

"But I received a call from a Mr. Russell whose cow was having trouble calving."

"Oh, that's my brother. He's the next driveway."

"Thanks for the bathroom. Sorry for the inconvenience," I said hotfooting it out the door. Minutes can make the difference between life and death for the calf, and here I'd just lost five minutes. Pulling up to the brother's farm, I saw his wife on the porch. "Sorry, I stopped at the other Mr. Russell's."

She laughed and pointed me to the pasture where her husband was waiting anxiously for me at the gate.

The cow was loose, and I could see something hanging out. I thought perhaps she already calved, but no such luck. He didn't have a head catch but we herded her into a small pen and dragged a rusty metal gate across the opening. This must be the older one, I thought to myself, as he was frailer than his brother.

"I've got a bit of trouble with my ticker," he said, a nice way of telling me I was on my own as far as catching and securing this cow. I walked around the pen and pushed on all the posts. All but one was too wobbly to hold a cow. I made a big loop with the end of the lasso and dropped it over her head. It fell off an ear. She swung around every time I missed and chased me over the fence. Finally, I got it around her neck and snubbed her to the post, but the rope was too long and gave her enough room to run back and forth sideways. If she did this while I had my arm inside her, she could break it.

"Sir, can you tighten the rope so her head is snubbed up against the fence when I get her closer?" She tried to kick the fat out of me, but in doing so, she ran closer to the post. And that got her still enough for me to palpate her. I gloved up with plenty of lube and stuck my arm in the birth canal. The calf was right there with the two front feet pointing out like they should. I stuck my arm in a bit farther. *Where was the head and why isn't the calf moving?* I reached in up past my elbow and felt the head turned back, twisted toward the tail. *These are tough to get right, and I may have to cut the head off,* I thought to myself.

"It's stuck because its head is turned back. I don't feel any movement. I think the calf's dead. I need to push it back inside to make enough room to turn the head around so that it can come out straight," I said as I pushed. Her contractions were working against me. With each contraction, my arm was crushed against her pelvis. The hot August sun was merciless, and sweat was popping out like BBs on my upper lip. I needed to stop these contractions, or I wouldn't get anywhere.

Pulling off my palpation sleeves I wiped my brow. A dark wet ring of perspiration, manure, and placental fluid stained the front of my shirt around my middle, and I felt beads of sweat trickle down my back. Quickly scrubbing the top of her spine, I cranked the tail up, found the divot and stuck the needle in for the epidural. I put a few drops of Lidocaine in the hub of the needle, and it was sucked into the epidural space. I injected 5 cc to stop the contractions. It went in smoothly.

Stepping back to my vet truck, I grabbed the chains and calf-jack. After assembling the long steel pole to the winch, I headed to the cow. The pen was not in regular use and thorny blackberry bushes lined the inside. Now, with the contractions stopped, I repulsed the calf's body back, and after ten minutes of intense effort, I managed to straighten out the head. Then I fastened chains on both legs, still slippery with amniotic fluid. To check if the calf was alive, I stuck my finger in its eye; it was unresponsive.

"I'm pretty sure the calf is dead."

The farmer just nodded grimly. The heat was getting to him.

I pulled but to no avail. I couldn't get the calf to budge, which meant I had to use the jack. The problem was that the cow was positioned with her butt against the fence, and I couldn't get the ten-foot-long calf jack attached to the chains on the calf. After much maneuvering, I finally got the cow moved, chains hooked up, and started cranking. She leaned forward into the dilapidated wooden fence in front of her—and then it broke. Down she fell through the splintering boards onto her knees. I kept cranking the calf jack. The calf was halfway out, and if it was alive, I wanted to get it out as fast as I could so it wouldn't asphyxiate. If the umbilical cord got squeezed against the cow's bony pelvic rim, the blood flow to the calf could stop.

The calf's head and shoulders were out, but now the cow was down, and the lasso tightened. She was choking to death.

From my position in the rear, I could see her eyes bugging out. I asked the farmer to loosen the rope, but it was so tight against the post that he couldn't. Now the cow was in respiratory distress.

I stopped pulling the calf and tried to get the rope off the cow, but it had twisted on itself, and the quick-release knot was not coming loose. The weight of the cow hanging herself made it impossible to get the knot untied. I asked the farmer to use his knife. Finally freed from her death noose, the cow's head dropped, and she gasped for air and fell the rest of the way to the ground.

Racing back to the calf, I didn't have room to pull any more with the jack, so I asked the farmer to help me by pulling a leg. The calf was almost out. We both pulled. With a last big heave, the calf came out. I flew backward and landed in the blackberries, a thorn embedding deeply into the plump flesh of my thumb. It was a big calf, but still. No corneal reflex. Dead.

It was covered with meconium, which is the first feces that is expelled in the womb if the calf is in distress, telling me it had been stressed and probably dead for a while, maybe even before I got the page. She was a lovely heifer, and her body was still warm. It made me sad.

The farmer tried to tickle her nostrils with some grass to get her to breathe, but it was no use. I should have done more heroics, but I knew she was dead, and I didn't have any strength left to throw her over the fence and pretend to resuscitate.

Mr. Russell said, "It was a nice calf."

I said, "No, maybe it was going to turn out to be a bad calf, a mean one," trying to lighten the mood.

"Yeah, maybe it would have hurt someone." He rubbed his chin.

Then I said, "It was a nice, big calf, though. I'm sorry."

"Happens," was all he said.

I palpated the cow to make sure there wasn't a twin. Nope, empty. The cow was still lying down on the rump brace of my calf jack, and when I tried to get her to move over, she jumped up. I would have liked to put some iodine boluses in her and given her a bottle of calcium to prevent a retained placenta, but she was up and wild. I knew there wasn't a sturdy post left in the pen to snub her to, so I heaved the gate away and let her go.

I helped the farmer drag the dead calf out to the woods for the scavenging coyotes and buzzards to eat. The cow stopped at the water trough to cool her parched half-strangled throat and watched us drag her dead calf away. I wondered what she was thinking.

Together, we walked up to the old farmer's house, slow like we were leaving a funeral. I was soaked through to my bra with placental fluid, meconium, and my own sweat.

"You want to come in for a pop?" Mr. Russell asked.

I was as thirsty as the cow. "Sure, but I'll just sit out here on your porch, if that's all right."

"Do you want a donut?" his wife asked through the screen door.

"Please," I said. My blood sugar was spent. She served it to me in a bowl with a fork and a crème soda.

"I saw you out there, dear," she said to her husband. "What were you doing in that hot sun? You have heart surgery next week."

"I'm fine," he said, popping a nitroglycerin pill.

"You didn't tell me you were having surgery," I said, alarmed.

"I'm fine," he smiled.

We sat in silence for a few minutes, both wiped out from the sun and strain. I pondered what I would have done if he had had a heart attack while we were pulling the calf. Noticing the bumper sticker on their Oldsmobile, "Be an organ donor. Give your heart to Jesus,"

I told them I liked it and that I was moving to Bolivia to be a veterinary missionary.

Catching me by surprise, he said, "I got saved when I went to church drunk."

Mrs. Russell replied, "Yeah, he used to drink something fierce."

"That pastor said Jesus would forgive my sins if I asked Him to come into my heart and change my life. Despite being drunk, I staggered to the altar. Crying, I knelt, asked for forgiveness, and gave my drunken butt to Jesus. The elders took me down to the basement and prayed out that drinking spirit's power that had ahold of me. I haven't had a drop since."

"Nope, not a drop in thirty years," his wife nodded with a smile as wide as the gates of Heaven.

"That's miraculous," I said.

"That is the power of the Holy Ghost. If I knowed the real Jesus I was running from, I would have gave my life to him a lot sooner. I guess it was a case of mistaken identity, just like you going to my brother's house today," he said retrieving something from the house.

I chuckled, recalling the brother and his chicken dumpling wife's expression when I asked where their cow was.

He walked back onto the porch with a Mr. Potato Head in his hand, "I used this teaching Sunday School last week. Lots of us build our image of God like He's a Mr. Potato head while sticking on a crooked set of eyeglasses and big nose. We don't take the time to read the Good Book and find out who God really is. There's lots of mistaken identity going around. If people knew the real God and the healing power of the Holy Ghost, everybody in the world would love Him. He's irresistible."

"Yep," I said wondering how accurate my view of God was. Plucking the last blackberry thorn from my arm, I rose and left, "Thanks for the donut and drink. Sorry about your calf. Make sure she sheds that afterbirth."

I was an hour from home, and it didn't take long for my sugar high to become a sugar low. I hadn't eaten anything decent all day, and I became "hangry," remembering I was on call until 7:30 in the morning. I got even grumpier when Mr. Russell's words drifted back into my mind, "I got saved when I went to church drunk."

I thought back to my own mother's struggle with the bottle and her senseless death from alcoholism when I was sixteen. Why didn't she know this powerful God that transformed Mr. Russell? She only knew the Jim Beam god, and he destroyed her life. Already low in spirits, the more I thought about it, the madder I got at God, "Why, Lord, did you help him and not my mother? In a stew, I nearly missed my exit home and honked at a person to get out of my way as if it were their fault. I drove home sulking, daring Him to call me out in the middle of the night for an emergency. I whined at God before my tired body pulled my brain into a fitful sleep.

As if God were giving me a peace offering, it was a quiet night with no calls to force me from my warm bed, except at 2 a.m., "Doc, you gotta come out!" A distraught woman on the other end of the line pleaded into the phone. I could barely understand her.

"Did you say your calf can't stand?" I asked, trying to clarify.

"Cat, my black tomcat is sick and won't get up," she cried.

"It could be a urinary blockage, but I'm sorry; we only treat large animals. You can take him to the emergency clinic in Christiansburg," I said, feeling badly for the women's cat but very happy to go back to sleep.

The next morning, I woke up at six, got ready for work, opened my journal, and wrote my rant to God. As I sat in silence, a Mr. Potato Head with big red frowning lips and black scowling eyebrows rolled into my head. *Is that my God?* I wondered.

I looked up descriptions of God in the Bible. God is love. God is good. God is faithful. Jesus wept. Jesus died. He forgives. Jesus saves. The Holy Spirit is our Counselor. He leads. He empowers. As I journaled, the pain faded like invisible ink. My mother made her choices, not God. My throat tightened, and tears came as I felt His holy love envelop me. He took my anger, confusion, and loss and held me in His compassionate embrace. I rolled the plastic frowning skull with the black eyebrows into my mind's furnace and watched it melt.

I thought back to my childhood bedlam and why I became a veterinarian. The Lover of my soul was always there, even when I didn't know it. He provided the pets that soothed my pain and brought me companionship during the dark times; beginning with the first batch of black puppies that swarmed me, tugging at my crooked braids and licking at my giggles with their warm milk breath.

PART II

THE EARLY YEARS

CHAPTER 7
SALISBURY, MARYLAND

"**D**o your Dream" was the motivational bumper sticker plastered on my desk when I was studying to get into veterinary school. I'd picked it up at the drug store next to the pediatrician's office when I was going through a spate of childhood illnesses with my son and daughter. It reminded me to hold fast to my lifelong aspirations. There are certain careers to which many children aspire, such as professional football players, cowboys, ballerinas, or veterinarians. But parents can't put in what God left out such as the ability and a passion strong enough to sustain them through the sacrifices necessary to attain the dream. I knew at an early age that I wanted to be a vet. However, I was slow getting there, taking a circuitous route. It would be four decades before I held my diploma.

People often ask me what made me want to be a vet. Was it the cuteness of a speckle-bellied pup, the warm purr of the family cat, or perhaps the gentle nicker of a pony greeting me from the stall? My answer is that all of these did coalesce into a deep affection for animals. But my first pet was neither warm nor soft.

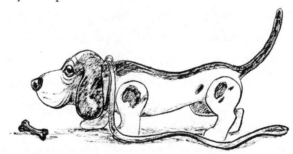

Gaylord was my first dog. He offered solace from my parents' thundery, gin-spiked marriage. Gaylord was a two-foot long, plastic, remote-controlled Basset hound, and I got him from my grandparents for Christmas when I was just four years old. Eventually, his little battery heart gave out, and his gear-driven brown legs seized up. When he stopped functioning, my parents held a funeral for him in our backyard with our neighbors in attendance. I cried as they threw the last shovelful of dirt into his sandy grave, the little pebbles making a tinkling sound as they slid down his plastic body. The neighbors stood solemnly at the graveside, sniffling softly into their beer cans. My family may have had its shortcomings, but being humorless wasn't one of them.

Our first family pet with a pulse was my mother's cat, Sam, a mean, tan tabby. He was not one to suffer fools gladly and often scratched the taste out of me when I dressed him in my sister's doll clothes. The next pet was my sister Jean's beautiful seal point Siamese cat named, originally enough, Baby. He was certifiably crazy, as Siamese cats can be, but lots of fun, so he fit in well with my family. Chasing my parents' cellophane cigarette wrappers around the room got Baby really throttled up. He would spring from the mantle and run across the tops of the wide picture frames around the room. My mother would run too, cursing and grabbing paintings before they crashed to the floor. And we wondered why she drank.

My own first pets with fur were Nappy (Napoleon Solo), a black-striped calico tom kitten, and Tilly, a black Lab-mix puppy. I loved them both with all my heart. When the emotional atmosphere in the house darkened with Dad and Mom fighting and drinking, I would wrap my arms around Tilly's neck and bury my face in the refuge of her warm, thick fur. She was always glad to be with me and provided a sense of escape and stability during the frightening chaos.

Otis Twilley, the landlord of the first house I remember, gave Tilly to me. The house was in Salisbury, Maryland, where we moved from Petersburg, Virginia, for my father's job with Texaco Corporation, shortly after I was born.

In addition to providing for four kids, my father spent his paychecks on gentlemanly pursuits—boats and bourbon. He could never save enough for a house, so we rented from Mr. Twilley, a widower who owned and operated the Otis Twilley Seed Company. He often visited for cocktail hour, or as my father called it, "Toddy Time." In those days, everyone dressed for the occasion. My mother would put on a cocktail dress and pearls. She reminded me of Lucille Ball when Ricky would come home.

I remember that Mr. Twilley was very kind to me. I guess he was lonely, so he let me hang around the greenhouse for some company. His only companion was a lovely black Lab who had a tryst with a local hound dog and as a result, she delivered a batch of puppies. They were the real reason I went to visit Mr. Twilley. It was pure puppy love for me, as I lay on the ground behind the greenhouse and let them flop all over me with their fat little speckled bellies, tugging my braids with their tiny teeth as they warmed my face with their milk breath. Mr. Twilley, having recently buried his own wife, perhaps felt sorry for me after attending Gaylord's funeral. Whatever the reason, he gave me one of the pups.

Mr. Twilley offered me kindness; he made me feel special, something I didn't receive at home, but that wasn't all—he also asked me to be on the cover of his spring seed catalog. That was affirmation I never knew before. For the photo shoot, dozens upon dozens of cantaloupes were stacked on shelves, creating a pyramid with a small opening in the middle. I stood behind the stack so that all you could see was my head. My dark brown hair stuck out in little pigtails all over my skull, and my fat baby cheeks gave my face the same shape as the melons. The 1963 cover of the Twilley Feed and Seed catalog was only of my head, right in the middle of a five-foot-high pyramid of hundreds of cantaloupes.

My southern father, never one to lose an opportunity for a racist slur, said, "Child, you look like a little pickaninny."

However, there was more affirmation when my budding modeling career grew exponentially when the size of my face went from one square-inch on the seed catalog cover to three feet tall on the back of Greyhound buses. Passionate about dogs, I was thrilled to have my picture taken with a real Greyhound for these nearly billboard-sized advertisements. In the 1960s, before air travel became affordable, the bus was the common man's mode of long-distance travel. Despite my own rickety family life, I was the face on the back of the buses, encouraging everyone to take a Greyhound bus to be with their relatives for the holidays.

Constant bouts of tonsillitis slowed my fledgling modeling career. Back then, the standard remedy was to yank out children's tonsils. I was tricked into having the surgery by my mother's promise of buckets of ice cream. All I got post-surgery was buckets of lime Jell-O and pain. I remember lying for days on the burgundy-and-white toile sofa in the formal living room with my cat, Nappy, and dog, Tilly, at my side, nursing me back to health while my mother nursed her cocktail in the kitchen and made more of the lime-green slime. Tilly stood guard beside the sofa, within arm's length, so I could caress her soft, black ears. I was a very active child, always running around with her nipping playfully at my heels. She did not understand her playmate's weakened condition but was there to protect me. Normally friendly to strangers and my siblings, now she would bark if anyone came to the door and even growled at my brother when he came too close to me. Naturally, this fierce protection endeared her to my heart even more, if that were possible. My sweet cat, Nappy, was constantly on the sofa with me, coiled up at my feet, keeping them warm and toasty. I was never alone with those two nursemaids looking after me.

My pets' warmth and companionship became a substitute for my parents' nurture. I have an old black-and-white Kodak photo of me at age four in my mother's lap. My two brown braids are frayed, and my bangs crooked. My lips are tight with determination. I am facing her, up on a knee, clinging to her dress and pulling myself nearer her chest, trying to climb into her heart, as it were, but it is out of reach. My dark, deep eyes reveal the parchedness of my thirsty soul. She sits in her satin cocktail dress, enduring my assault, sipping bourbon from a crystal tumbler, while grabbing for me with the other hand to keep me from falling. She was a sensitive woman, battered by a dangerous world and her own husband. She gave me all the love she had; it was not perfunctory, but it was scraped from the bottom of her own empty soul and was a paltry offering. I was like the starving African child, trying to suck from the flat breast of her emaciated mother.

My mother's psychoses and addictions occupied all the space in her soul. As an adult, I can understand that now, but as a small child, I merely felt lost, frightened, alone, and rejected. Her disposition was a bit jumpy to start with. After falling off a horse in college, she began to fear horses. Somewhere along the line, she also developed a terror of birds and would duck and run whenever one flew over her head. She had a minor car accident and never drove again. What for some people would be mere put-offs turned into phobias for her. Granted, it was World War II and every important male figure in her life was off fighting for his life and for our very existence. When the entire world is at war, that's reason enough to be jumpy.

Her fear of the world around her implanted itself firmly in her soul when, in high school, she received the news that her greatest hero, her father Colonel Alexander Quintard, was captured by the Japanese and was a prisoner of war.

Facing an uncertain financial future and with a gaping hole in her heart, my mother graduated from Mary Washington College. A year later, still struggling with not knowing if her father was alive, she met and married my silver-tongued father, a dashingly handsome man with an acerbic wit, a hot temper, and a job. He did a spell at William and Mary College before going into the US Navy and then working for Texaco. They had us four kids in rapid succession. By the time, I—the youngest—was born, the war was over and my grandfather had returned. Though he was over six feet tall, he weighed less than one hundred pounds, having survived the brutal Bataan Death March. By then, my mother was already deeply in the bottle, fighting depression and addiction to Valium, and still reeling from her older sister's suicide eleven months earlier.

Years later, I learned some of this background and understood that her depression and suicidal tendencies flowed through her veins as deeply as the iron ore in the red clay of her ancestral Powhatan County. The pain and mind-numbing elixir found its receptors deep in her soul. Her genetic predisposition for drink, like a tentacle from hell, would not loosen its grip for decades until it dragged her to an early grave.

Now, as an adult, I can understand a little of her pain, but I never fully learned what happened to shape my father's personality. I know now that he struggled with his own father's death the year before I was born, and at his mother's funeral, he told me that she never loved him and that a neighbor, not his own parents, named him Pierce.

This certainly explains why he was not a well-adjusted, loving husband or father. I can see that now, but as a helpless child, I could only see the anger and violence, and his love affair with Jack Daniels whiskey. He loved us as well as he could, but he was emotionally distant, volatile, and narcissistic. Animals became my consolation prize.

Their warm, unconditional love was my Balm of Gilead, the substitute for the parental love that I craved.

My tonsillectomy was followed by two more plagues, and the prolonged ill health and convalescence brought me even closer to my pets. The week following my tonsillectomy, I had an itchy rash, then clusters of blisters covering my entire body. It was chicken pox, which focused mainly on my face and back. The prickly, intense itch made me want to ask Job for a shard of his broken pottery to scratch myself.

Following on the heels of chicken pox, I got the mumps. With lymph nodes under my chin swollen to the size of grapefruits, my father called me Mama Cass, after the great, jowled singer who was the star of The Mamas & the Papas band. While my father and siblings mocked me, Nappy and Tilly were my constant companions. When I was at my lowest point, wondering if I would ever enjoy good health again, Tilly crawled up on the sofa and sat scrunched up beside me, looking into my face with her anxious brown eyes of concern. She licked my swollen cheeks with her wet, pink tongue. Then she burped a big, smelly dog burp right in my face. It was just the sort of bathroom humor that five-year-olds love, and it brought the first smile to my face in months. I hugged her close. Through my afflictions, a bonding happened in my soul. My pets took care of me, and I would take care of them. That's when I decided that when I grew up, I would become a veterinarian.

Looking like an early childhood disease poster child, my fledgling modeling career flamed out as quickly as it began, just a year after my cover girl shot on the seed catalog. That same year, Texaco transferred my father from Salisbury to Annapolis, Maryland. When we moved, I experienced loss for the first time, and my little heart was broken.

CHAPTER 8
WILD ROSE SHORES–ANNAPOLIS, MARYLAND

*Outside of a dog, a book is man's best friend. Inside of a dog it's too
dark to read.*

—Groucho Marx

*What fairy tales give the child is his first clear idea of the possible defeat
of bogey. The baby has known the dragon intimately ever since he had
an imagination. What the fairy tale provides for him is a St. George to
kill the dragon.*

—G. K. Chesterton

The moving men slowly backed up the green-and-yellow Mayflower
truck to our Salisbury rental house. They carried the ramp to the
front door and neatly loaded all our worldly goods into the van. All
our possessions, except the two things that my sister and I loved the
most: my sister Catherine's doll house, made by our grandfather just
for her; and my beloved dog Tilly. My father left them both on the
curb. He said there wasn't room for them and to stop bellyaching or
we would get the belt.

I was five years old and powerless to voice any objection, but that
was the moment I developed a bleeding heart for abandoned dogs—
and a hardened heart toward my parents. For years after that move,
I collected stuffed animals and lined them up on my dresser like an
altar, with candles and flowers. I prayed for all discarded animals and
for Tilly, that she didn't starve and wasn't standing out in the sleeting
rain shivering with her little black tail curled between her hind legs,
and I sobbed into my pillow.

The move to Annapolis was painful, but I quickly grew to love the place. We rented a house in an older neighborhood called Wild Rose Shores that sprang up along the salty shores of the lovely Aberdeen Creek. The depth and movement of God's creation opened my soul to a whole new world that brought peace to my heart and soothed the pain of missing my Tilly. Our rental house was a stone's throw from the water and had its own small dock. It was my first experience with the ebb and flow of tides and marine life. I treasured sitting on the dock and watching the tide go out. The fiddler crabs, sensing my presence, scurried into their wet, muddy holes, while the green-grey snails slowly slimed their way up the cattail stems.

Being on the creek to the South River that empties into the Chesapeake Bay fueled my adventuresome spirit, and I grew to love everything about the water. My brother Pete taught me how to skip stones on the creek. He was a good instructor, beginning with oyster shells—even a dog can skip an oyster shell—then working up to flat stones. I was athletic, and he taught me to compete, to play ball, to crab, to fish, and to survive. His love and attention filled the vacuum in my heart left by my parent's lack of emotional nurture and began to shape a seamless gender identity in me. I found that boy's games were a lot more fun than girl's games. My sister Jean and I were opposites. She had a Barbie set, and she and her friends would stay inside and play dolls for hours on end. Ordinarily, I wasn't included in their "big girl" play, but one rainy day, Mom made Jean let me join them. Jean and I didn't get along so well, not since she made mud pies in her Hostess Easy Bake oven and then told me how good they tasted and made me take a big bite. On this day, she gave me the job of putting on Barbie's shoes. I tried cramming the tiny, deformed foot into the pink high-heeled shoes, unsuccessfully. Wedging her stiff feet into her shoes takes expertise and practice, neither of which I had. Jean laughed at my clumsiness, and so did her friends. Embarrassed, I threw the Barbie across the room.

On my next birthday, I asked for a GI Joe. This early swap in gender roles, from the more peg-holed girl and boy roles, dissolved any boundary lines in my mind regarding what I could or should be doing versus what I wanted to do or was capable of accomplishing. It is an attitude that has served me well in the less traditional role of becoming a large-animal veterinarian, which in the past was a male-only field.

I preferred the fresh salt air and the beauty of the creek. I needed space to run and play, and my accepting and doting brother was better company than my sister and her friends. The atmosphere inside our house tended to be chaotic and stressful, so I escaped outside as often as I could. But things were not always tense, and I have happy memories of many summer outings motorboating with my parents up to Mike's Crab House.

My father bought a small wooden Chris-Craft boat with a black outboard Mercury motor that he kept tied to the dock by our house. On Saturday nights, my siblings went out with their friends, but I got in the boat with Mom and Dad and headed to the crab house that was built on top of a dock on the South River. The first smell that greeted us as we tied up the boat was the fresh garlic bread coming right out of the oven. We sat at newspaper-covered picnic tables, and as my feet dangled from the bench under the table, I loved seeing the green water between the spaces of the dock boards lapping against the pilings. It all seemed quite swashbuckling, arriving by boat to eat on a pier with no real floor beneath us. I pictured myself as a pirate and loved the adventure.

Our parents taught us the art of "picking," that is, of getting the meat out of the hard-shelled crabs, using wooden mallets to crack the claws and rusty metal crab knives to dig out the hidden meat. We picked blue crabs by the bushel. After a short swim in drawn butter, the succulent white meat took a quick dip in the little hills of Old Bay seasoning we sprinkled on the newspaper before being savored in our mouths.

Like many alcoholics, my mother had a sweet and tender side within her, as well as many good qualities. Unfortunately, these were often submerged in a sea of bourbon where our relationship could not swim. Seeking her approval, I found food was a common ground where we connected. We shared an epicurean camaraderie in eating the slocum, the yellow-green goop in the edges of the top shells. After poking through the thin, brown membrane in the corners of the shell, we scooped out the bounty and, with a quick finger flick from shell to mouth, happily slurped it up. The silky pâté of the sea looked, smelled, and tasted like it had been drawn from the murky depths of the Chesapeake Bay. Slocum, Limburger cheese, and liver were delicacies that my mother and I alone truly appreciated. The rest of my family lacked our silver palates and scorned our sense of taste. This affinity created a special bond between us, one that I would lose just ten years later. Her passing left me with a raw, lonely vacuum in my soul, and with no female model, I was left to piece together my own feminine identity.

It just isn't anyone you can eat Limburger cheese, liver, and slocum with, and even if you could find that unique person with the same taste buds, no one could ever replace the warm smiles and love shared by a mother and her daughter.

My mother seemed to enjoy my company because we liked the same foods. My father, on the other hand, only seemed to enjoy me when I was performing for him, like when we took the boat home after the crab dinner. I was quick and nimble, so Dad had me jump from the boat onto the pier as he docked. Grabbing the bow line he tossed, I would secure the boat to the cleat on the piling. Dad's confidence in my performance made my little heart swell with pride and started me down the slippery path of equating what I did with who I was. Performing for his love, instead of being accepted for just being me, was yet another factor that drove me to my pets, who loved me unconditionally.

My parents did give me an appreciation for the water; they also helped me to develop a good sense of humor. Our family's sense of humor was unsurpassed, and to this day, my siblings can make me laugh harder than anyone else in this world. Sarcasm ruled, and my father, with his acerbic wit, was the life of every cocktail party. My mother no doubt developed her sense of humor to fight the bouts of depression that often darkened her mood. Her lightning fast, funny responses to life's situations were brilliant. For some reason, fear was funny, and scaring people made us laugh the hardest. And my father, whether telling us ghost stories or pulling pranks on someone, was the master.

But the vein of cruelty in my parents' wit brought me sympathy for those who were fearful or humiliated. A few weeks after a Crab Shack outing, my mother called me into the living room. In those days, children needed permission to enter this room. Formal living rooms were like museums and smelled of lemon Pledge.

As I obeyed my mother's call and bounded into the room, a life-sized gorilla came roaring after me. Terrified, I threw the stuffed mouse I was playing with as hard as I could at him and ran out of the house, wetting my pants in the process. It was my father in a gorilla suit, and he scared the bejesus out of me. I felt alone and made fun of by the very ones who were supposed to be protecting me.

It turns out that scaring the snot out of me was the dress rehearsal for another prank with the gorilla suit planned for the weekend. It was Pete's birthday, so the whole family boated to the Crab Shack. When the Schlitz Malt Liquor was overserved, Dad pulled out the gorilla mask he had stuffed in Mom's pocketbook. He watched the waiter clear the table beside us. This dark ebony-skinned man in his once-crisp white apron and white hat bussed tables for years at this crab house and masterfully piled the shells, empty bottles, and soiled newspaper two feet high on his big tray.

Waiting until the waiter's back was turned, Dad donned the life-sized gorilla mask, then said, "Hey boy, get me another beer!"

"Yessira," the waiter replied slowly, sweat dripping off his powerful biceps as he turned around and got a full view of the gorilla within arm's length of him.

How a big, old, black man could move as fast as he did, I don't know, but it was as if he saw a haunt. All we could see was the whites of his eyes and the tray flipping heavenward as he made haste off the dock! We were all covered in crab carcasses and stale beer, but we didn't care because we were dying laughing. I, however, felt mixed emotions. I knew the same terror and the resulting shame of being tricked by that gorilla.

After that night, Dad was *persona non grata* for a while at the crab house, so we caught our own crabs off the dock by our house. We tied chicken necks to a string fastened to the dock and let them hang into the green salt water. Periodically, we checked the string to see if there was any tension. If there was, we slowly pulled the line in and scooped up the crab with a net. Crabs were plentiful back then, and several hours of crabbing yielded a bushel, enough for our family. Mom would boil them in water with Old Bay and a bottle of Schlitz malt liquor added for flavor. We cooked shrimp the same way. Our cats, Sam, Nappy, and Baby, sat under the table and batted our legs with their paws until we gave them some. Now that I had no dog, I bonded more closely with the cats, secretly slipping them seafood morsels.

Besides crabbing, we also fished off the dock. This pastime led to a decisive event in my life. A week after our big crab catch, Sam came up to the house with fishing line hanging out of his mouth. He swallowed the baited hook that I must have left on the dock. After blaming me and cussing me out, Dad took Sam to the vet for surgery. He didn't want to pay for Sam to stay overnight so he brought him back heavily sedated. In 1965, cat anesthesia wasn't as safe as it is today, and Sam was administered a whopping dose. Dad left Sam in my charge and told me to pump his heart if it stopped. That was a heavy responsibility for my little six-year-old shoulders, and I was petrified Sam would die. But I took my job seriously, watching him like a hawk and gently shaking him every now and then to make sure he was still alive. I didn't really know what to do if his heart stopped beating, but there I sat, eyes glued to his chest watching it rhythmically rise and fall with every breath. This went on for hours until he came fully out of the sedation. Seeing him so helpless and feeling that if he died it was my fault, deepened my desire to help animals. It was my first vet case, and I was sure I wanted to be a veterinarian.

Despite my renewed closeness to cats, I still missed my dog, so when a dirty, charcoal-colored poodle wandered up to our doorstep, I was thrilled. The name *poodle* comes from the low-German word *pudel* for "splashing about," and judging by his matted hair, he had been splashing about in the creek, no doubt going after ducks. Dad took a liking to him, started feeding him, and named him Charlie.

Charlie's black, curly hair was not clipped, and he was full of cockleburs. I decided to comb out all the tangles and debris, so it would be soft and wavy. When I approached him, Charlie started panting, hunched his back, lowered his tail, and cowered in the corner. Avoiding all eye contact, he looked for an escape route, yawning to reduce the tension. Sensing his nervousness, I tried to cuddle with him like I did with Tilly. But he panicked and snapped at me, drawing blood as he scraped his white teeth across the soft skin of my tanned forearm. No doubt he was poorly socialized and tossed out in our neighborhood because of his unpredictable temperament. Some abused dogs panic when humans get too close, and the only way they can communicate their fear and tell people to back off is to bite. Dogs become fear-biters in their formative puppyhood if they experience trauma during the fear-imprint stage, at eight weeks to sixteen weeks. Contrary to what people would assume, these are usually the more sensitive, tender-hearted dogs, not mean dogs.

I loved him and took care of Charlie, but he disliked children and bonded with Dad, who gave him countless table scraps and affection. Charlie liked to doze off at his feet while Dad watched the popular comedy, *The Honeymooners*. It was the 1960s, and men were supposed to be strong and rough, ruling their households with an iron fist. A man who pantomimed slugging his wife was considered funny, and this made *The Honeymooners* the hit comedy of the day. In one episode, Jackie Gleason, who played the starring role of the husband, threatened to knock his wife to the moon. "Send her to the moon!" Dad yelled, startling Charlie from his nap. The dog leaped up and bit my father, and my father grabbed the wine glass on the floor next to his armchair and threw it with all his might at Charlie. The glass smashed against the sliding glass door and shattered. I was terrified he was going to kill Charlie. Bolting through the door, I ran out with Charlie to safety.

A few weeks later, on a hot summer day, Dad returned from the liquor store and said he accidentally left Charlie too long in the car, and when he came out, the dog was dead. In disbelief, I ran to the dock with my stuffed dog and wept bitterly into his cloth side. I sat there for hours looking out over the peaceful green creek. Then the wind picked up, the water became choppy, and whitecaps started forming on the creek. A storm was whipping up, not only on the water but also in my father.

Dad loved Charlie, and that night he drank to dull the pain of his own murderous negligence. Mom had hidden some of the whiskey, and he wanted it. She held out, even after he got his belt and started beating her. I cried as I heard the arguing and slaps, powerless to stop it. I was the only child at home that night, and he called me in as a playing piece. He smacked Mom around in front of me and then did the unimaginable: he pulled out his .45-magnum pistol and threatened to shoot her if she didn't tell him where the booze was. I clung to her leg, begging her to tell him, pleading for him not to kill her, and trying to run interference from the belt. Mom was strong in her own way and never would back down if he wasn't torturing me as well. She finally gave him the booze, and I fled the room, my soul terrorized. This event, coupled with the second canine tragedy in my own formative puppy years, caused me to become a fear-biter: distrustful, edgy, hypervigilant, lashing out at the unsafe, confusing world around me, and protecting what was left of my tender soul from anyone who got too close. I was becoming a tough survivor but at the cost of a calloused heart.

My childhood was like a checker game, with the pieces of red happy memories and the black sad pieces constantly jumping one another. The following week was my birthday, and Dad and Mom took us to the Chesapeake Bay Inn. This was a lovely historic inn with white tablecloths, candles, and warm yeast rolls. Everyone ordered steaks except for me. I ordered the buffalo burger because I loved the wild spirit of the banshee. On reflection, I'm sure the burger was just a regular hamburger off the child's menu, but back then I felt empowered, like I drank the blood and ate the flesh of a real buffalo. I fantasized about galloping bareback on a horse across the plains. I was an "Injin!"

The week after Charlie's death, we drove to Powhatan, Virginia, where my grandparents and cousins lived, and stayed at Medway, the sprawling white asbestos-sided house my grandfather built. While a prisoner of war, he dreamed of building Medway on the banks of the James River. At the end of World War II when freed from the Japanese prisoner-of-war camp, he broke ground, built the house, and put in a pond. It was secluded at the end of a long, wooded driveway and had a beautiful view out the front door clear across the river to Goochland County. Holidays and summertime always called us south to Medway. The woods, river, and fields of Medway, Jamie the Collie, his stray bride, Pocahontas, and the black tomcat, Chewnie, all breathed life into my wounded soul.

Granny showed her love to me by reading me poetry and fairy tales, such as Robert Louis Stevenson's, *A Child's Garden of Verses,* and Rudyard Kipling's *Jungle Book.* My favorite character was Kipling's Rikki-Tikki-Tavi, from the story of the Great War where Rikki-Tikki-Tavi, the red-eyed mongoose, fought, and single-handedly defeated the hooded Death Nag, the cobra, and his mate, Nagaina, saving the lives of the human family in the Indian bungalow.

As G. K. Chesterton so wisely writes in *Tremendous Trifles,* "What fairy tales give the child is his first clear idea of the possible defeat of bogey. The baby has known the dragon intimately ever since he had an imagination. What the fairy tale provides for him is a St. George to kill the dragon."

There were many dragons in my life, and I was happy to find St. George was slaying them, if only in my fairy tales. It would be years before I found my true Dragon Slayer.

The first day at Medway, I went to play with my cousins, dressed as an Indian chief, complete with feathered headdress. In the field beside their house were two horses grazing peacefully. When I caught sight of them, I stopped dead in my tracks and stared. *Now that is what a real Indian would ride,* I thought. Delighted by the sight of the majestic steeds, I raced over and stood in awe by the old wooden fence. "If God made anything more beautiful, he kept it for himself," (author unknown) is an apt quote for that moment.

The two horses were surprised by the feather-headed four-foot chief galloping toward them. Lifting their heads in curiosity from the lush pasture, they ambled to the fence. Stony, a cranky gray gelding, was used to receiving sugar cubes from my cousins when they came up to his fence, so he nuzzled my hands inquisitively with his big whiskered muzzle. I basked in the feel of his warm lips caressing my fingers. He smelled my face, the exhale from his mighty lungs blowing my bangs and feathers out of my eyes. The sweet grassy smell of his breath enveloped me. I closed my eyes in worship.

"A lovely horse is always an experience. . ... It is an emotional experience of the kind that is spoiled by words," wrote Beryl Markham, aviator, first woman jockey in Kenya, and author.

Stony, angered at finding no treats, flattened his ears, pawed the ground, and shook his head sideways at me. Not understanding this god's demand for a sugar cube offering, I smiled at him and reached to stroke his neck. He responded by smacking open his lips and nipping me right in my little round belly, leaving a slimy green grass stain on my white t-shirt. It was his way of telling me to bring him a treat next time. No worries, the bite did not bother me at all. It was obvious to me that he loved me, and I was star-struck. I cherished that t-shirt, not allowing my mother to wash out the green imprint of horse teeth when we returned home to Annapolis. My lifelong love affair with this magnificent creature had begun.

At the end of the summer, I started first grade and made a good friend who was not of the four-legged variety. We met in PE class. She was the only girl in the class who could keep up with me, wind and fire, just like me. We were terrors on the playground, running around, chasing the other girls, and playing on the jungle gym. Our friendship deepened, not through words, but through throwing the ball together and playing horses. A couple of months later, she invited me to spend the night at her house.

The fact that she was black was something that completely escaped my notice. But the significant color difference between me and my best friend did not escape the notice of my southern father, "Hell, no!" he said, sitting me down for a stern lecture. His words were like the song from the musical *South Pacific,* "You've Got to Be Carefully Taught". The song meant that racism was not innate, but something you were taught.

Dad drummed it into my dear little ears. I felt I had missed some huge social lesson, the memo to hate all the people my relatives hated. Dad rarely had a conversation with me that consisted of more than "Get my cigarettes and another beer," so the fact that he sat me down and spoke to me was significant and young as I was, I understood that the topic was of huge import to him. He was not one you talked back to, especially if he had been drinking. He had a brown leather belt that he would pull off, snap the flat sides together for effect, and then use it on us or Mom, leaving welts. Anne Lamott in her book, *Bird by Bird,* writes about how children respond to the lies of their parents:

> And you nodded, even though you knew that these were lies, because it is important to stay on the adult's good side. There was no one else to take care of you, and if you questioned them too adamantly, you'd probably get sent to your room without dinner, or they'd drive a stake through your ankles and leave you on the hillside above a Mobil station. So you may have gotten in the habit of doubting the voice that was telling you what was really going on. It is essential that you get it back.

My natural sympathies and ability to love were aborted. I doubted my own voice under my father's dominance and prejudice. Who wants to be staked on a hillside above a Mobil station? I had to obey, but doubting my own voice cast my soul into confusion. The vibrant colors of an intimate friendship pulled in one direction, toward the joy of being with my best friend, but the dark fury of my father's prejudice clouded the relationship and forced me to end it just to survive.

It was a strange sensation, a pulling apart of my soul, a split. Two halves, my true heart dulled, and a false persona emerging. I would have to put down many layers of self-protection, developed many times over, just to survive my childhood. Denying my needs, my heart's longing, being voiceless and powerless to resist and fight for my God-given desire for intimacy caused me to put my heart into an emotional lockdown. I was made to think that its longing was bad, and these emotions were not to be trusted. It would be years before I would stop "doubting the voice that was telling me what was really going on" and begin to get my own voice back.

But children can be remarkably resilient, and I soon made another friend at the bus stop: Lucy, who lived across the street. That weekend Lucy had a slumber party, and Dad allowed me to spend the night at my white friend's house. Three nights later, I had a terrible headache but was too terrified of my father to wake my parents. Instead, I went and woke up my dear sister Catherine, my oldest sister, who was often my primary caretaker. Also afraid of our parents, she gave me two aspirin and told me to go back to bed. I spent a sleepless night in excruciating pain. The next morning, I was too weak to walk. I remember my father carrying me into the doctor's office. He rarely hugged me or carried me in his arms, so it was comforting despite the pain.

"Can you touch your chin to your chest?" the doctor asked gravely.

"No." I couldn't, the pain was too great.

"You need to take her to the hospital immediately," he said, and off we went. At the hospital, they put me in a bed, and the nurse tried to draw blood. I didn't think sticking me with a needle would really help things, so I rolled from one side of the bed to the other out of her reach. She got a big, burly orderly to pin me down. They found a tick under my armpit and thought I had Rocky Mountain spotted fever. But when the blood tests came back, it turned out I had bacterial spinal meningitis, and I was going downhill fast.

The next day, my parents weren't around to comfort me, and these strangers hauled me into isolation without explanation. In horrific pain, I felt sheer terror and total abandonment. They tied my arms and legs to the bed and stuck in the IVs. Now in quarantine, only my parents and the medical staff were allowed in. Everyone had to wear green face masks and gowns. After a few days, I saw my grandmother from Powhatan through the small glass window in the door. She and Granddad put on a brave face and waved at me, putting their hands together as if in prayer.

The doctors were running antibiotics as fast as they could through the IVs in my scrawny arms. After those veins collapsed, they did a cut-down on my ankle and continued to run them full bore. The prognosis was poor, and I continued to fail. Then the hallucinations started. The bedside monitoring machines to which I was attached began to take on the shape of my pets. Tilly was back, and I felt comforted. That was the last thing I remembered before slipping into a coma. The doctor told my parents that although there was always hope, he could offer them no encouragement.

Much to everyone's surprise, I regained consciousness a few days later and promptly tore down the oxygen tent, fearing I would suffocate under the plastic. I also ripped out my IVs. That brought the nurse flying into my room, but she wasn't mad. In fact, she had a big smile on her face and tears in her eyes. I asked for a pizza.

A week after I came out of the coma, I was moved from ICU isolation onto the children's floor. My mother didn't drive, and Dad was busy working, so they did not visit me every day. Despite my family's craziness, I missed them. Lonely, I determined to regain my strength quickly to go home sooner and ran up and down the halls like a banshee. The doctor released me a week early—on Christmas day!

At home, my grandmother, Jean Quintard, told me that everyone at St. Luke's Church in Powhatan, where they were parishioners, prayed for me to get well and that God answered those prayers. With the literal mind of a six-year-old, I believed in this God, a personal, powerful God who could bring me back from a death coma. It was a solid, thank-filled belief, with cords securing deep into my soul the certainty that there was a mighty God out there who could kick butt.

I was getting stronger by the time we left Wild Rose Shores and moved to our house in Annapolis near the Naval Academy stadium. I would need this strength and more as I met my first felonious friend. But as Winston Churchill said, "We have not journeyed . . . [all this way] because we are made of sugar candy."

Neither had I.

CHAPTER 9

THE BOOT CAMP OF DELINQUENCY

No man can be called friendless who has God and the companionship of good books.

—Elizabeth Barrett Browning

In my opinion, a horse is the animal to have. Eleven-hundred pounds of raw muscle, power, grace, and sweat between your legs—it's something you just can't get from a pet hamster.

—Author Unknown

I skipped my last oyster shell on Aberdeen Creek. The owners of our rental house decided to sell it. Dad found another house in Annapolis, about three blocks from the Naval Academy stadium. The house was small and sat at the intersection of two busy streets, Howie and Summer, with an ivy-covered hill for a front lawn. There was no water, no woods, and no privacy for me because I shared a room with Jean.

My father kept his boat at a marina since we were no longer living on the creek, and the high marina fees necessitated my mother getting a job. She applied for a position at the local library, and being so well-read, she thrived in her new job.

"I don't have any friends here," I complained to my mother.

"No man can be called friendless who has God and the companionship of good books," she said, quoting Elizabeth Barrett Browning. "I brought you a horse book from the library: *Mustang, Wild Spirit of the West,* by Marguerite Henry." I gobbled it up, and every other horse book she brought me. I guzzled down *Misty of Chincoteague, Black Gold,* and *Justin Morgan Had a Horse,* all with the artful illustrations of

84

Wesley Dennis, which drew me into the action and held my rapt attention. Walter Farley's books, The Black Stallion series, captivated me. Mom tried to expand my genre and brought me other animal books. The first books that broke my heart were *Old Yeller* and *Charlotte's Web,* which both brought me to convulsive sobs on my bed.

In the fall, I entered the third grade at Germantown Elementary, my fourth new school in four years. Because of our family's many moves, I was reticent at making close girlfriends. And being athletic, I enjoyed the more physical games the boys played, and they didn't demand intimate relationships.

The school was a half mile from our house, which was too close for me to be picked up by the school bus, so I walked. By November, it was a cold trek, but when my birthday rolled around, I was in for a surprise. My parents told me to follow them down into the basement. I hesitated, being a bit leery of my parents' pranks and of basements.

In Salisbury, we had one of those creepy basements—damp and spiderwebby, dark with one light bulb hanging from a frayed electrical cord, and stuff piled around in the corners where a legion of bogeymen could hide. I remember my mother telling me, "Mary, don't play in the basement because there is a bad draft down there that will make you sick." Mothers seemed to worry more about drafts in the 1960s than they do now.

My big, brown, four-year-old eyes got as large as saucers, "Really? We have a bad giraffe in our basement?" I asked incredulously.

"Yes," she said matter-of-factly, like every house in the neighborhood had a bad giraffe living in the basement, preying on small children, and causing them to fall ill. I was terrified.

Several weeks later, she asked me to run down to the basement and get her some potatoes. Scared of the bad giraffe, I shook my head no. Frustrated she said, "There is nothing down there that can hurt you. Now run downstairs and grab me some potatoes before I get a switch."

Tearing up, I said, "What about that bad giraffe you said would make me sick?" She laughed and embarrassed me by telling the entire family at dinner.

Now, at the mature age of eight, I no longer believed in basement giraffes, but I worried about falling victim to another one of my parents' pranks as they blindfolded me and led me down the stairs. The blindfold removed, I saw before me a lovely banana-seat bike with curved handlebars. It was speed, freedom, and independence all wrapped up in one pink bike with tassels flowing from the handlebars. Who wouldn't love that? Such joy, yet life was such a conundrum. Sometimes my parents were grand, but I never knew when it was safe to trust them.

With my new wheels, I explored the community. I met a brown-haired girl sailing down the streets on her bike. I followed her around, and over the next week, she showed me all the different routes in the neighborhood. Her name was Sarah Freddy. She was only a year older than me but had an older brother, so she was many years older in worldly experience, and she took me on as her felonious apprentice.

Her father was fighting in Vietnam, and her mother worked, so she was on her own, as I was. Soon after we met, she asked me if I wanted to wrestle. Before I could respond, she snatched me half bald, laid a full-nelson on me and pinned me to the ground. I fancied myself a brave Indian, but she was a squaw who could rip out the enemy's heart and eat it while it was still pulsating. From then on, she would pounce on me at random like Cato in the *Pink Panther* movies and take out her pent-up anger toward her brother on my scrawny frame. Most days I was beaten up, but I learned to fight and grew tough and mean under her bludgeoning. I was angry, too, and fighting was a good release. The next two years, I was enrolled in her boot camp of delinquency, which singed my conscience. With no one at home when I returned from school, I was free to do as I pleased, but as Augustine said in his *Confessions,* "The liberty I loved was merely that of a runaway."

Even though having spinal meningitis brought me close to death's door and drew me into a solid belief in a powerful God, this belief had little impact on my sensitivities concerning the morality of my behavior. God was up there, and I was down here and under her tutelage, I was hoping that never the two worlds would meet. I don't remember going to church when we lived in Maryland, but my sister Catherine said we did go and that she was president of the Episcopal Youth Group. Because the priest almost got defrocked when the kids were smoking pot at a youth group retreat, and because I screamed and kicked and wouldn't go into Sunday school, my family stopped going to church.

I spent more time with Sarah. She taught me how to start my dad's push lawnmower. It was the kind that had a crank that you wound up and a switch you released to get it started. Our toes turned green as we cut the tall grass barefoot. This was before all the worries about safety, so there were no shields to keep us from getting our limbs whacked off, but our parents were oblivious. There was something empowering in this, two girls entering the world of volatile gasoline, smoky exhaust, howling motors, and cutting blades. We crossed over the invisible line into the male domain before we even knew that there was one.

In addition to Sarah, I made another friend, Helen, who lived across the street. At school, we had a science project together, and I got the duckling. Helen and I played with the downy soft duckling quite a bit, perhaps too much, because he died. I decided we should have a funeral for him and bury him in our backyard and invited Helen to participate. I fashioned a cross out of sticks and put it on the mound of dirt. She made a Star of David and put it on his grave. It was my first introduction to other world religions. I had never seen the Star of David before, and I asked her what it was. She told me and suggested that perhaps the duckling was Jewish. She seemed as sure of this as I was sure he might need a cross. "Who knows if ducks are Christian or Jewish? And why can't they just be both, anyway?"

Now duckless, I pined for a dog of my own, and my parents finally relented. They took me to the pound, and we looked at all the dogs waiting to be adopted. I wept at the sadness of it all and wanted to adopt every one of them. Dad saw a lovely Old English Sheepdog named Baxter in a corner run.

"Is that purebred up for adoption?" Dad asked, always one to sniff out a deal.

"Yes, sir. He's somebody's dog, but he ain't been claimed, so he's yours."

With that, we loaded him up in Dad's light-blue company car and took him home. I gave him a bath, which was no small feat since he was a huge, long-haired dog. Baxter stood about two feet tall at the top of his shoulder, with a white-and-gray coat and ears flat against his head. He was full of energy, with a docked tail and hind end taller than his front end, giving him a clownish bear-like quality. He and I spent that summer down at the Naval Academy stadium, just about three blocks from the house, where we galloped around until both of our tongues lolled out of our mouths. Then we flopped down on our backs in the green grass and watched the fluffy clouds float by as I read books on dog care. I was now certain I wanted to be a dog veterinarian.

Meanwhile, my mother was happier now that she worked, and my parents seemed to be getting along better. On Sunday nights, Dad would pop a batch of popcorn on the stove, sprinkle it with Lawry's Seasoned Salt or Old Bay Seasoning, and drown it in melted butter. We would watch *Mutual of Omaha's Wild Kingdom*. I was fascinated by the wildlife and dreamed of one day going on a safari. Little did I know that the knowledge I gained by watching this program would lay a foundation for the work I would one day do, saving elephant calves in Kenya.

We also watched *The Wonderful World of Disney* that came on after *Wild Kingdom*. I remember watching *The Three Lives of Thomasina*, a charming movie about a cat, a daughter who loses her mother, and her atheist veterinarian father who returns to faith in God when he prays for his dying daughter to live and she does. The cat, too, had many lives and supernatural experiences which caused me to reflect on life at a higher, mystical plane. I began to think about God again for the first time in many years. Life was good.

Pete graduated from high school and moved to Medway to live with Granny and Granddad while he attended Virginia Commonwealth University. He was the first to alert Mom and Dad to Granddad's progressing dementia. My parents discussed what could be done to care for Granddad and, unbeknownst to me, were making plans to move.

But I had more to learn from Sarah before we moved again. She filched her brother's BB gun and taught me to shoot, and we shot out my neighbor's sidewalk lantern. She also talked me into skipping school. But that wasn't all I learned.

In the fourth grade, we started smoking and stealing. At first, we just took the half-finished cigarettes our parents left in ashtrays and smoked them down to the filter. Mom wrote me notes and sent me to the store to buy cigarettes for her. On these cigarette runs, I would get a pack for myself as well. Sarah taught me how to shoplift, so when I went to get cigarettes, I would snag a candy bar off the store shelf when the owner wasn't looking.

That summer, on a nearby creek, we stole a rowboat and took it to another inlet on the river. We became blood sisters, pricking our fingers with a fish hook and rubbing the blood together like savages. It was 1970, and we paddled our stolen boat into the Severn River and sang the latest Tom Jones song, "Daughter of Darkness." Little did I know how aptly that song described us.

Sarah's lessons were educating me in one direction, but Providence provided a glimpse of a better way. In the fall, my family went down to Powhatan for the annual Homecoming at St. Luke's Church. Walking into church, I looked at the ivy growing up the front of the ante-bellum brick church and the ancient oaks in the churchyard. The building's trim was white with green shutters flanking lovely stained-glass windows. Behind the altar, the circular colored-glass window depicted an open Bible.

At nine years old, I only cared about the food and seeing my cousins. Little did I know that the history of my family's ties to this church would form my lifelong attachment to St. Luke's as tight as the lichen in the crevices of the chiseled names on the gray tombstones. St. Luke's was my family's spiritual entrance and exit platform, from cradle to coffin; eight generations were baptized, married, and buried there. We sat with our grandparents, Colonel "Alec" Quintard and Jean, in the third pew on the right side of the church. My father told us that if you sat on the left side, you wouldn't go to Heaven. Our family friends, General "Chux" Collins, and his wife, Memaw, sat in the second row, with their grandkids in front of us. The grandchildren knew to behave surrounded by all that brass.

Homecoming, as the name implies, was when everyone who grew up in the church but moved away for education, employment, marriage, or to escape the invisible barriers of a small town "comes home." Folding tables and chairs were set up in the grass, and the women of the church brought out a continuous bounty of delicious dishes from the parish house kitchen: deviled eggs sprinkled with paprika, thin slices of salty country ham on homemade buttered biscuits, and mounds of crispy fried chicken so good they made you want to suck your fingers off. Flakey-crusted, deep-dish chocolate chess pie, was the best thing I ever put in my mouth! The accompanying buckets of sweet iced tea, lemonade, and a cooler of sodas was there to wash it all down. An occasional yellow jacket, diving into the Sprite cans, surprised the unsuspecting visitors from the city.

The cornucopia of food was only exceeded by the cornucopia of friends. Not only had all the related Jervey and Moncure cousins arrived, but also generations of family friends, including the Richardsons, Montgomerys, Mitchells, Kennons, Evans, Coles, and Baileys—not blood relations, but our great-grandparents, grandparents, and parents and their children's friends. Each successive generation shared the family secrets, joys, and tragedies for decades. This created such a spirit of delight and thread of connection to my roots; each year these reunions brought a belongingness to my soul.

We moved continually, and I had no sense of what community love could mean, nor did I really know to what I belonged. St. Luke's Homecoming gave me a vision of what was good and tethered my free-floating soul to the connectedness of extended family and friends.

After Homecoming, we visited the Collins's for cocktail hour. He was a retired World War II general, and Connie was a big-hearted officer's wife. She always put out ruffled Lay's potato chips with French onion dip, peanuts, and black olives. He mixed the Scotch, bourbon, or gin. They were friends with Granny and Granddad, the Collins's children, the Gunther's, were friends with my parents. We children also enjoyed wonderful friendships with the Gunther's children. The goodness of my heritage was a great gift, but there was another. The Collins's granddaughter Pat Gunther was my sister Cat's good friend, and Pat was keeping her horse at the Collins's farm, Holly Hill, for the summer. Seeing my love for horses, Pat asked if I would like to have a ride on her horse, Rhett Butler. Of course, I said yes, and was elated as they lifted me onto his back and led me around. He was a lovely, big, bay Thoroughbred, standing over sixteen hands, and I held onto his mane for dear life, white-knuckled and joyful, scarcely glancing at the six-foot drop to the ground. My hips swung rhythmically with his four-beat walk, and I had a huge, fried-chicken-eating grin on my face. Euphoric, I begged them to let me stay on him forever. It grew dark, and they had to make up a story about him having night blindness to get me off his back. I cried. It was a transformational ride. Even though all we'd done was just walk in circles, it was the greatest thrill of my life up to that point. Recalling it now, these words come to mind: "In my opinion, a horse is the animal to have. Eleven-hundred pounds of raw muscle, power, grace, and sweat between your legs—it's something you just can't get from a pet hamster." (Author unknown).

It's been said that some people are alcoholics before they ever take their first drink. The same is true of horse people. Before they ever take their first ride, there is a horse-shaped hole in their hearts, waiting to be filled by an equine. Churchill said, "There is something about the outside of a horse that is good for the inside of a man."

Little did I know that within a year I would say goodbye to my blood sister, be confirmed at St. Luke's Church, and get my first horse. Well, not exactly a horse, but Duke, an 11.3-hand Shetland stud pony.

My childhood checkers game would continue, and in the next few years, these red happy memory pieces of my life were about to be double jumped by horrific black ones, but those gifts of St. Luke's would remain in me like a north star until I could look up for direction.

CHAPTER 10
MOVE TO MEDWAY

Children's talent to endure stems from their ignorance of alternatives.

—Maya Angelou

Alzheimer's is no respecter of person or rank. My grandfather Colonel Quintard survived the Bataan death march during World War II but now fought an enemy more evil and deadly than the Japanese prison guards. My grandmother did not drive. So, in the fall of 1969, my parents moved us three hours away to our grandparents's house, Medway, in Powhatan, Virginia, so they could help care for my grandfather. A few months later, I was in the backyard with him when he lit a firecracker but forgot to let go. It exploded the flesh off several of his fingertips. Dad decided to put him in the Veteran's Hospital in Salem, Virginia. I sat with Granddad in the back seat on the four-hour drive to southwest Virginia, petrified that at any moment Granddad would open the car door and step out onto the fast-moving highway. We dropped him off at the hospital without his precious wife, whom he called Boots, by his side. Several months later, he passed away. At his funeral, our neighbor, Sarah McGree, told me that he was the finest man she had ever known. At eighty-one years old, he was buried with his Distinguished Service Medal at St. Luke's Episcopal Church with a full military gun salute.

It was three years since my cousin's horse, Stoney, bit me in the stomach. I loved the country and delighted in the move to Medway, dreaming I could be with Stoney. However, our first winter there, the pond where he drank his water had partially frozen over, and when he walked out to the middle, he crashed through. The icy, brown water filled his gasping lungs before he made it to shore, and my dreams sank with him to the pond's muddy bottom.

But, that spring my sister, Catherine, borrowed a lovely chestnut Thoroughbred named Fox from Francis Baily, an old family friend. Sadly, several months later, Fox jumped a cross rail, stumbled, and fell. He fractured his shoulder, and Catherine broke her collar bone. We wept as our vet, Dr. Britt, put him down.

Shortly after the accident, Catherine was graduating from high school, and her interests turned from horses to college. When her graduation day arrived, our brother Pete came home from college to attend the ceremony. He arrived on the morning of the evening ceremony and, looking for a diversion, decided to take me fishing. My hero worship of him that formed during our time together in Annapolis had never waned, and I was eager to go—even though we were told that there was a convict loose. We lived downriver from the James River Correctional Facility, and occasionally prisoners escaped. One of our neighbors at John Tree Hill, the farm next door, would not let her children camp out with us in the springtime because, she said, it was "convict season." Apparently, she was right, and one had hatched that spring day.

Unfazed, Pete strapped on my dad's .45-magnum pistol to protect his little sister, and off we went. After fishing for a couple of hours, we returned to Dad's Lincoln, and I heard a loud pop. I thought Pete lit a firecracker.

"Mary, quick, go get help. I shot myself."

"Right, Pete, you can't fool me," I said jovially, having been tricked by my brother enough times to know better.

But as I came around the side of the car, I saw his ashen face and realized this was not a prank. The pistol slid out of the holster when he bent down to get into Dad's low-riding Lincoln, landed on the ground releasing the trigger, and unloaded a .45-magnum bullet from a foot away directly into his back.

"Run, get Max," he breathed out.

I flew across the field to Max, our cousin's house. Unglued by the prospect of my brother's death, I burst through their backdoor, breathless, red-faced, and sobbing. Max had been drinking and was three sheets to the wind but managed to drive Pete the forty-five minutes to the closest hospital. I was only twelve years old, but his wife, my mother's first cousin, Kim, gave me a beer to drink to calm my nerves as we waited for news of Pete's condition.

"No, Max. The emergency room, not the morgue," Pete said when he saw to which hospital wing Max was pulling up.

Within the hour, he was on the table, and the surgeon removed the slug that entered at Pete's hip, traveled up his back and lodged under his shoulder blade. Miraculously, it had missed his spinal cord and every major organ.

"I was pretty lucky," Pete said later, fingering his memento, the removed slug.

"You weren't so damn lucky; that bullet could have gone anywhere in Powhatan County," my father quipped.

Cat said sarcastically that Pete always tried to upstage her, and this was the final trump, making both of my parents miss her graduation. She was glad to get out of the chaos of the house and within two years of going to college, was married to Charlie Akins, a wonderful man from Tennessee. But she still helped me find an outlet for my passion by introducing me to a neighbor, Hip Alan, who bought and sold ponies and had a fondness for young girls. Suitability of horse to rider was never a consideration that clouded the sale. In my case, it was difficult to determine who was greener, the horse or rider. Never was the old saying, "Green and green make black and blue," truer than in my early riding years.

Mr. Alan taught the neighborhood kids, Susan, Anne, Evelyn, Laura, Sally, Jean, Cabell, Terry and Julia to ride from the back of his bay Tennessee Walking horse named Brandy. This was before helmets became standard safety equipment, and we considered saddles optional. Centered riding meant keeping a leg on each side and your mind in the middle, and there was a good deal more "yahooing" than "horse whispering." Mr. Alan gave you a leg up bareback and swatted the pony on the backside with a shovel. If you stayed on, you passed to the next phase: trail riding. On the trails, he carried peppermints in his pocket because he liked to hold our hands. As we took the mint, he would grab our hand and not let go. Trotting past us, he pulled us askew or off. Bareback, we had no stirrups to brace ourselves, so we developed legs of steel and perfect balance. No one broke her neck, although we did get a good taste of that dusty, red Virginia clay. Will Rogers was right when he said, "The only thing hard about riding is the ground."

I began riding one of Mr. Alan's very naughty but handsome Shetland ponies, a blood bay named Flip. He reared up often and occasionally flipped over backward.

I also rode Duke, an 11.3-hand (four inches in a hand), liver chestnut Shetland stallion. I was afraid of him because he would sniff noses with the mares, squeal, and strike out with his front hooves. Then he would curl up his upper lip in the Flehmen response and dance wildly around, attempting to breed any mare in season. Mr. Alan kicked him in the belly and swatted his extended penis with a switch until he behaved himself.

Christmas was approaching, and I begged my parents for a horse of my own. My birthday was in November, and they surprised me with Duke. My heart was set on Flip. Raised in a family where it wasn't safe to share your feelings honestly, I feigned joy and then went out to Duke and cried disappointed tears into his mane. It would be the first of many times he patiently stood while I hugged his thick, cresty neck and dried my tears on his long, flaxen forelock. Although initially, he was not the pony I wanted, he became my succor, my life and my world, my best friend and confidant. His rich, deep, earthy horse smell filled my heart with joy as I sank my nose in his wooly winter coat. I determined that any species this divine was worth giving my life to care for, and, at the tender age of thirteen, I set my ambitions on becoming a horse vet.

That Christmas, I asked for horse-care books. The Saturday night before Christmas, I heard Mom and Dad engaging in their characteristic fighting in the den, right below my bedroom. Then Dad yelled, "Get the hell down here, Mary!"

He wanted Mom to tell him where she hid the bourbon, but she wouldn't.

Panicked, I ran down the stairs. Brandishing his hunting knife, he went into the closet and pulled out the bag of our Christmas presents.

"Tell me, or I'll cut up her presents," he snarled, grabbing a gift with my name on it.

Mom was silent, torn between her addiction and the love for her child. He sliced through the wrapping paper. I saw it was a horse book for me. He started to carve up the front cover of my new horse book. My horrified look caused my mother to cave in and blurt out the location of the whiskey. He threw the book into the closet while I ran outside into the cold night air. Once again, I ran to Duke and buried my face into the warmth of his fuzzy winter coat. His reassuring nicker and unconditional love enveloped me with comfort.

Duke became my refuge, not only from my father's drunken rages but also my mother's and grandmother's depression and suicide attempts. At fourteen, I found my mother wrapped in a bloody sheet after slitting her wrist. I got help and then ran out to the pasture to find Duke. Throwing his bridle on him, I leaped on bareback and took off down our sandy driveway, tears streaming down my cheeks at the insanity of it all. The rhythm of his small hooves in the sand brought freedom and relief to my tormented soul as each stride took me farther from the bloody bedlam. Benjamin Disraeli knew what he was talking about when he said, "A canter is a cure for every evil."

That Christmas, Jean Silvey's parents bought her the naughty pony Flip. Mr. Alan delivered him Christmas morning with a huge red ribbon tied around his neck and a shiny black Western saddle with little red-and-white rosettes and a matching bridle. I wasn't jealous. By now, after daily sloshing water buckets and tossing hay to Duke, we bonded. I loved him, and he loved me. My life would never be the same, never completely fulfilled without a horse in it.

I propped up a little cedar tree in one end of his stall that Christmas, cut up old Christmas cards for ornaments and tied carrots and apples onto the tree for him to munch on. His Christmas dinner was a flake of hay and hot bran mash with loads of Brer Rabbit black-strap molasses.

Duke taught me more about horse behavior than any two-footed instructor. The lessons I learned from an 11.3-hand Shetland stud pony saved my life many a time, years later, when I was a practicing veterinarian.

I rarely conversed with my parents, and my mother realized the only bridge to my silent heart was horses. So, despite her fear, on one occasion, she decided to ride with me. My mother acquired her courage from the same source as the Canadian humorist Stephen Leacock, who once said, "It takes a great deal of physical courage to ride a horse. This, however, I have. I get it at about forty cents a flask, and take it as required."

Whether it was from her fortifications or my being overexuberant in giving her a leg up, I don't know, but she managed to go up and over the other side onto the ground, without ever making it into the saddle. That was the first and the last time she attempted to ride with me. But, she supported my passion and even tolerated it when I led Duke in through the screened porch and into the dining room. She was laughing too hard to swat me with the hairbrush as she occasionally did for my antics. I swung him around when she caught sight of me and nearly took out the curved glass on the china cabinet, high-tailing it out before she had time to change her mind. Maya Patel once said, "Small children are convinced that ponies deserve to see the inside of the house."

Over the next few years, Jean and I outgrew our ponies. But sadly, Mr. Alan did not outgrow his desire for young girls. I will never forget the night he took some of us to his cabin and stuck his hand inside the front of my jeans and groped around. I felt shocked, shamed, and violated by one who I trusted as a father figure. He lured us in with his kindness and our love for horses, and then betrayed many of us, leaving us feeling powerless, confused, and scarred. Years later, his lust finally landed him in a courtroom, and he was formally charged with child molestation. If you ever think someone spending time with your child is too good to be true, it probably is.

But joy of joys, there were good forces pulling toward health and Heaven about a half a mile from Mr. Alan's because the Fleischmans moved in with both a gaggle of kids and a herd of lovely Welsh ponies. Mommy Fleischman was truly amazing and took me under her tutelage. She was a fabulous horsewoman who fostered my love of veterinary medicine by teaching me how to spray the ponies' wounds with the antimicrobial Gentian violet and treat the vile-smelling thrush in their hooves with copper sulfate. More than a dozen of us would mount up and gallop down the light cut where the electric company cleared a path to Trix Jones General Store where our parents had charge accounts. A couple of us held the ponies while the others ran in to get the health food of middle-schoolers: Charms Pops, ice-cold Dr. Pepper, Mallow Cups, and Mary Janes.

One day cantering home with a sour apple Charms Pop in my mouth, we ran through a nest of angry yellow jackets. Alice's pony, Poppy, stopped, dropped, and rolled. I was riding their gray pony named Cracker Jacks, who bucked so hard I did a summersault over his head, pulling his bridle off and crushing the hard candy between my molars as I slammed into the solid ground. He bolted home, and I had to ride double back with Alice.

That summer, we watched the 1972 Summer Olympic equestrian events while eating Mommy Fleischman's cheese dream sandwiches, made from her ripe garden tomatoes, mayonnaise, and cheddar cheese. I fantasized about riding in the Olympics and walking to the podium to receive my gold medal. Little did I know that one day I would work for gold medalist Joe Fargis and silver medalist Conrad Homfeld. The jumping events thrilled me, and I wanted to learn to jump. Duke was big in heart but small in stature. I needed something bigger. But that cost money and my parents were lukewarm about my equestrian passion.

Then God brought us a gift from England to Powhatan: Mrs. Pat Betts. She and her husband, Jon, bought my great-uncle Colonel Jim Jervey's farm, Level Green. Pat was a British Horse Society instructor, and she gave us free lessons. She became my mentor and my role model. Every night I thought up new horse questions to ask her just to talk to her on the phone. She was my source of stability and joy. I rode Duke over to her house bareback and put her baby Yvonne on in front of me, and we would canter around their house.

By now my feet hung down past Duke's knees, so Pat helped me get my second pony, named Shadow. She broke Shadow for Linda Phillips, who owned a farm down the road on Route 7–11, and arranged a free lease for me to keep her at Medway. Dad would only pay for feed for one pony, so I had to sell Duke to the Remington's, who lived at Calais, a lovely farm on the James River about 2 miles from Medway. Dad said the farm had belonged to my great uncle before he lost it in a poker game. Sixty dollars bought Duke, my soul mate. I rode him to their house. My mother said she would come pick me up when I got there. Holding back my tears, I told her I would rather just walk home alone.

It was a long, sad, Dukeless walk, my heart breaking.

The next morning, the Remingtons called: Duke was not in his pen. I looked out the window: he had returned to Medway. This went on for about a month until Mr. Remington said he had enough and gave me Duke back. Having two ponies doubled my joy, and I took them both down to the banks of the James River and let them graze as I sat on their backs, reading my horse books. The sounds of the swift river coursing past, along with the horses tearing off the grass and grinding it with their strong teeth as I read have stayed in the "unconscious library of my memory," to borrow from the Welsh journalist Lewis John Wynford Vaughan-Thomas, who wrote:

> Again the early-morning sun was generous with its warmth. All the sounds dear to a horseman were around me—the snort of the horses as they cleared their throats, the gentle swish of their tails, the tinkle of irons as we flung the saddles over their backs—little sounds of no importance, but they stay in the unconscious library of memory.

Shadow was a good-looking 14.1-hand Welsh pony, black and fast. As Shadow and I flew around her riding ring, Mrs. Betts yelled in her thick British accent, "Mary, you have an electric bottom, please slow down!" But going through the woods and across the fields, I opened her up full throttle, thrilled by Shadow's speed. My eyes watered as the wind whipped across them and blew through my hair. It was a sliver of time when I could outrun the devils in my home life.

Cat and her husband, Charlie, discovered a small horse show a few counties over and signed me up. But I had no show clothes. Mrs. Betts was kind enough to lend me her brown paddock boots, jodhpurs, and a tweed riding jacket. My mother and Cat took me to the Town and Country tack shop and bought me a velvet helmet and riding shirt, called a ratcatcher, with a collar. I had a silver stock pin from my great-aunt Abbot.

The day of my first show, I bathed and groomed Shadow until her black coat shone like a polished crow feather. Terrified of going into a trailer for the first time, she balked when we tried to load her, dug her toes in, and then started rearing. She reared so high that she caught her hooves on top of the trailer, and I thought she was going to break a leg. Charlie was a former rodeo rider and knew how to load horses. He hooked a winch up to her halter and dragged her on.

At the show, Shadow shied at the brush jump in the first class and ran out. The next round, she cleared it fine, and we placed fifth. I also pulled a few ribbons in the flat, nonjumping classes. I was thrilled: four ribbons in my first show! I was intoxicated. I was addicted to the horse show competition at my first show. This was a measurable way to determine my performance, my ability, and in my heart, my own worth. Winning became my passion.

That summer, we went to the District 4-H horse show, which was mandatory if one wanted to show at the Virginia State Fair. My mother came to watch me but hid behind the bleachers, too afraid I was going to crash to watch me jump. Despite our backyard ponies, all the Powhatan kids qualified to go to the State show that fall at the fairgrounds in Richmond.

Those were the glory years when the horse show was during the state fair. Years later, it would move to a different location, and the next generation of kids would never know the thrill of showing horses during the day and cruising the midway at night, enjoying the food, rides, and exhibits. How we loved the food! Greasy Italian sausages, seared black on the outside, saddled with green peppers and onions caramelized on the well-seasoned grill that no doubt had not been cleaned since the 1864 World's Fair. There were elephant ears made from deep-fried sweet dough, sprinkled with powdered sugar that left you with sticky fingers, and wads of pink cotton candy that dissolved in your mouth, candy apples that pulled out your fillings, and everything was washed down with fresh-squeezed limeade. Visiting the Virginia Tech Dairy Science booth, we milked a cow and ate homemade vanilla ice cream. Years later, I would volunteer at the same Block and Bridle Club stand where I ate my first lamb BBQ.

When the sun went down and the stars came out, it was time to ride the double Ferris wheel. From its high point, we saw the entire fairgrounds: the exhibit halls, the horse show ring, and the full midway with its fancy lights drawing us like moths. The rides and the white-knuckling thrill of the Zipper called us to its rickety seats. Its strong vertical G-forces did not just empty my pockets of change but even pulled my necklace off over my head. Its twists and drops had us regretting the fair food as we saw it for a second time.

The bustling smorgasbord of people, with every color of skin and shape of tattoo, crowded the midway, creating an air of danger and excitement for us country girls.

But we were there for the horse show, and the first class was Fitting and Showmanship, which judged how well horse and rider were groomed. I stood proudly in the ring, despite my borrowed riding apparel and pony. Shadow, with her fraying braids blowing in the breeze, seemed just as proud to be there as I was. The judge, Marion DuPont, touched her elegant blonde bun and, smiling, said kindly, "We all need a bit of Dippity-do hair gel when it is windy, now don't we?"

I did not place but was thrilled that a judge spoke to me. Faring better in the jumping class with a clear round, I pulled a sixth-place ribbon. I rode as well as the riders who placed above me but was outclassed by their fancier, expensive show ponies. At that time, showing was still fun for me, especially the costume class; we dressed up Shadow as a P-51 Mustang plane, and I was her pilot. We attached an aluminum foil propeller to her noseband and two large cardboard wings, coming out from under my saddle. I got seventh place, but the experience did little to prepare me for the next year's costume class, where I nearly got killed.

We beamed as we showed our ribbons to Frank, a horse trainer we hired to haul our ponies home. The few ribbons we won left us proud of our accomplishments but also sowed in us a drive to perform better in the future. We would return the next fall with horses instead of our backyard ponies. And my own life would be irrevocably changed as well, by tragedies I could not have imagined.

CHAPTER 11

BITTERSWEET

A woman needs two animals—the horse of her dreams and a jackass to pay for it.

—Anonymous

F rank, the man we hired to trailer our horses home from the fair, was impressed with my riding ability and asked me to ride his horse Black Knight in some local shows. Thrilled at the opportunity to ride a horse and have someone else pay the show fees, I leapt at the chance.

By now, both my parents were alcoholics, and I had no nurturing, love, or support at home. My thirsty soul sucked up his attention, praise, and gifts. It would take me decades to see that this is a classic pattern of seduction older men use to lure in hurting young girls.

As abuse often does, it started gradually, his arm around my shoulders, a hand squeeze. Then one night, when we turned the horses out in the pasture, he grabbed me and kissed me hard on the lips. He was thirty-four years old, married, and the father of three boys. I was a naïve fourteen-year-old child with an empty parental love tank, sucked in by his attention, but now I was shocked and confused.

A few months later, we put Duke in with his horse, Black Knight; they fought, and Duke kicked him, leaving a deep gash. We drove to his barn for some wound ointment. It was a Sunday, and no one was there. He pinned me against the doorframe and kissed me all over, lifted my shirt, and felt my breasts. I had no place to turn. I certainly wasn't going to tell my drunken, violent father. The results could have been catastrophic. My mother had already served a round in the Westbrook mental hospital for depression and alcohol use; telling her might cause a return visit or worse. I did not want to lose my chance to ride, so I told no one. Almost every afternoon, he came to Medway to watch me ride. Every night, Frank called me. Mom caught on and was angry, but she was waging her own losing battle with prescription drugs and alcohol and did nothing. One night, while we were driving in his truck, he was very sullen. When I asked what was wrong, he grabbed my hand and put it on the rise in his pants between his legs. I was stunned. He pressured me to perform oral sex. I was grossed out, confused, and felt trapped.

A few months later, Dad lent me money, and I bought a chestnut mare to show, which I named Bittersweet. Little did I know how fitting the name was. I showed Bittersweet every weekend that summer, and in the fall, we returned to the State Fair. All of us neighborhood kids moved up from our scruffy ponies to horses. My cousin, Evelyn, found a big Appaloosa mare. The show began with the jumping classes, and Evelyn went first on her horse. They entered the ring, started trotting nicely, transitioned into a smooth, controlled canter, and cleared the first fence beautifully. Then the mare slammed on her half-ton brakes. Wild-eyed, nostrils flared, her panicked snorting could be heard all the way back at the in-gate. Terror seized her at the sight of the double Ferris wheel, turning behind the ring. Throwing herself into a full-throttle reverse, she propelled backward until her massive hindquarters were planted against the fence she had just jumped and she could go no farther. All four of The mare's striped hooves were fear-frozen to the ground. Evelyn had to dismount and lead her, trembling at the end of the reins, from the ring. This was a bad showing from our country crew, but not nearly as dreadful as my performance the next day.

That year, 1975, the blockbuster movie *Jaws* just hit the theaters, so for my entry in the costume class, I dressed up as a diver being eaten by a shark. I covered Bittersweet with an aqua blue horse blanket to which I had glued paper fish. I cut a large paper barrel into the shape of a shark head, complete with jagged white teeth. I was the diver, with a snorkeling mask over my face. Sitting on the horse with the shark-head barrel over me, it looked like I was being eaten by a shark. The only problem was that Bittersweet was not accustomed to the sorts of shenanigans to which we had subjected Duke and Shadow. They were unflappable ponies, but she was a more sensitive Anglo-Arabian horse.

We started out fine, walking around the ring. Then a kid dressed up as a jockey came breezing by, and Bittersweet started to trot. The barrel was so high around me that I could barely hold the reins, and riding bareback, I had no stirrups to brace against. As Bittersweet trotted, the barrel started bouncing up and down on her back and the blanket with the fish on it started flapping. She spooked. Terrified, she bolted around the arena, once, twice, three times, at a dead gallop, fish flying off the blanket and me hanging on for dear life.

The ringmaster stopped the entire class and called all the entrants to the center of the ring, out of harm's way. Bittersweet just wanted out. She sprinted around, hugging the wooden sides of the ring, her panicked hoofs no longer on the sandy soil but half-scaling the boards at full throttle, trying to escape. I heard mothers gasping in the stands. Someone lunged for the reins but missed. Another lap. Finally, Frank ran into the arena, grabbed a rein, whipping us around and almost flipping us over. He snapped the lead shank chain over Bittersweet's nose to control her, then led us trembling into the center of the ring. My face mask fogged up so I couldn't see, and sweat stung my eyes as it rolled off my forehead. I stood there embarrassed, with horse and rider both shaking.

My life mirrored this performance. Being in my family was like riding a runaway horse. It wasn't that I liked being in the relationship with Frank or the favors he pressured on me to perform, but he was the only one around to grab the reins— "any port in a storm," as they say. I fled to an unsafe refuge and, like many an abused child, felt powerless to change the situation. As Dan Allender writes in his book, *The Wounded Heart,* abuse often offers unfair choices for a child to have to make. I sacrificed my body and soul on the altar of survival and was left burdened with the shame of a false complicity.

Bittersweet and I did not win anything at the show. Disappointed in my performance, I returned to the crazy swirl of an alcoholic home. But my mother was gone. Dad neglected to tell us that he committed her for the second time to Westbrook mental hospital to help her deal with her demons. She was there for several weeks, and during that time, she made a ceramic goose. It was quite pretty. She had an artistic, sensitive vein, and it was beautifully expressed in painting this handsome goose. The work she did in rehab seemed to be taking hold, and emotionally she was doing better than she had in months. Unfortunately, the years of bourbon and prescription drugs took their toll, and her liver was shot.

My mother had a small, black, curly-coated, poodle mix named Cricket. Cricket loved my mother, and my mother loved that silly little dog. They were inseparable. If my mother went up the stairs, Cricket would follow. When my mother came down, the dog was on her heels. If my mother went into the bathroom, Cricket sat patiently outside the door. While she was cooking in the kitchen, with the dog under her feet, my mother would often cuss at Cricket while doing gymnastics to avoid stepping on her. Cricket was loyal only to my mother and didn't care much for the rest of us, not that she was mean or would bite or anything. It was just that her heart was fully consumed by a devotion to my mother alone.

Cricket seemed to understand the gravity of my mother's condition more than I did. Despite my mother's final attempts at sobriety, she had cirrhosis of the liver, and as there was no cure for her, her skin yellowed. During her last few weeks at home as she declined, my mother lay on the sofa in the living room with Cricket faithfully at her side. When my father took her to the hospital, my mother gave Cricket a little hug. Unbeknownst to me, it was a final goodbye. Cricket stayed on the sofa day and night, barely eating, anxious for her return and mourning her absence.

Two weeks later, I took Bittersweet to the Walden Pond Horse Show and won grand champion. Dad told me to go to the hospital and show my mother my prizes. I had no idea how grave her condition was, and Dad gave no indication. My dear, jaundiced mother smiled at me through her pain when I showed her my silver trophy and championship ribbon. She leaned over and told Frank to take care of me, doubting my father's inclination to do so. The following week, my mother hemorrhaged from her mouth and nose and passed away. I was sixteen years old and alone.

I was in the kitchen when the call from the doctor came. I overheard Dad's reaction; heard him dial my brother and tell him to come out to Medway. Thirty minutes later, Dad met Pete at the door and told him Mom died. They wept in each other arms. As I retreated to my room, I saw Rose Watson ironing in the kitchen. She was the housekeeper at Medway for as long as I could remember and was my mother's friend and confidant. Tears rolled down her dark chocolate cheeks and splattered on the white linen tablecloth. Normally, I would run over and playfully untie her apron, but not today. She was preparing the dining room table to receive the mounds of food the neighbors soon brought. In the South, grieving is soothed with good cooking—a ham, deviled eggs, and a pecan pie would be the first offerings of love and sympathy to arrive from the cousins and friends.

With no one to comfort me, I disappeared into my bedroom and sat stunned in the overstuffed green toile chair, staring at the upholstery. I wanted to climb into the calm setting portrayed on the surface print: decorations of French farm girls picking apples; a boy napping against a hay wagon. I never saw my brother, father, or Rose cry before, and the trifecta of grief tsunamied my soul. Confusion, disbelief, and denial ricocheted around in my head like misfired bullets.

In shock, I stared blankly at the horse show ribbons on the wall, thinking how little it all mattered. Seized by a convulsive sob that rose up from a primal place, hot tears flowed as I kicked the bed at the senselessness of her death. My gut muscles contracted and throat tightened, as the realization that she was gone sank into the sinews of my soul.

Her coffee-brown eyes, my eyes, would never brighten at my presence again. Our inside jokes, Rudyard Kipling stories, and the epicurean camaraderie were all gone. The only caregiver, advocate, and role model for womanhood I knew was no more. Her love, humor, and hopes for me to become a veterinarian were soon to be buried in a premature grave, an irrevocable loss. I damned my father, the impotent doctors, and a distant God; none prevented this tragedy. As an adult, I can understand that my grief was intensified because of the life that could have been and the mother-daughter relationship that never really was.

I stared at the wall covered by satin horse show ribbons. I thought my good performance would win my parents' approval and love. But now, none of it mattered.

On top of the walnut dresser stood my Best Defensive Player trophy for basketball. Not only on the court but in my very heart, I was the "best defensive" player. This layer of toughness was what enabled me to survive these tragic years. But the defensive scarring of my soul would also mean that, for years to come, my protected heart could not enjoy the intimacy I craved.

At her funeral, two days before Christmas, 1975, I sat in our family pew at St. Luke's, across from my forty-nine-year-old mother's casket. I wondered where she had gone. Was there a Heaven? Was there a hell? Where was she? Where would I go? I walked back from her graveside, praying she was finally resting in peace. My teenaged friends met me in the churchyard, and in a huddle hug, we wept.

People brought mounds of food to Medway for the reception after the funeral, and Cricket ran for cover. Somehow, she knew the life her soul orbited around was gone for good. She hid under Mom's bed and whimpered softly.

After Mom died, I realized that she kept our family intact despite her illness, cooking meals and keeping the house together, preserving Medway. Now, it was every man for himself. There was no such thing as grief counseling back then, and no one in the family even admitted Mom was an alcoholic. My sister Jean was busy working, and Dad was out seeing other women.

I poured myself into my riding. Frank fed me, took me to nice restaurants, and bought me clothes and horses. One weekend, we went to the York River Yacht Haven for fishing on Dad's boat. Afterward, Frank and I left before the others, and he took me to his rental house where he showed me *Playboy* magazines. I was badly sunburned, and he started putting aloe lotion on my legs and kept going up. I remember lying on the bed, watching car lights coming by the house and thinking that if that were Dad, he would kill Frank. Part of me wished he would.

With no one to confide in, I told no one. Virginity stolen, trust violated, I did what I thought I had to do to survive those awful years, becoming sarcastic, arrogant, and impenetrable. I rarely spoke to other adults. A friend of Frank's at a horse show glanced at me and said, "Still waters run deep, dark, and dirty." Contempt for men, shame, and defensiveness began to fill in the shucked-out portions of my heart.

One day, a few months after our precious mother was laid to rest, my sister Jean went to pick up our dear Rose Watson. With our mother gone, Rose was the mainstay of our lives, frying chicken for us, cleaning, doing the laundry and holding the household together. There was no answer when Jean knocked on the door, so she got a neighbor to unlock it. Stepping inside, they saw Rose's cold, black body sprawled lifeless on the old oak floor. The neighbor said Rose loved my mother dearly and died of a broken heart.

Two weeks later, Catherine and her husband were coming home at night and didn't see the small, black dog in the driveway. Perhaps Cricket went out in the night, still searching for my mother, or maybe we had carelessly left her out in the dark. Whatever the case, they hit her. Waking me up, they showed me her little black body, still warm. A small stream of blood flowed from one nostril as she lay lifeless. I trembled and felt like I might throw up.

"I'll tell Dad for you," I told them, and we went back to our rooms. I wept into my pillow, heartbroken. Cricket's strong thread connecting me to my mother was broken. When Mom went to the hospital, the only anchor in our lives was pulled up. Without her in the house, each of us acted out our pain in rebellion, but not Cricket— she stayed steadfast at her sofa vigil, faithful to the end.

Dad returned an hour later from a cocktail party. I told him the news. His gin and grief sent him into a violent rage. "Go get them," he hissed.

He lit into Catherine and Charlie, saying horrible, unpardonable words. Then he grabbed Mom's lovely goose off the mahogany sideboard and violently slammed it down on the dining room table. The goose shattered, embedding pieces of the ceramic she painted with her last artistic touch into the white linen tablecloth Rose laid out for the funeral reception.

Cricket, the goose, and a piece of me all shattered amid the violence. I stopped crying that night. Death's necrotic hand caught me unaware, again. Once more, I couldn't avoid Dad's violence and verbal spewing. I vowed never to be caught off guard and vulnerable again.

The only area of my world I controlled was my riding, and I was driven to win. Scaling up from Pat Betts's borrowed jacket, paddock boots, and free lessons, I was now taking lessons from professional trainers Jimmy Lee and Joe Fargis and showing in a tailor-fitted Pytchley riding jacket, dark charcoal gray with light blue pinstripes and fox-head buttons. Pat's paddock boots were replaced by expensive, custom-made Dehner field boots with laces at the ankle, spur rests, a capped toe, and fully lined, with my name in gold letters on the inside. My old, deep-seat Argentine saddle with knee rolls was traded in for a new flat equitation saddle with my brass nameplate on the cantle. Training hard, I trotted across the Calais fields, without stirrups, day after day, to perfect my form.

I set my heart on the goal of every Olympics-bound junior rider, to win the hunter seat equitation, US Medal and ASPCA Maclay finals at Madison Square Garden. Qualifying required earning a certain number of points and placing first in an equitation class at an American Horse Show Association rated show. I won the silver medal on my dapple-gray mare, Fiddlesticks, who I picked up cheap from the vet because of a chronic hoof condition. I just needed three more points to qualify for the finals, and this was the last year I was eligible. But something in the horse van spooked Fiddlesticks when returning from a show. She threw a fit and fractured the splint bone in her leg. She needed surgery and was out for the season.

Three points short of qualifying, and it was over. Fiddlestick's splint bone, my heart, and the ladder rung I was climbing up to equestrian greatness fractured. A dream snuffed out makes the heart sick, and my soul was crushed. The top medal I hoped to win at the equitation class at Madison Square Garden had become my idol, but as C. S. Lewis said, "Idols always break the hearts of their worshippers."

With the money I made from selling Bittersweet, I bought a young chestnut Thoroughbred named Look-A-Here, (Luke) who I was training. He was too green to do the equitation jumping classes, but I could at least take him to the Virginia State 4-H Horse Show that fall. He won reserve champion. I was surprised that Dad came to the show. He told me he was having open-heart surgery the following week. It was the early days of those surgeries and risky. The very real possibility of being an orphan rocked me. But Dad proved to be one of the miracles of modern medicine.

I hated my father on one level, but he was my father and part of me loved him. Growing up, we got the belt for misbehaving, and my father's slim slivers of praise were meted out only when I did something well. I lost the ability to separate my performance from who I was. Long gone were those carefree days of riding up to Trix Jones's store with my friends. I left them behind, along with the ponies and my innocence. I no longer rode for fun. I rode to win.

Winning, I felt like a champion. Losing was devastating. When it happened, it wasn't just that I lost a class at a horse show. No, it was that *I* was a loser. My identity was now dependent on winning and looking like I had it all together. I built my fragile self-image with

Izod shirts and blue ribbons. On the outside, I looked as polished as my custom-made boots, but on the inside, I was just as hollow.

In my fourth and final year at the Virginia State 4-H Show, Luke and I won Grand Champion. The trophy was a silver champagne cooler with my name engraved on the side. I had come a long way from my borrowed show clothes and Shadow's fraying braids. It was my highest achievement. But for every victory, I had wholesaled a piece of my body and soul along the way.

Amy Grant's song, "Ask Me," is about a sexually abused little girl, who asks where was God in the middle of her shame? I too wondered if there was a God up in the heavens, and like the girl in the song, it would be years before His mercy would bring me life again.

That same year, Dad did the unthinkable and sold my beloved Medway. True to form, on moving day, he forgot to tell my sister Jean. She came home to a vacant Medway. She swore she heard someone in the basement that night—doubtless the ghosts of the relatives gathering the pieces of their hearts before Medway passed out of the family for a season. Dad moved us thirty minutes away into a townhouse in Midlothian, which I despised as much as I did my father. The next fall, I kicked the dust of that place off my shoes, packed my new suitcases, and left for Virginia Tech with dreams of becoming a horse vet.

In eighteen years, the tender little girl, so full of wide-eyed innocence and passion, was transformed by her violent, unpredictable world, a world where she learned that love could be lost or betrayed but certainly was not dependable. Every childhood jab was a lesson, teaching me to survive by splitting from my true self into a tough, performing self. Little did I know that a merciful shaft of light was about to shine on the pain of my past. Someone who also endured betrayal, loss, and death was about to step into my world. His light was soon to transect the darkness of my heart, softening it, and making it bright again.

CHAPTER 12

VIRGINIA TECH–GOD STORY

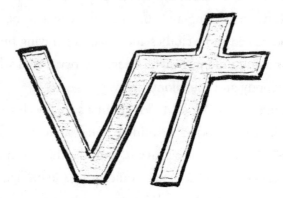

If God were small enough for us to understand, He would not be big enough for us to worship.

—*Evelyn Underhill*

...and if you spend yourselves in behalf of the hungry and satisfy the needs of the oppressed, then your light will rise in the darkness, and your night will become like the noonday.

—Isaiah 58:10

The impressive Blue Ridge Mountains were the backdrop behind the Virginia Tech dormitories, welcoming me with their autumnal grandeur in the fall of 1978. Standing outside West Ambler Johnson dorm, I saw the tears welling up behind Dad's sunglasses as he and Jean hugged me goodbye. During the summer, I read to my father a nice letter from my future roommate introducing herself. His response was, "Like hell; I'm not sending you to college to live with some nigger from New Jersey. I have friends at Tech," he said pausing, his face distorted with the purple prejudice of hate. "I'll get that changed so fast it'll make your head swim in circles." And he did.

Entering my dorm room, I heard my new roommate speaking in a fast, unintelligible language. Alicia was an engineering student from Puerto Rico. I was an animal science pre-vet student from Virginia who never heard anyone speak a foreign language. That was just the beginning of the new experiences I was to encounter.

I struggled from day one in my coursework, which included two crippling subjects for me: College Math I and General Chemistry. To my mind, general chemistry is just math trying to disguise itself with elements. When I was in high school at Huguenot Academy, I had a fabulous English teacher, Mrs. Rogers, and placed out of freshman college English. But my math and chemistry teachers were sports coaches, and they gave me passing grades because I played basketball and cheered, "Offense sells the tickets, but defense wins the game."

Compounding the problem was the fact that within a few weeks of the start of the semester, I was selected to be on the Inter-Collegiate Horse Show team, which required me to skip classes to compete in horse shows around the state. The other academic drain was missing two weeks of classes, due to traveling on the horse judging team.

The summer before I started college, I won a place on the Virginia State 4-H horse judging team and was to represent Virginia nationally in judging contests at Keystone International in Harrisburg, Pennsylvania, Quarter Horse Congress in Columbus, Ohio, and the Arabian Nationals in Louisville, Kentucky. Our judging team partied both on the road and back on campus. One night, we imbibed enough sloe gin fizzes to fortify our rebellious hearts and walked to the X-rated movie theater, but even as drunk as we were, it grossed us out and we left just after the film began.

The very next night, there was a rap on my dorm room door. It was Cindy and Julie, who worked with a campus ministry called The Navigators. They asked my roommate and me if we would take a spiritual survey.

"Are you interested in a Bible study?" Cindy asked.

I laughed to myself, thinking that sounded way too spiritual for an Episcopalian, particularly given my current hangover. I politely declined, wanting to enjoy all the fun and freedom of my freshman year. Anyway, it had been years since I thought much about God.

Seven years earlier, after our move from Annapolis to Powhatan, we attended St. Luke's Episcopal Church, but I had only one spiritual conversation—ever—and it was with my mother after a neighbor girl dragged all her friends, including me, to a Mennonite Church youth revival. The speaker shared about praying and asking Christ to come into your life. Some of my friends did just that, but my fearful heart shied away. When I returned home that night, though, I ran straight to my room, bereft.

I did not understand why I felt spiritually orphaned. I had felt a sacred place in the church where something beckoned to my heart with the promise to fill up the neglected places in my soul. I was drawn to its tender warmth like a moth to a flame but feared being burned alive because the only intimacy I knew ended in the shattering abuse of my body and soul. The inability of my alcoholic parents to show unconditional love and nurture left me famished, and what-ever was in the church that night felt like love and nurture. I sensed a lover's embrace that was within reach, but I just couldn't respond. It was like Michelangelo's fresco painting of the near-touching hands of God and Adam. Earlier that night, God reached down to tenderly touch me, but I pulled my hand away.

Dazed by a sense of loss, I felt as if I had let something very important pass me by. Something I couldn't define, something spiritual, supernatural, and frighteningly powerful was out there. I sensed I needed the deep peace and love, even wanted it, but an internal battle raged. I resisted and won the scuffle but felt like I lost some cosmic war. Several of my friends walked to the front of the church and said some prayer, a prayer that affected them mightily. They wept tears of joy. But I couldn't deal with all that raw emotion and slunk out the back of the tent. I was a tomboy, a strong survivor, and a self-determined, independent fighter. But my tough, ice-cold choice left me confused, empty, and afraid, and on my bed at home later that night, I broke down.

Overhearing my sobs, my mother came in. Barely able to articulate my emotions, I told her about the evening. Seeing her normally unemotional and distant daughter undone, she feared drugs or a cult was the culprit for my uncharacteristic behavior. After all, just a few weeks earlier at Huguenot, our headmaster called all the students into the auditorium and informed us, "Marijuana has raised its ugly head in our student body! It will not be tolerated!"

It must be that marijuana stuff, she thought, because only drugs could make me confide in her. Fearing the worst, she told me I needed to go to confirmation classes at St. Luke's and called our priest.

That spring, I attended the classes for confirmation, and we recited the words to the Lord's Prayer and the Nicene Creed from the 1928 *Book of Common Prayer.*

THE LORD'S PRAYER
Our Father, who art in heaven,
Hallowed be your Name,
Thy kingdom come,
Thy will be done,
On earth as it is in heaven.
Give us this day our daily bread,
And forgive us our trespasses as we forgive those
Who trespass against us.
And lead us not into temptation,
But deliver us from evil,

For thine is the kingdom,
And the power, and the glory.
For ever and ever. Amen

THE NICENE CREED
We believe in one God,
the Father, the Almighty,
maker of heaven and earth,
of all that is, seen and unseen.

We believe in one Lord, Jesus Christ,
the only Son of God,
eternally begotten of the Father,
God from God, Light from Light,
true God from true God,
begotten, not made,
of one Being with the Father.
Through him all things were made.

For us and for our salvation
he came down from heaven:
by the power of the Holy Spirit
he became incarnate from the Virgin Mary,
and was made man.

For our sake he was crucified under Pontius Pilate;
he suffered death and was buried.
On the third day he rose again
in accordance with the Scriptures;
he ascended into heaven
and is seated at the right hand of the Father.

He will come again in glory to judge the living
and the dead,
and his kingdom will have no end.

We believe in the Holy Spirit, the Lord, the
giver of life,
who proceeds from the Father and the Son.
With the Father and the Son he is worshiped and
glorified.
He has spoken through the Prophets.
We believe in one holy catholic and apos-
tolic Church.
We acknowledge one baptism for the forgiveness of sins.
We look for the resurrection of the dead,
and the life of the world to come. Amen.

When I completed them, the bishop confirmed me, and I took my
first communion, surrounded by the fragrance of lovely Easter lilies
at the St. Luke's altar.

But there was a twelve-inch distance between memorizing something in my head and learning it by heart. As we said the words before
the bishop, it was like the adults talking in the Charlie Brown movies,
"WAAAA Wa WAAA Wa WAAAA." I said all the right things, but my
world was so chaotic, I didn't grasp their meaning. Walking up the
dogwood tree-lined sidewalk to the church, I wanted to change from
my stealing, smoking Sarah Freddy days, and I thought perhaps confirmation would keep me out of the detention house. My godmother,
Betty Sue Scott, gave me a little gold cross and prayed for me until
the day she died fifty-seven years later. Charlie Kennon, my godfather,
a good and godly man, prayed for me as well.

Later that spring, at St. Luke's Lenten supper, I shyly shared how God healed me from spinal meningitis. It was in front of about 100 people, including parents and peers, and I choked up as I spoke. My sister's friend, Debbie, kicked me under the table, giggling at me. The emotion of the moment caused me to burst out in tears. I went home mortified and vowed never to share about God again and ran to Duke for comfort. My heart felt the words that J. D. Salinger wrote in *The Catcher in the Rye*, "I'd rather have a goddam horse. A horse is at least human for God's sake."

When my mother died, I stopped attending St. Luke's, except for the obligatory Christmas and Easter services. The lingering questions regarding her death still plagued me as I headed to college, "Was there a Heaven? Was there a hell? Where had my mother gone? Where would I go?"

Regardless of my inner turmoil, I was not ready to accept this Bible study invitation from some stranger at my door, but my room-mate did. The women came by once a week and held the sessions in our dorm room. Feigning disinterest, I observed from my top bunk. I noticed that they had a sincere love for one another and a genuine-ness I did not have with my drinking buddies. There was something about them that was just different. I couldn't put my finger on what it was, but it both repelled and attracted me.

Alicia also started going to their rallies, which were weekly meet-ings with other students on campus. She always seemed so happy when she returned, and it irritated the crap out of me. Competing that fall, I had won top honors in the national judging contests, but academically, my performance was less than stellar. Missing weeks of classes, poor study habits, partying, and Frank's visits left me barely hanging on to D's in math and chemistry. Getting into veterinary school is extremely competitive, and I began to see my lifelong dream of becoming a veterinarian crumble. Final exams were upon us, and

Alicia, seeing my panic, dragged me to the Catholic Mass in Tech's War Memorial Chapel. It was the first time I prayed in years, and in desperation, I pleaded, "God help me be able to copy the exam answers of the student beside me, so I don't fail chemistry and math, Amen." Sometimes help comes in mysterious ways. I did pass, but only by the skin of my teeth.

Returning from Christmas break, I determined to make a new start. Alicia and the girls continued to have their Bible study in our dorm room. My mother's death caused me to wonder about the after-life; this curiosity drew my interest as I listened from my bunk bed.

Alicia told me that there were some cute boys at the Navigator rallies, so I finally went. Yes, there were two handsome guys there, and it was a nice-enough group of about fifty students, but it was not for me. They sang songs, none of which I knew, but the most disconcerting thing was that they talked about God like they knew Him, like Jesus Christ was their friend. I determined not to return.

The next week when Cindy and Julie came, I had an excuse ready. They saw through it and asked why I did not want to go. Irritated that they were picking at the scab of my soul, I shot back, "People were talking about God like they knew him, like some genie in a bottle. I bet they were on drugs or something."

"Would you like to know God personally? We could share the Navigator's *Bridge to Life* illustration. That shows you how," Julie said kindly.

Too taken aback by the thought of it, I could not think up another excuse fast enough.

"Sure," I said, and the three of us sat down on the cool tile dorm floor of 7021 West A.J. The devil must have choked on his chew, as he swallowed his tobacco wad, watching this scene unfold and sensing his power over me begin to loosen. Julie pulled out a piece of note-book paper and handed it to Cindy. Placing it horizontally, Cindy drew a line across the top connecting the words *God* and *man*. Above the line, she wrote the word *spiritual* and below the line, the word *physical*.

"God created us to have a love relationship with Him—to be with Him physically and spiritually forever, walking with Him in the Garden of Eden, talking like we are now," Cindy explained. "But Adam and Eve messed that up by choosing their own way instead of God's. They got booted out of paradise, breaking their physical and spiritual relationship with God in the garden, and that is when death entered the world."

She drew a wedge transecting the line and wrote the word *sin* in it. Then she crossed out the words *physical* and *spiritual*.

I was totally out of my element, but happy that I at least recognized Adam and Eve's names and remembered the story of the Garden of Eden.

"Yep, heard of them," I said, trying to act cool and in control. Intrigued by their explanation of how death got started in the first place, I reflected on my own struggles with my mother's fate, wondering what happens when we die.

"So do you think there is a Heaven and a hell? Is there life after death? After all, the mortality rate is 100 percent . . . well, except for Elvis," I said, wanting to somehow lighten up these heavy questions and not seem so interested.

Smiling at me, Cindy drew a big crevice or chasm, with man on the left ledge and God on the right ledge and eternal separation or hell at the bottom of the chasm. Then she wrote that "sin" word again in between the two cliffs.

"You like writing that word, don't you?" I asked, thinking that most of these Bible thumpers were fond of the word, *sin*, and *hell* as well.

"Do you know that sin is actually an archery term?" she asked. Not waiting for my answer, she continued, "In the olden days, when they competed, they used a string to measure the distance from the bull's eye to where the arrow landed. The distance the arrow fell short was called sin."

"A sin string," I quipped.

"The bull's eye represents perfection, anything less than hitting the bull's eye is called sin," Cindy continued. "In spiritual terms, God is the bull's eye because He is perfect and holy. So the distance we fall short of being holy and perfect is called sin. Why don't we look at what the Bible has to say about all of this?" she said and handed me her opened Bible with highlighted verses.

Oh great, a Bible thumper who uses a highlighter. I didn't think you were supposed to even write in The Holy Bible.

"Would you please read these verses in the book of Romans?" she asked, pointing to the page.

Somehow, "Hell, no" just didn't seem the appropriate response, so I said, "Sure" with an it-isn't-going-to-kill-me tone.

After reading just three verses, I learned that everybody sins, and because of that, we all are going to die, and after that, we were all going to face judgment.

"So where is the good news here?" I asked, sensing I was in trouble.

Ignoring my question and looking me straight in the eyes, she asked, "Where do you think you are on this illustration?"

Screwed, I thought to myself as I pointed to the bottom of the chasm where she wrote eternal separation, *hell.*

"How do you think you could get to the other side, God's side, where you would have eternal life with Him?" she asked.

"I guess by being a good person," I said.

Damn, screwed again. I certainly haven't fallen prey to that temptation.

"Mary, God loves you and sent Christ to die on the cross for you and forgives everything wrong you have done in your life." Cindy said it with such love that I was undone. "He gave us the gift of eternal life to be with God forever. Where would you like to be on this illustration?" she asked kindly.

I pointed to God's side with His forgiveness, love, and eternal life.

She drew a cross as a bridge from one side to the other with *Christ* written over the word *sin*.

Now Christ was on the illustration, clearly bridging the gap from my side to God's side, forgiving all of my crap. It seemed so clear, simple, and suddenly inviting. She asked, "Do you want to ask Christ into your life, to forgive you, love you, and bridge the relationship with God?

I felt as if something was wooing me, something freeing and warm, drawing my heart; it was irresistible. It would be difficult to calculate who was more surprised, me, Cindy, or all of the company of Heaven when I said a soft, "Yes."

Cindy looked at Julie. No one had ever said yes with Cindy, and she didn't know what to do.

Julie stepped in and said, "You need to surrender your whole being. It's not just a mental assent; it's *everything*. He promises in Revelation 3:20 that He is right here, standing at the door of your heart and knocking. You have heard His voice. If you open the door, He promises to come in and be with you and you with Him. Jesus knocks at the door of our hearts, but he is a gentleman and won't barge in without an invitation. The door handle is only on the inside, and you have to open it by praying for Him to come into your life."

"I don't know about praying," I said, shrugging my shoulders and wondering how serious she was about that "everything" bit.

"Prayer is just talking to God like we are talking now. Would you like me to say the words aloud, and then you can just repeat them after me?" Julie asked with a reassuring smile.

This time I knew that there was nothing else for me to do. Choked up, I nodded yes.

Having no idea what I was doing, I bowed my head, surrendered, and asked Him into my life. Together we said, "Dear Jesus, thank you for dying on the cross to forgive my sins. I accept you into my heart. I give you my life. Please come and change me. Amen." I winced and shut my eyes just in case there might be a lightning bolt.

Sometimes the best way to get somewhere is by taking a leap of faith. That night, I took the leap. A warm feeling filled my chest, a seeming cease-fire from some of my inner fighting and questions and a peace I never knew before. I knew I would be with the Lord when I died; something small, solid, and unexplainable deep within me shifted.

You have come a long way, baby, I said to myself a week later as I lit up a Virginia Slims cigarette. Just then Cindy's voice rang out in the hallway.

"Crap," I breathed through my teeth, quickly tossing my cigarette out the seventh-floor window and fanning away the smoke as I opened the door. *What made me throw out that perfectly good Virginia Slims menthol? Was I feeling embarrassed, guilty, and ashamed? What an odd sensation!*

Cindy stopped by to follow up on our conversation. "Do you have any questions?" she asked.

Did I have any questions? My whole life was a question.

Every night for the next two weeks, she came by, and I plied her with questions and arguments. My scientific mind was not going to accept things at face value. If Cindy could not prove it, I questioned it. I soon realized the scientific method is a poor grid for determining supernatural truth. It was like using an E. coli filter to catch a prion; just because you could not catch it, didn't mean it wouldn't kill you. I did not want to become my stereotype of born-again

Christians—polyester suits, little goody two-shoes, "holier than thou,"—but I did want Christ. My moods were like a horse's ears. When a horse is intent on something, their ears are straight up and pointing forward. If something makes them angry, they put their ears back. I shifted one ear forward and one ear back, constantly, during those early months of my journey with Him.

Cindy put up with me being a Push-Me-Pull-Me: come close, I love this newfound peace and joy, but go away, I don't believe this stuff. I liked to argue, anything to keep this newfound faith from coming in too far too fast. When things were getting too personal, I would ask her questions to take the pressure off my own flinty heart and try to stump her.

She did her best to defend the God she loved. But finally, she asked, "How do you defend a roaring lion?"

Looking at her stupidly, I said, "I don't know. How do you defend a roaring lion?"

"You don't have to," she said as she handed me a Bible of my own. "Read the book of John yourself, and then we'll talk."

Me? Actually, read a Bible—by myself? I didn't know if I was ready to put that much skin in the ring.

"OK, I snapped back, "I can do that." *So why am so I upset? This Jesus stuff is starting to rock my boat.*

Remembering how Granny prayed for me when I had spinal meningitis and read her Bible daily, I called and asked her what she thought.

"Mary, dear, every well-read person has read the Bible," she said, "It is the most-read book in history."

Well then, I'll read the damn thing, if only to be well-read! I opened it. *Thin pages, small print, and no pictures—this ought to be fun,* I thought sarcastically.

Not only did I read my new Bible, but I also got hooked into a *Lessons on Assurance* Bible study with Cindy, Alicia, and some girls on my hall.

The next week, one of my horse-judging buddies asked me after class if I wanted to go out partying that night. I said without thinking, "No, thanks. I'm going to a Bible study."

Her eyes lit up. "You, ha-ha, funny. You almost had me going there for a second. I thought you were serious. I can't see you ever becoming one of those Jesus freaks. See you tonight," she said, laughing her way down the hallway.

Walking across the drill field back to my dorm room, I heard in my head, as clear as a bell, "There is no God. Who are you kidding? This is all some fake, made-up crutch. Give it up. Skip that Bible study thing." The wild hyenas of doubt ambushed my newly formed faith like it was a wounded antelope calf.

That night, I shared with Cindy, "I have some concerns about all this Christianity stuff." I told her the words I heard that afternoon, "I just need to figure out some things, you know, like the miracles, resurrection, virgin birth, and stuff like that."

"Good timing," she said. "Tonight, we are studying about assurance of victory and about how Satan attacks our thoughts."

"Right, the horned guy with his little red pitchfork?" I asked, incredulous.

"Not exactly. I doubt he has a pitchfork," she smiled, "but he does exist and tempts us, discourages us, and causes us to doubt our faith. Mary, picture a dog on each of your shoulders. Whichever one you feed is going to grow bigger. Feeding your old nature, that dog named Doubt will grow bigger. If you feed your new creation by reading the truth of God's word, that dog will grow bigger."

The next week, just as I left for spring break, Cindy stopped by and handed me a well-worn copy of C. S. Lewis's, *The Screwtape Letters*.

"Read this over your break. It's a funny, fictional story of how the enemy tempts us," she said.

I opened the cover and read her inscription:

Dear Mary,
I am praying for you, Ephesians 1:17, 18.
171 keep asking that the God of our LORD Jesus Christ, the glorious Father, may give you the Spirit of wisdom and revelation, so that you may know him better. 18I pray that the eyes of your heart may be enlightened in order that you may know the hope to which he has called you, the riches of his glorious inheritance in his holy people,

Love in Christ,
Cindy

I knew she prayed for me and that she loved me; both were true. The thought of disappointing her if I turned away made me sad.

"Thanks," I mumbled, brushing a tear from my face. Wanting no more dialogue, I turned and got in my Mustang.

Was it worth it? Maybe it was just a crutch. Horribly conflicted, I drove home to Powhatan for Easter break. Down Interstate 81 North I sped in my little convertible, pondering it all. Cutting across to Highway 460, I cried out, "Jesus, are you really real?"

Just then, for some reason, I glanced to my left and saw Bonsak Baptist Church. My eyes followed the tall, white steeple to the top, where the setting sun reflected brilliantly off the cross. Breathtaking.

I pulled over.

The words of Jesus that I read in John that week, flooded into my heart: "I am the way, the truth, and the life. No one comes to the Father except through me." And, "Your heart must not be troubled. Believe in God, believe also in me."

Wow, I guess two can play at these mind games. Jesus's words and the beauty of His setting sun caused my doubts to vanish. I smirked at my own pride, thinking that I was smart enough to figure out what St. Paul called "the mystery of the Gospel." As the English Anglo-Catholic writer Evelyn Underhill said, "If God were small enough for us to understand, He would not be big enough for us to worship."

That Sunday, I attended St. Luke's Easter service, and the old hymns I sang my entire life were now electrified with meaning. On my way back to school, I sang them from my heart as I again passed that old cross:

"Welcome Happy morning!" age to age shall say:
    Hell to-day is vanquished, heaven is won to-day!!"

Then, I belted out,

Jesus Christ is Risen Today Alleluia!
    Our triumphant holy day, Alleluia!
    Who did once, upon the cross, Alleluia!
    Suffer to redeem our loss, Alleluia!
    Hymns of praise then let us sing, Alleluia!
    Unto Christ, our heavenly King, Alleluia!
    Who endured the cross and grave, Alleluia!
    Sinners to redeem and save, Alleluia!"

I believed and meant every word I sang.

Over the next months, as I burned through the pages of that little brown Bible, it wasn't so much that I took hold of the Scriptures as that they took hold of me. I thought I was strong and could resist, but just like Mary Magdalene, I fell in love with Him. I was no longer just following a religion, I was deep in a love relationship with this Jesus

Christ. I felt I was living the words sung by Mary Magdalene in the musical *Jesus Christ Superstar.* I was changed and I felt like a different person. It was as if by some magical spell, a God spell, my heart was warming, and my attitudes changing on numerous fronts.

But I was still involved with Frank, and as the time rolled around for his monthly visit Cindy prayed that I would not go. She even came over when he arrived, thinking her prayers and presence would make me change my mind. But I just waved goodbye as I got in his gold Corvette. My exuberant sharing in the car about my newly found faith was met with stony silence, only exceeded by the ice-cold stare when I chose to sleep in another bedroom. The following week, when he called, we both knew it was over. I wept over the small sink in my dorm room, splashing water over my face, so Alicia would not see my tears.

Despite his lust, Frank cared for me when no one else in the world was there. His humor sustained me through the tragic times. His belief in me and his finances enabled me to become a champion rider. But he stole my childhood innocence and robbed me of a piece of my soul.

Going to bed that night I felt both loss and freedom, sadness and joy—a confused amalgam of emotions. Doubts plagued me: Had I done the right thing? I knew he would keep everything we owned together; I would lose it all. It was a costly decision: my life in the horse world as I knew it was finished.

Sorrow spent the night, but in the morning, there was a new spring to my step, a freshness in my soul, an unexpected and strange tranquility. Jesus showed up. If I was happy, Cindy was overjoyed when I told her the news.

That spring the church where Cindy was taking me, was doing baptisms in the Roanoke River, and we both decided to take the plunge. I was baptized as an infant, but I wanted to make an outward profession of my new, inward faith. Besides, I thought, if once was good, two times would be better. Each of us stood before the church and gave our testimonies, telling our spiritual journeys, and sharing a meaningful verse from the Bible. We both chose Isaiah 58:10, ". . . and if you spend yourselves in behalf of the hungry and satisfy the needs of the oppressed, then your light will rise in the darkness, and your night will become like the noonday." That became my life verse, through which I would filter my important decisions.

On the day of the baptism, the first candidate stood up and told the joke about a little boy being baptized: "The preacher bent him over backward in the clear river water and when he brought the dripping boy up, the preacher asked, "Son, did you find Jesus?"

The boy said, "No." So the pastor dunked him under again and asked, "Boy, did you find Jesus?"

"No," he replied. Exasperated the boy said, "Preacher, I didn't see him this time, either. Just how long has he been missing?"

When my turn came, I trembled as the church elder came up to baptize me, and it wasn't just because Dr. Kingston was my organic chemistry professor. There was something sacred happening, and I felt its import. Tears came to my eyes as I shared my spiritual journey and how different my life was from the night I prayed on my dorm room floor. Cindy joined me in the river, and we were baptized together. Hallowed space surrounded us as we hugged, dripping wet in that cold mountain water.

That day, I committed my life to "spending myself" on behalf of the spiritually and physically hungry. Carrie Underwood's song, "Something in the Water," rang true for me, because now I was changed. I was stronger.

If my old horse buddies saw me baptized, they would have sung the words from the Randy Travis song, "Pray for the Fish". The fish wouldn't have enough room to swim with all my sins in the river.

I continued studying the Bible with Cindy and meeting with her one-on-one. That summer, I attended a training program with the Navigators at the University of Maryland. Each of us found jobs wherever we could, but in our free time we did topical studies, looking up all the verses pertaining to certain themes and made life applications.

All went well until we came to the topic of forgiveness, which brought me up short. *Frank? My father? Really, Lord?*

I read Corrie Ten Boom's book *Tramp for the Lord,* about how she and her family were arrested by the Nazis for harboring Jews and were put in concentration camps. She recounted how Christ enabled her to forgive when she was powerless to do it on her own. She said that those who could forgive their former enemies were able to return to the outside world and rebuild their lives, no matter what their physical scars. Those who nursed their bitterness remained invalids. Or, as Richard Rohr says, "If we do not transform our pain, we will most assuredly transmit it." I still had anger toward Frank but asked the Lord to help me to forgive him. The Lord seemed to want me to go talk to him in person. I'd heard it said that not forgiving someone is like drinking rat poison yourself and waiting for the rat to die. At the end of the summer, I called Frank and asked if we could talk. Surprised, he agreed. I drove to his new place and asked forgiveness for my part in our relationship and told him I forgave him for his. He brushed me off. Then he handed me an envelope with my brass nameplate from the saddle I rode, and we parted company. I knew forgiveness was not based on his response. I did what the Lord asked of me, and that was enough. I would drink no poison.

Nikki Giovani, the Distinguished English professor and poet, said after the Virginia Tech shooting in 2007, "Forgiveness is not for the recipient. It's for the aggrieved. We cannot have someone who hates us, define us. That's what forgiveness does, it defines who you are."

I felt free from my bitterness and was beginning to embrace my new identity, my new belonging, and His love for me. Over the summer, my desire to go deeper in my relationship with Christ had grown. This new relationship drew me like the comforting logs of a wood-burning stove, warming my soul. At times, its flame erupted in an intimate passion, greater than any lover. But most of the time, it was a steady, slow burn: a transforming fire. If I drifted from Him, I would feel the chill.

Cindy encouraged me to co-lead a Bible study with her and to share my faith. I will never forget the thrill of the first person I led into a relationship with Christ. It was exhilarating, like a spiritual buzz. Seeing someone come to know Jesus and eternal life in Him, I rejoiced with the angels in Heaven. I led another woman to Christ but was unmotivated to get together with her and follow her up like Cindy did with me. A week later I was reading Acts 10 where the Lord showed Peter a vision about all the animals coming from Heaven and being acceptable because God created them. He went on to say that God does not show favoritism, but every person in every nation is loved by Him. His word was an ice pick, breaking through the frozen ice cubes of prejudice that my father placed in my heart. The first women I led to Christ was white, the second black. Immediately I recognized my reticence to spend time with her because she was culturally different than me. As the Holy Spirit convicted me, I wept. I asked the Lord to remove any prejudice instilled in me from my childhood.

It wasn't just blacks whom my father did not like, he said any man with a beard was an animal, and any ugly woman would make a train jump the track. Anyone with poor grammar or bad manners he called tacky times or trailer trash. Effeminate men he said were "light in their loafers." I was angry at how blind I was to my own bias and all the ways I was conditioned to hate all the people my father hated. I asked the Lord to forgive me and change me. I remembered Dad forcing me to give up my best friend in first grade because she was black. I wondered where she was and how she was doing. I thought of Rose Watson, our housekeeper at Medway. Thinking of missed relationships, times I lost when I could have loved and been loved, saddened me.

Grieved, I realized that I embraced many lies about people who were different than I was. I gave all the misconceptions to the Lord. I felt a lifting take place. Generational bondage of hatred was gone, and in its place, the warmth of a new freedom, truth, and love was born. Little did I know that He was preparing my heart for future ministry in South America and Africa, and with international students from around the world.

Time passed quickly, and before I knew it, it was the last day of the last semester of my last year at Virginia Tech. The excitement of graduation day, however, was overshadowed by a cloud of uncertainty. In just a few days, I would graduate from my Virginia Tech womb. So many times, when studying for exams, I wished they were over, but now that they finally were, I wanted the time to extend. I realized college life wasn't so bad, especially when you looked at the alternative—work. College was spitting me out, scarcely more prepared than when I entered, except that now my soul was fortified. I was changed, stronger in His strength, not my own. I deeply believed in a God who loved me and had a plan for my life. Good thing, because I sure didn't have a clue.

I went to the campus bookstore to buy a few souvenirs to remember my time as a Fighting Gobbler. I'd always loved books and couldn't resist strolling through the aisles smelling the freshly printed pages. Happening upon the row of textbooks for the newly opened vet school, my heart sank. After years of trying to establish a vet school in Virginia, the state legislature finally approved the opening of a teaching hospital at Virginia Tech. All my life I dreamed of being a veterinarian, and now that there was a school in Virginia, I wasn't going. I sat down on the carpet between the aisles and flipped through the impressive, expensive books: *Miller's Anatomy of the Dog, Large Animal Surgery,* and *Adams' Lameness in the Horse.* I couldn't help myself. Filled with melancholy, I sat for a long time, my throat dry and eyes moist.

Had I missed God's calling? Was I letting this opportunity pass me by? Why did I feel this sense of loss? My grades improved since freshman year, but they weren't good enough to get into vet school because there was such a backlog of applicants. Those who didn't have straight A's weren't accepted. Was I lacking faith? I knew that nothing was too hard for God and that if He wanted me to be a vet, He could get me into vet school.

However, after finishing four years of college, I was tired of studying. Studying was never something I enjoyed. It didn't come easily to me. Years later, I would find out that there was a reason that I struggled academically: attention deficit disorder.

I decided to work with healthy animals instead of sick ones. I would go into the horse business. Joe Fargis, my old trainer, now had his own barn, so I headed down to Petersburg to see if I could get a job. He made me an offer, which I accepted, but not before I cashed in on my grandmother's graduation present: an airplane ticket to visit my cousins at Medway Ranch in Texas.

CHAPTER 13
A DETOUR FROM MY DREAM
MEDWAY RANCH, AUSTIN, TEXAS

Texas is a state of mind. Texas is an obsession. Above all, Texas is a nation in every sense of the word.

—John Steinbeck

Some folks look at me and see a certain swagger, which in Texas is called "walking."

—George Bush

Right after graduation, I packed my blue Mustang convertible to the gills and sped out of Blacksburg. As I headed north on US-81, I glanced in my rearview mirror and wondered if it was not just Virginia Tech, but also my dream of becoming a veterinarian that faded into the distance. The thought gave me a sinking feeling in my gut. Fortunately, I had no time to get mired down in my regrets. I was headed to Texas. Two days later, butterflies swirled in my stomach as I boarded my first airplane.

My mother's sister, Shep Wyatt-Brown married an Episcopal priest who was assigned to a Texas parish after graduating from Sewanee. Their family drove up to visit our grandparents at Medway in Powhatan, Virginia, every summer. The oldest cousin, Alexandra Shepherd, nicknamed "Ecky," married a Texas oilman and named their Austin property "Medway Ranch."

The economy was booming, and my cousins lived as large as the state. After arriving in Houston, we flew in a private plane to their ranch in Austin. The handsome young pilot even let me fly the plane briefly.

The finishing touches were being done to the ranch house when I arrived. It was a replica of our great-great-grandfather Boss Shepherd's hacienda in Batopilas, Mexico. He built it after serving as governor of Washington, DC, and he lived there while in the silver mining business. The newly built house was on a section of the Colorado River known as Lake Austin. It was a spectacular a 5,800-square-foot ranch house, with white stucco sides and a tile roof made crooked to look like the old Batopilas hacienda. It had two large wings on either side of a huge central room. Opening the front doors, we were ushered into the great room with gorgeous aged oak paneling with intricate carvings of wild game bought from the old New York Stock Exchange. At one end of the room stood a twenty-foot stone fireplace where two overstuffed dark brown leather sofas engulfed me in their embrace. At the other end of the great room was a banquet table. Little did I know that in the years to come, I would eat scrumptious dinners there with visitors from around the world. These cross-cultural exchanges would create a spacious place in my heart for internationals and help prepare me to live overseas in the future.

About 100 yards out the front doors stood the matching stucco horse barn with a three-bedroom apartment above it. The apartment had a fireplace, a small kitchen, and double doors that opened onto the second-story deck that faced the river.

Soon after arriving in Texas, I realized that it was not just the people but the entire state of Texas—including the food—that swaggers. The mesquite-smoked beef brisket was the best thing I ever stuck a tooth into, and the enchiladas and tamales at Rosie's had the power to make one forget the Alamo. When I first saw their bumper stickers—"Everything is bigger in Texas!" "I wasn't born in Texas, but I got here as fast as I could," and "Don't Mess with Texas"—I thought all Texans were braggarts. But soon I realized it is just who they are. Their entire way of life swaggered, and I loved it!

The warm Southern hospitality of my Texas relatives made this shy new graduate feel right at home. The excitement, adventure, and "bigness" of Texas captured my heart and I did not want to leave.

Still starry-eyed, I returned to Virginia to start my job at Sandron, Joe Fargis and his partner Conrad Homfeld's show-jumping stable. Mucking stalls, feeding, grooming the horses, and setting the fences for them as they schooled their mounts in Virginia, as well as at the Madison Square Garden and Hampton Classic horse shows was an excellent education. Little did I know I was working with the best of the best. Two years later, Conrad would win the silver individual medal in show jumping at the Los Angeles Olympics, beaten only by Joe, who won the gold. In the next decade, the two riders would be inducted into the Show Jumping Hall of Fame, along with the two horses with whom I worked, Touch of Class and Balbuco. The experience, being a part of a top-ranked show barn, was invaluable, but I knew I didn't want to be a groom for the rest of my life, and trying to get Medway Ranch out of my mind was like trying to unboil an egg.

I was thrilled when, after five months as a stable hand, I received an offer from Ecky to manage Medway Ranch in Texas. It seemed like the best thing that could have possibly happened at this point in my life. I prayed about the decision and sensed the Lord's leading, but I had never lived that far from my family or from the godly women who mentored me in my walk with the Lord. I worried without them I would fall away from the Lord. My friends prayed with me regarding the decision and gave me the names of the Navigator staff in Austin.

My self-doubts about going into the unfamiliar badgered me until finally, after much prayer, I pressed forward in reliance on God. He showed me before that He was the author of my faith; now I would trust Him to be its sustainer. At twenty-two years old, I moved to Texas to single-handedly take the ranch from losing money to becoming a profitable enterprise. Little did I know that in the next few months I would meet rattlesnakes, scorpions, and tarantulas.

My cousins lived in Houston, four hours away, so much of the time, I lived by myself in the apartment above the ten-stall barn. My first morning, I sat on the apartment's second-story deck, which cantilevered out over the pasture. Facing the Colorado River, I watched the mist rise off the water as it snaked its way through the ravine. Like a daily apparition, it reminded me of the mystery of the Holy Spirit, and I could sense the presence of the Lord close to me as I read His word. Looking out at the horses grazing peacefully in the fields of Bermuda grass, I thanked God for the opportunity to manage His breath-taking creation.

I read Matthew 25:21, "His master replied, 'Well done, good and faithful servant! You have been faithful with a few things; I will put you in charge of many things. Come and share your master's happiness!'"

Working in Virginia, I felt I was faithful as a groom but had little responsibility. When I took up management of Medway Ranch, I felt that He put me in charge of many things, and I was sure I'd hear God say, "Well done!" but after the first six months of averting near-disasters, I was not quite so sure and I wondered if I would ever share the Master's happiness.

My troubles started immediately. Having slept through most of the only beef production class I took in college, I had little knowledge of and no hands-on experience with cattle. The ranch foreman wasn't pleased that a recent college graduate was the cause of his pink slip and left just hours after I arrived, giving me only some brief feeding instructions for the livestock, "Get in Neutral; you'll learn a lot about trucks keeping her running. Most of the gravy's done been driven outta her," he muttered, pointing to a dusty tan pickup truck. "There is the bull; keep that feeder full," he said, pointing to the behemoth as we drove past.

"How much grain does he get?" I asked, partly needing to know, and partly trying to make conversation.

"As much as he wants," he chuckled. He drove off the driveway and up a steep hill where the cows hid behind some cedars, "They get five bags of alfalfa cubes."

We drove back to the barn in silence. I followed him into the office, where he plopped some files on the desk, "Here are the Paint mare records. They are all due next month." He turned to get into his pickup truck, holding his hand out to me, "Here are the keys to everything and the ranch credit card. Good luck getting this place to make money," he growled as he spun out the driveway.

"Thanks. That is what I got hired to do, and I am, by God's grace, going to do it," I said into his dust.

The first morning, I loaded the truck with the alfalfa cubes and navigated the slippery path to the hill where the cows waited hungrily.

"It can't be that hard to feed cattle," I muttered as I drove "Neutral" so named because even when in gear she drove like she was still in neutral. She was a Chevy flatbed dually whose odometer, air conditioning, and all other indicators of life had long since given up the ghost. Jumping out of the truck, I confidently shook the bags of the four-inch, green cubes onto the pebbly ground. Hearing thundering hooves, my eyes flashed up and saw the entire herd of twenty cows with their calves stampeding me!

I dropped the bag and tried to get away. But in my haste, my feet spun out in the gravel like a cartoon character, and I fell before their pounding hooves. I covered my head and waited to be trampled to death. Thinking I should have met Jesus by now, I opened my eyes and saw the herd stopped just short of me and was devouring the alfalfa cubes. I sat up on what I thought was going to be my grave, laughed, and thanked the Lord for His protection.

With one chore behind me, I went to feed the expensive horned Hereford bull named Big Red, but this time I wasn't so fortunate. His auburn hide strung tight over a ton of muscle and two-foot ivory horns set on his massive head, he gave no hint that he was one to suffer fools. His steel feeder, ten feet tall and five feet wide, needed to be filled weekly. After loading the feed bags on Neutral's back, I opened Red's pen and drove in. I thought he would be happy I fed him, but as I emptied the last bag I heard a snort behind me. Glancing over my shoulder, I saw Big Red draw one of his super-sized front legs back and paw the ground. The last thing I saw before scrambling onto the top of the feeder were the whites of his eyes and his horns cocked sideways about a foot from my behind. When I drove into Red's pen, it delighted me to see my first roadrunner and jackrabbit dart across the pasture, but their speed didn't compare with mine as I scrambled up the side of the feeder for dear life, just as Red's horns crashed into its side, nearly rattling me from my perch.

Having dispatched me, Red then sank his massive muzzle into the feed, satisfying his vast rumen. He gave me an occasional menacing glance as sweet molasses drool dripped from the corners of his bovine mouth. The truck was too far for me to jump on its roof, and it was hotter than a jalapeno atop the metal feeder that was baking in the Texas sun. Sweat trickled down my back as I waited for Red to finish. Fifteen minutes later, he sauntered off. I watched him until he was out of sight, then I scampered down the feeder and bounced off the ground like a pogo stick into the truck, just in case he made a hasty return. As I drove Neutral out the gate I had left open, I saw that my troubles weren't over. Red was nowhere to be seen. He escaped! I went to get Pat, the only horse on the ranch who knew how to work cattle and prayed as I saddled her up. I was a preppy girl from Virginia who knew nothing about how to lasso a bull, but I hoped that Pat knew how to drive him back. The rest of the day I searched the 450-acre ranch unsuccessfully. Despondent, I headed to the barn, wondering how I would tell my cousin that within thirty-six hours of my arrival, I lost their $20,000 prize show bull. Glancing through the still-open gate into the bull pen, I berated myself for leaving it unlatched in the first place. There he was, head in the feed bin. Apparently, he doubled back when I was riding around the ranch. The Lord proved once again to be my protector and provider, a lesson He would brand on my soul in the four years I managed the ranch.

Over the next few months, I gained the cattle experience I sorely lacked. But it wasn't just the cattle that were worrisome. The horses also presented a problem. Before his hasty departure, the foreman said the paint mares would foal soon. The first foal born was an all-white filly. But within hours of her birth, she was writhing in agony. The vet diagnosed lethal white foal syndrome, having inherited the lethal color gene from each of her parents. Born with an incomplete GI system, the filly had to be put down. Over the next few weeks, the rest of the seven mares delivered, mainly solid-colored foals, with only two paints from the entire crop. With such a low ratio, I was sure to lose money quickly. I lamented with the prophet Habakkuk that even if there were no livestock in the pens, I would be joyful in the Lord and trust Him.

Since the breeding operation was unsuccessful, I decided to turn the broodmares into riding school horses and use them for teaching lessons. The summer after my freshman year at Tech, I taught at the Level Green riding school in Powhatan and learned how to run a camp. My cousin, Darrell who lived in Austin, provided the first students by bringing her daughter and her friends.

I advertised in the local paper, put brochures in the schools, bought some radio time on the Christian station, and sent out press releases to the newspapers and TV stations. The lesson schedule filled up quickly as did the summer day camp called "God, Kids, and Horses."

As in any successful operation, Medway Ranch's achievements were a team effort. I found two talented riding instructors through friends at my church. They loved the kids and were dedicated to the profession. The ranch owners believed in me and allowed me the freedom to operate the ranch as I thought best. But what mattered most to me, though, was that we saw people's lives changed on the ranch. Through hearing about the love of Christ at the camp, many students and employees asked Christ into their lives, and their lives were transformed. Juan is a good example; I met him at a shoe store while buying some work boots. He wanted a change from selling shoes and I needed a strong man to work on the ranch, so I hired him. When he came to the ranch, he knew little about God, kids, or horses, but he was peerless when it came to drinking and reckless driving. He even flipped his Volkswagen on a nearby bridge! I never trusted him enough to let him haul livestock, but once I sent him with the trailer to pick up railroad ties for the riding ring. A few hours after he set off, a car salesman called and asked if I had insurance. When I said yes, he retorted, "Well, that's good because you are going to need it. Your employee turned too sharp and clipped a Mercedes and pulled that car into two other cars. Then he backed over my fence!" Fortunately, our insurance covered it all, but I talked to Juan, "When I hired you, you told me that you were a Christian, but I have seen little evidence of it in your life."

"Yeah, I try but I just keep screwing up," he replied looking at his feet.

"Well, we can't do it on our own. We need the Holy Spirit's help."

"May I share this Holy Spirit booklet from Crusade with you? I asked opening to the first page.

"Sure, go for it," Juan replied.

"We can be a Christian, but not have Christ on the throne of our lives or be filled with the Holy Spirit. Then we end up trying to live a godly life in our own strength, which is frustrating and, frankly, just doesn't work. We must surrender our lives and ask the Holy Spirit to fill us. The word *fill* means to control, like to be filled with rage, but of course, He fills us with Himself. When the Holy Spirit guides us instead of ourselves, we begin to change, and we receive some gifts: love, joy, peace, patience, kindness, gentleness, and self-control. You have wrecked two vehicles in your short time here at the ranch, and I think you could use some self-control. It isn't a one-time filling, but daily you ask God to direct and empower you. Would you like to pray and ask the Holy Spirit to be your counselor, power, and guide?"

"Yes, I feel something is lacking in my life," Juan said, a tear slipping down his cheek, as he closed his eyes, prayed, and asked to be filled with the Holy Spirit. When he opened his eyes, a huge smile spread across his face, and he fairly skipped out of my office.

Over time, many things in Juan's life changed. As he gave up trying to live a godly life in his own strength, he started to drink in moderation, his driving improved, and he began to grow in His love for God, going to church and attending a Bible study. The following year, I noticed some rock piles stacked about five feet tall around the ranch. I asked Juan, "What's up with the rocks?"

He said, "I raised some Ebenezers."

"What?" I asked, intrigued.

"I read in the Old Testament how Samuel, after winning a battle, wanted to make sure the people of Israel never forgot what God did for them. So he put up a stone pillar and called it Ebenezer, which means 'Stone of Help.' They are my Rocks of Remembrance because I don't want to forget God's faithfulness to me and how He refreshes my soul."

"What a wonderful response, a grateful heart, is evidence that the Holy Spirit is filling your life!" I replied, thinking those rock piles will be monuments of thankfulness on the ranch until the Lord returns.

I had much to be thankful for as well. God answered so many of my prayers. Before leaving Virginia, my friends gave me the Navigator staff contact, Theresa, in Austin at the University of Texas. We connected my first month at the ranch. She gave me the encouragement in my walk with the Lord I hoped to find. That fall she asked me to lead a Bible study with some students on the UT campus forty-five minutes away. I met with several of the women one-on-one. There was one student who became my roommate at the ranch, helping with the camp and later went on to be a missionary in Cameroon, Africa. Another roommate became a missionary in Thailand.

In the spring, Theresa and I decided to have a summer training program at the ranch, like the ones I attended in college. There were two rental houses on the ranch we used for accommodating the fifty students from all over the state of Texas. Theresa and the program staff shopped and prepared the food. The students labored half a day and then did Bible studies and ministry activities the rest of the time. It was a joyful and powerful time during which the students deepened their faith and got many projects completed on the ranch. Seeing the student's spiritual growth made me want to do more ministry work in the future.

Over the summer, Theresa determined that the Lord called her to be a missionary in Lusaka, Zambia. At the time, I didn't know where Zambia was and never imagined that within five years, I would also live in Africa and go visit her in Lusaka.

Several months after the students from the summer training program left, I was alone in my apartment one night when I heard a noise in the bedroom beside me. The entrance to that room was from the outside barn loft. I picked up my rifle, walked out into the hall, and flipped on the light switch with the barrel. The door that led to the room was shut, and as I stood there, a moral debate swirled in my heart—if I opened the door to find someone with a gun, either I would shoot and probably kill him, or he would shoot me. The implications of taking another person's life stopped me in my tracks; just then the handle to the bedroom door turned before my eyes.

I don't need to make any moral decision—I'm outta here! Heart pounding, I flew down the stairs and out of the barn. I drove to my nearest friend's house ten minutes away, arriving in my nightgown.

Bob, a beefy former Marine, armed himself to the hilt with a knife, shotgun, and pistol. I thought of the bumper sticker, "Texans don't call 911." Standing in the hallway in my apartment, Bob very carefully turned the handle, then swiftly kicked the door open wide. There, standing beside the door, was Simon Single Socket, the one-eyed ranch cat. I don't know how he got in, but he perched himself on top of a chair and was trying to turn the door handle open. It was my rehearsal for the security breaches I would experience when living in Africa and South America in the years to come.

I chose Psalm 20:7, "Some trust in horses and some in chariots, but we trust in the name of the Lord our God," for our ranch verse and made brochures, business cards, and posters advertising in as many places around Austin as possible.

I was learning to trust God for my security, but trusting Him for my success and my core identity was another matter. To me, the two were inseparable. It would take me years to learn that *success* is not a name of God. I was driven to succeed, and I didn't know why. My childhood experiences created a fragile self-image, and I based who I was on how well I managed the ranch. By the end of the first two years of my work, I was proud that Medway Ranch was a thriving training and showing facility. I worked nonstop, my motto being, "It is better to wear out than to rust out," never realizing that either way, I would be out.

It would take me decades to see that although I wasn't an alcoholic, I became intoxicated with the liquor of my labors. My parents dulled their pain with bourbon; I outran mine with busyness. It was my gin, always seeking a greater challenge, a better high, by turning the ranch around and starting new programs. Money, power, and success were the anesthesia for my wounded heart.

I denied the past, and my instincts and habits took over. If Frank's abuse, my father's rages, or my mother's death crossed my mind, I shut it out through work and activity. Dan Allender in his book, *To Be Told* says:

> Not only do we deny the tragedies of our past, but we are also willing to make others pay for the hurt. We are combative toward the tragedies that shattered our shalom, or else we are blind to them or merely dismissive of them. In order to understand our passion, though, we must have access to the moment of the shattering that set into motion both our core paradigm for how we see life and our core determination

of how we live it. Tragedy shapes our deepest passions, and our passions shape who we are and what we will become. It is in the midst of affliction that we become our truest or most false self.

The tragedies of my past shaped who I was, and I based my core paradigm for how I saw life and my core determination of how I lived it on my achievements. I had to perform successfully to be okay, to love myself, and to be loved by others, including God. My thinking was that He loved me like my earthly father did, which was only when I did well.

I was in denial of childhood heartbreaks and in full construction mode, building a successful self. It would be decades before I could bear the reality of the old wound. That said, without accomplishments, I was unlovable. Truly accepting and embracing my true self like God does, fully and unconditionally loved, was at that time as far out of my reach as the Milky Way stars I saw from my barn deck.

I needed to face my emptiness first, but I cut myself off from this self-contempt piece with its shame. Unknowingly, I split myself in two. There was my young Mary self, who survived a chaotic and even violent as well as neglectful world. She fragmented into her false selves, by the grace of God, to survive. Little Mary built a sense of "self" around her abilities, initiation, and successes. This little girl, so unseen, so unsafe, so unprotected, didn't believe she was loved. She didn't believe she was lovable. That was my core wound. It's easy to see now where my defenses were built. I thank God now for those defenses because I would not be alive today without them. But, this Performing Mary believed without her, Little Mary might not exist. Her belief was: *What I do is who I am.*

But, we all must have an intact core sense of self to be whole, healthy people, and this false self or selves I created was holding God and others at bay. This driven Mary was robbing the true Mary of love because she couldn't relax enough to stop performing and let Mary be seen and loved as she was, without performing for God or anyone else. Imperfect, but whole and loved.

At the beginning of my first two years of frenetic work at the ranch, I lit a candle. As I began the third year, I lit the other end, and it was only a matter of time before they would meet in the middle.

CHAPTER 14

LEAVING MEDWAY RANCH

Sad enough to bring a tear to a glass eye.

—Anonymous

The previous ranch foreman spent entirely too much money on the Hereford herd, and it was impossible for me to turn a profit on them. After discussing this with the ranch owners, we sold the herd to cut our losses. Full of joy, two years after arriving at the ranch, I left to deliver the cows and Big Red to their new owner in Waller, Texas. Neutral cheerfully pulled the heavy stock trailer up the last hill on the driveway until she lost speed. A bead of anxious sweat dripped down my neck as she slowed further. I downshifted, and she chugged. I downshifted again, and then she stalled out. I put my foot on the brake, but the load was too heavy and the trailer full of cattle pulled the truck backward as it slid down the gravel hill.

Cancel Christmas, I thought and yelled, "God, help!" as the trailer jackknifed off the side of the hill. At the bottom of the hill was a pond, or a tank as Texans call it, big enough to swallow us all. The headline of the next day's paper reporting the grim accident flashed into my mind: "24-Year-Old Ranch Manager, Gooseneck Trailer Loaded with Cattle Found at Bottom of Ranch Tank. No Survivors." The article would be sad enough to bring a tear to a glass eye. Just in time, the big rig stopped its perilous slide into the pond. The God-brakes kicked in. Neutral started again, and this time she crawled over the top and made it over the rest of the hills to Waller—except for one. Two miles south of the middle of nowhere, Neutral died. With no working instrument lights, I didn't know the truck overheated until steam came out the air conditioning vents, and by then it was too late.

Getting out of the cab, all I saw was an ancient-looking house trailer at the end of a long-overgrown field. I sat for about thirty minutes waiting for a car to pass by, but no one was on that desolate road. I walked toward the trailer, thinking the Texas Chain Saw murderer was surely the owner. As I rapped on the dilapidated screen door, I heard a shotgun lock and load. The door creaked open to reveal a man who looked like the dog kept him under the front porch. His coveralls seemed cooked in Crisco. His beard and fingernails were long and yellow.

"Whoa, no need for the gun," I said.

He stared at me like a cow stares at a new gate.

"Who are you and what the hell do you want with me? You with the gov'ment?" he hissed.

"No, sir. My truck, with a load of cows, broke down. May I borrow your phone?"

"I'll call, damn it," he grunted.

"No worries. I'll wait in my truck, sir," I said, as I backed out of his front yard. He waved the shotgun in the air, friendly as a bramble bush.

When the tow truck arrived, the mechanic quickly fixed the problem, and I was on my way. The rest of the trip to the new owner's ranch was uneventful, and I returned home.

At the time, I was just relieved to be rid of the herd and especially its most expensive member. Little did I know that working with that ornery bull and band of cows at Medway Ranch would prove to be invaluable training for the time when I would, by a series of miracles, become a practicing veterinarian. But that was in the future.

Once the cattle were off the ranch, I was free from the feeding routines and focused on the horse business. I pushed on, opening a tack shop, training a show team of students, and increasing profits through buying and selling horses. My farrier told me about Creasy Smith, a horse trader.

"He's honest as far as traders go, which is to say that he wouldn't hesitate to steal the nickels off a dead man's eyes. Kinda like that story about the father and daughter who went to buy a horse. The horse trader showed them an old horse walking nicely around his familiar ring. 'Folks, he is a fine horse, he just don't look too good,' the horse trader said.

"The father bought the horse, but when they got him in his new home, he bumped into things. The vet came out and said he was nearly blind. When the father called the horse trader and demanded his money back, the old timer said, 'Nope, no refunds. I told you he didn't look too good.'

"Creasy hails from that same horse-trader school of ethics. His horses come with a thirty-second, thirty-foot warranty, but you know what you are doing and can get some good deals outta him. Here is his number," he said handing me the shoeing bill with Creasy's number scribbled on it.

I called Creasy and told him I needed horses. The next month and every month thereafter, he showed up with a trailer load. He always told me that they were from Oklahoma, shown by a 4-H kid and were sound. Some of the horses had a hitch in their giddy-up and were too unsound for the riding program. If any showed potential, we haggled over the price. The ranch hands would gather around just to watch the bargaining.

I learned to negotiate by watching my father wheel and deal over boats and cars growing up. For the first time, I appreciated my father's example. Despite our distant relationship, Christ was softening my heart toward him, and I began to forgive, appreciate, and love him as he was, not how I wanted him to be. I invited him and my brother to the ranch. Dad brought me a tee-shirt that said, "Somebody in Richmond loves you." He talked me into buying some land in Powhatan in hopes I would one day return to Virginia. I appreciated his attempts at our relationship. But, my heart knew to guard itself against his sarcasm and criticism and not to expect emotional closeness.

I applied my father's negotiating wisdom and enjoyed matching my wits with Ol' Creasy. I bought many horses from him, some better than others. One memorable purchase was a lovely dapple gray Thoroughbred we named Ezekiel. I got him for a song, knowing he needed surgery on his back legs to fix his stifle joints. After his surgery, one of my riding students, Angela, begged to take him to her place for the summer until he recovered.

After being groomed, pampered, and led around all summer, he was as gentle as a lap dog and returned sound. Now it was time to mount him and get him going for the riding school. He was fussy about the bit being in his mouth and goofy when I put the saddle on him, but Ol' Creasy assured me he was shown by a 4-H'er. He seemed a bit nervous, so I asked the student to hold him while I mounted him in the ring. With my left foot in the stirrup, I was in mid-air, about to bring my right leg over the saddle, when he reared and jerked away from her. I landed catawampus in the saddle.

It didn't matter how I landed because I wasn't going to stay there very long. I tried to pull up his head, which he swallowed between his knees. But it was too late—he exploded, and I was unloaded. As I lay on the ground with the wind knocked out of me and a handful of Ezekiel's mane still in my hand, it dawned on me—he was never broken to ride.

Angela, fearing for her life, scampered up to the top of the fence, out of harm's way. Her mouth was still open like she wanted to say something, but there were no words. When I finally caught Ezekiel by the tattered remains of a broken rein, I said sarcastically, "Next time, we should lunge him first" and quoted the poem "Riding Lesson" by Henry Taylor, including the line about when you realize they are going to throw you, then you should get off.

Fortunately, after several months of training, Ezekiel turned out to be one of the best show horses at the ranch, and I sold him, and many others, for a nice profit.

I was always thinking up new activities. Our students rode in the local Fourth of July parade. They rode to the Texas state capitol building, raising money for the 1985 Mexico earthquake victims through World Vision.

It was the spring of my third year at the ranch, and I volunteered at the Special Olympics in Austin. I met one of the staff and told her I was interested in doing a therapeutic riding program, "If you supply the kids and the expertise with the disabilities, I'll supply the horses and riding lessons."

"Deal!" she said excited at the prospect.

With that agreement, we started providing lessons for those with disabilities. It was a fulfilling time for me, for the riders, and for the many volunteers who helped. The program won the Mayor's Award for Meritorious Service. These, and other successes, got the ranch featured in the Austin paper and by the local TV station.

Of course, any business is likely to succeed when its manager works fifty to sixty hours a week, rarely takes a vacation, lives on site, and takes calls seven days a week. I was driven to succeed, outrunning the pain of my past and, like most workaholics, headed for burn out. I met the challenge of turning the ranch into a thriving riding school that honored God and made money. That done, there were no more hoops for me to jump through or so I thought. I had attained my goal, and that's all I could see at the time.

But, instead of feeling fulfilled and enjoying a well-earned rest, I was empty and tired. With no new challenge to keep me busy and even though there was never a dull moment at the ranch, from a rattlesnake in my file cabinet to one on the dashboard of the truck, not to mention tarantulas in the feed bin or scorpions in my apartment,

I was bored. The gyrations of my professional performance did not satisfy my soul. I had fed my ego and gained the world, so to speak, but I'd buried my soul in the double-entry columns in the business day-book. I was successful, but I really didn't know who I was.

My restlessness was compounded when the ranch veterinarian, Dr. Wade Bradshaw told me, "I am going to Nepal to be a missionary with World Concern, to show the love of Christ through treating the villagers' livestock."

Hearing this sent ripples through my soul. *Had I given up my lifelong dream of being a vet? What was I doing with my life, anyway? Was teaching kids how to ride as valuable as being a missionary overseas? I've done everything here; shouldn't I be moving on to some bigger and better challenge?* Subconsciously, I asked, *was there still another bar to jump to be fully loved by God and others?* The old performance mode was working overtime!

I attended a presentation at the University of Texas by a Navigator missionary, Marcia Elliot, who worked in Indonesia. She challenged me to consider mission work. It seemed a pretty high bar since I had only flown once and had never left the United States, but if it was the next hoop to jump though spiritually, I would go. I booked a flight to Indonesia. I didn't have a passport or even a birth certificate but was determined to get all my papers in order and go. Landing in Yogyakarta at three in the morning, and then seeing geckos on my bedroom walls was my first eye-opener. The next day, the smells, sounds, and hordes of begging children accosted my senses. At dinner that night, I ate one of the extremely hot peppers on my plate, so hot that it served only as a garnish since even the Indonesians didn't eat them. I could barely breathe and couldn't speak for ten minutes. Rice was the only thing on my plate that I could recognize, and we ate it in some form or another for every meal. I rode on the back of the missionary's motor-cycle through the insane traffic of the city, hanging on for dear life as I sat side-saddle in my skirt and nearly was bounced off at every ubiquitous pothole. We flew to Bali where the beaches were beautiful, but I felt a darkening of my spirit, like an oppressive cloud hugging me, as we passed the sacrifices to their gods or evil spirits on the sidewalks, in the rice paddies and on the beaches. We drove out to a village deep in the rainforest and watched the witch doctor put two little girls in a trance and lead them over hot coals, barefoot, unhurt.

The cross-cultural experience with its spiritual warfare, poverty, and different languages, food, and customs was too much for me. I did not feel the Lord leading me to be an overseas missionary, but I was still looking for a change.

During my fourth year at Medway, my friend Theresa with the Navigators moved to Zambia, so I attended a Bible study led by some women on staff with Campus Crusade for Christ, an international evangelistic ministry, at Bari's house in Austin.

Merry, one of the leaders, and I hit it off. She had a quick, fun laugh, and I loved the way she would chortle—her brunette head shaking—at my ranch adventures. Spending time with her, I felt safe. Her dark coffee eyes seemed to see into my soul, and a deep connection began to form between us. I could share some of my feelings, and she affirmed me, telling me she was proud of me. Her insightful questions drew me out. Her words became big in my ears, as I allowed her to speak deeply into my life.

She was not afraid to ask me hard questions about the guys I dated. She also challenged me about my friendship with a woman who kept her horse at the ranch and wanted to spend an inordinate amount of time with me. When I described the relationship to Merry, she warned me about co-dependent relationships. I was hurt, as I thought I was doing well just to have a close friendship. It would be three years and a spiritual tumble later before I understood the wisdom in her words about emotional dependency.

Merry knew I wasn't happy and that I was searching. She wanted to help, and she gave me what she knew in the contexts she understood. She opened her Bible and had me read Matthew 9:37, "The harvest is plentiful, but the laborers are few." I agreed with her that there were many people who needed to hear about the love of Christ and too few people sharing it. Then she drew a chart on paper and showed me 2 Corinthians 4:18, "So we fix our eyes not on what is seen, but on what is unseen. For what is seen is temporary, but what is unseen is eternal." She wrote *Temporary* at the top of one column of the chart and *Eternal* on top of the other column.

"What are some things that people give their lives to that are temporary, that do not last forever?" Merry asked, and filled in the column with my responses: jobs, education, money, possessions, and power. Then she asked me, "What can we invest in that does last forever?" and wrote my answers in the second column: God, His word, people.

"Where are you spending most of your time, Mary?" she asked with her friendly, piercing eyes. "That's a rhetorical question—something for you to ponder and put before the Lord," she added kindly.

Merry then had me turn to the parable of the talents in Matthew 25:14–30. Three servants were given five, two, and one talents (money) to invest for their master. The first and second invested and doubled the money, but the third servant was afraid of the master and buried his single talent in the dirt. So, the Master gave the last servant's one talent to the first servant. Merry drew a table and filled it in to illustrate the parable, turning to me and said, "Mary, do you feel that you are fully investing your talents for the Lord?" she asked, and without pausing for an answer, she asked me to consider whether I could be using my life more fully for the Lord by working in full-time ministry. Then she challenged me go on full-time staff with Campus Crusade for Christ.

I loved the work at the ranch, seeing the horseback riders come to Christ and having Bible studies and ministry outreaches, but I was restless. After much wrestling in prayer, I applied to join the Crusade staff. I wanted to do all I could for the Lord and Merry, and it seemed this was the next step.

My time at the ranch had been fast-paced, one performance recital after another, but I hadn't known the people very well—except on the surface. It takes real sharing on both sides before people really connect, and I had walled my heart off long ago. Merry and I connected on a deeper level, and I wanted to perform for her as much as for God.

I believed He was calling me to go into full-time ministry. However, I failed to notice that working in full-time ministry in the Crusade modus operandi didn't really fit the outdoor, animal-loving, veterinarian wanna-be. If any doubts surfaced, I squelched them, and after raising financial support to cover my costs, I left the ranch. My Christianity was real, but in a way, superficial. My faith in God and experiences with Him were very deep and genuine. But my "performer self" mixed herself in here. There was a genuine relationship with Christ, but there was also a religious Mary. The religious Mary gave some definition to my identity as I sought a core sense of self. Religious Mary, however, was not my truest self—not yet. We all must die to our religious constructs a million times as we journey with Christ. Religious Mary believed that she could control life by being "faithful" enough. I needed a healthy, intact core sense of self to be whole. I needed to shed my false selves that held God and others at a distance.

I was assigned to the adult ministry of Crusade in Washington, DC. It was wonderful to be back on the East Coast, closer to my family, and I loved the ministry with some fantastic women, but I missed the ranch and horses. Some of the dysfunctions from my childhood began to surface in my unhappiness. Like the old Indian proverb, "We can outrun that which is behind us, but not that which is within us."

CHAPTER 15

DC—THE FALL

Washington is a community of Southern efficiency and Northern charm.

—John F. Kennedy

Outside of the killings, D.C. has one of the lowest crime rates in the country.

—Mayor Marion Barry

My four years of adventure on Medway Ranch ended when I joined the Crusade staff, raised my financial support, went to training in San Bernardino, California, and was assigned to work with career women in Washington, DC. I drove from Austin, Texas, to DC, arriving Memorial Day weekend, 1986, in an aging brown Buick donated to me for use in my new ministry. I had to part with my worn-out '66 Mustang and my two dogs. My heart broke, knowing that sacrificial service meant parting with the things I loved.

During my first foray into the city, Patti, one of the staff women who helped me navigate the DC streets exclaimed, "Lord save us!" I had turned my porky Buick the wrong way down a one-way street and made a sprightly exit before an oncoming bus could hit us; but, failing to decipher the myriad road signs and the complex diamond grid of the lettered and numbered streets, I turned the wrong way down yet another one-way street.

In the same way, I would soon learn I was just as lost trying to decipher my emotional signs and the complex grid of childhood shame that rose to the surface with my move to DC. A nebulous need propelled my actions forward without my understanding or conscious permission—a holy desire for intimacy, to love and to be loved. Initially the excitement of the call to full-time Christian work muffled the cries of my heart and the culture shock of city living. In that moment of my life, ministering to women in DC seemed like the best way to share the unfathomable love of Christ with others; the same love that so radically transformed me. Unfortunately, my mind began to divorce my secular ranch work from callings that seemed more sacred. It would take me years to see that all our work matters to God and that His kingdom is breaking in everywhere, not just through Christian professionals.

I loved leading Bible studies with many remarkable women on Capitol Hill. They were fun, witty women who wanted to know God better. Being on staff had me in a position of authority that stroked my fragile ego, allowing me to keep my wounded heart at a distance from those I led. I thought that I needed to be an example of holiness, with the false view of godliness that meant I struggled little. I did not share deeply from my heart or expose my past wounds. The women were so lovely and teachable. Even though I was unable to be very authentic and transparent with them, they still shared openly about their own struggles as single women in DC. I met for hours with each of them, listened to their stories, prayed for them, and directed them to His word.

My heart broke for them as they opened their lives to me. One woman confided her distrust of men and her gender confusion, both resulting from being repeatedly raped by her brother growing up. Another told me of her despair over being single and her struggles with pornography and masturbation. Others shared the scars of broken relationships after giving their hearts and bodies to men who had taken their virginity and discarded them as carelessly as a used

Kleenex. Still another confided about the nightmares she had after having an abortion. She never told anyone her story because she was afraid of being judged. I told her that Jesus did not condemn her confession but forgave her, and she wept as I told her how dearly God loved her. Her suicidal thoughts diminished as she experienced God's merciful grace through post-abortion counseling. As I cared deeply for these women, they brought joy to my life. I was not a professional counselor, but pointing them to the Lover of their souls and praying for them caused them to begin to heal and grow in their faith. Despite my own shortcomings, the group thrived. There is a saying, "Even a blind pig finds an acorn every now and then."

But, within a year, the shine of the new ministry and city life dimmed. Performing in my one-woman ministry show simultaneously excited me and left me feeling empty and exhausted. I worked to gain God's love and acceptance, although I could never have admitted it. I built up my self-importance by boasting of my ministry success. One of the staff, thinking me puffed up, quoted Winston Churchill, "There, but for the grace of God, goes God."

It wasn't my pride, but my lack of knowing my true self as His beloved that made me strive for results.

The enemy of our soul has been at his tricky ways for eons, and he knew my vulnerabilities far better than I knew them myself. Satan strung his bow and shot his flaming arrow deep into the emptiness of my thirsty soul. C. S. Lewis said, "God whispers to us in our pleasures, speaks in our conscience, but shouts in our pain: it is His megaphone to rouse a deaf world," and I was about to get an earful.

I left my wheelhouse at the ranch where I used my gifts of entrepreneurship, leadership, and love for animals to take the new, glossy position in DC. The transitions of my state of mind, with the vocational and geographic changes, mimicked nature's shifting seasons. Leaving Texas, I sensed loss like sadness of summer ending, and anticipation like one experiences looking forward to the brilliant fall colors. I moved from the spacious beauty of ranch life, with the horses that anchored my soul, to the drain of the frenetic city life, with its traffic, politics, and people preoccupied with power. A subtle grief crept in as my life changed. Joy came with the anticipation of moving to Washington, but the charm of city life and new ministry, like the passing enchantment of the fall colors, soon faded. My friendless soul became like a dying winter leaf, slowly floating through the air to the frozen ground, where its outer edges curled up, gray and brittle. The next two years would be the most difficult in my spiritual journey, and I would end up in a state of decay like a lifeless winter leaf on a compost pile.

The summer after my second year on staff, I flew to Colorado to take some Bible classes. I needed an inexpensive place to stay for three months, so I asked the seminary if they knew of any places I could rent. I was given Jill's name, an interior designer, who rented rooms in her house to seminary students. Jill was a tall, cool glass of sweet tea. Southern, kind, beautiful, with jet-black hair and eyes the color of dark roasted coffee beans. We were opposites in many ways; in contrast to my ranch background, she did not have a tomboy bone in her body. Rather, she was cultured, witty, well-read, worldly-wise, and most importantly, she was renting a room in her beautifully decorated house I could afford. Our conversation came easily, and I enjoyed getting to know Jill. It was nice being around someone who wasn't part of my work.

Most people said that I was outgoing and friendly, but my girl-friends didn't know me intimately enough to detect the invisible wall I erected when someone started to get too close. I wanted to be above reproach, so I was careful not to become too intimate with men and get into trouble; never did I imagine I could get in trouble with another woman.

Growing up, I built stone walls to protect myself, mortaring the rocks together with the red Powhatan clay from my past abuse. I didn't recognize my lack of self-disclosure, but Jill did, and her words slipped under my protective walls and weaseled their way through the defenses of my heart. They offered an invitation to a deeper relationship.

"I think I am pretty easy to get to know," I replied, my pride rising when she tried to excavate under my defensive walls.

"Definitely," she said sarcastically. She saw the Empress with no clothes and she laughed at her. I was undone. Jill persisted in getting to know me with her insight and barbed wit and called me out on my habitual distancing. I knew I needed to grow in my interpersonal skills, so I purposed to be more open and vulnerable. She was a great conversationalist, and when she reached a soft place, she gently pried, pulling out broken shards from my difficult past. We spent hours together talking and hiking in the Colorado Rockies. I felt heard and understood, and even nurtured. I didn't have to pretend that I liked the city or that full-time Christian work was the most fulfilling thing I ever did. I told her how much I missed my dogs and the horses at the ranch. When I deflected or acted like I was in control and super-spiritual, she made fun of me. Her jabs broke through my falseness, and made me mad enough to respond with thoughts and feelings that were authentically mine. I began to trust her.

With Jill, I could relax and let out the hidden sigh I held in all my life. Being in a relationship with her was like resting in a peaceful place at the bottom of that sigh. I shared about my mother's death, and she held me as I wept the first tears in many years. Her embrace did more than just console me; it met some primal need for affection. There was a sacredness in the space after that cry where something mysterious happened between my body, soul, and spirit that brought me comfort, partly because I felt safe with her and partly because God used my tears to rinse out some of my grief and bring me His peace. I felt loved, and I began to love her.

With my mother dead, I needed a feminine role model. Jill showed me how to tie scarves and match outfits for my new city-girl role. In the kitchen, where I was not very comfortable, she taught me how to make enchiladas and lasagna.

Our conversations were the short stories of our lives we read aloud to one another. Each chapter was welcomed, accepted, and acknowledged. She opened her heart to me, while we sat on her overstuffed white couch, lingering in the place of mutual acceptance, understanding, and care. I was frustrated with my boss and tired of the city life, and she listened to my rants. She was recovering from a recent divorce and I listened compassionately to her heartbreaking story. We shared the hurts from past relationships and abuse; no topic was off limits because the trust between us had grown so deep. I felt unconditional love, and my thirsty soul began to blossom. I was making A's in my seminary classes, and she told me I was smart, witty, and beautiful. My parents rarely complimented us children to help us develop a core self-image, so her affirmation filled the empty pockets of the little girl in me. My tough heart softened. As intimacy deepened, we became intertwined, like two indistinguishable vines, inseparable. We shared our clothes, books, food, everything. I went from erecting protective walls to having no boundaries, from independent to emotionally co-dependent. We patched the holes in each other's hearts with temporary paste, wounds which could only be healed by the spiritual Balm of Gilead. But, as the fake pearls made of paste soon disintegrate, so would our relationship.

I had a God-given need for nurture and intimacy, but the emotional dependency that formed, combined with the lighter fluid of hormones, was a volatile mix. Legitimate needs were being met in an illegitimate way. She cared about me, drew my heart out, loved me, and seduced me. I don't know how it happened, but when we first held hands and hugged, it was life-giving. However, the relationship continued to evolve from there. One day, I came home and she came into my bedroom. The next thing I knew it was sexual. Afterward, I was confused, even nauseated. It was raining. I got up and walked outside for hours, the pouring rain and guilt pelted me, soaking me to the skin. I was shocked and devastated. The emotional dependency had knit our hearts together, but as in any relationship, physical intimacy melded our souls. My trusting body craved her nurturing touch, my heart thirsted for the mother love I never had, and these longings drove me headlong to a crash resulting in an overwhelming shame. The confusion that ricocheted around in my head was unbearable. I did not understand any of my internal drivers from the wounds of my childhood, and nothing was reconciled by a single walk in the rain, no matter how hard it pelted me.

I wrote in my journal, "My worst fears have been realized." I had convinced myself that the emotional enmeshment wasn't bad, even though I looked to her to meet my heart needs, instead of looking to the Lord. She was my emotional idol, and as C. S. Lewis said, "Idols always break the hearts of their worshippers."

Undone, I needed to come clean, so I flew to Austin to admit to the Crusade leadership what happened. It was like standing before the Sanhedrin, "You must move back to DC and limit the relationship."

It felt like death. My head told me to separate, to maintain boundaries, and pull apart—but every fiber of my heart desperately wanted to maintain the intimacy. I knew if we were to ever have a healthy relationship in the future, there needed to be some time apart.

The rip in the relationship left me breathless and bereft; the sense of loss and humiliation felt incalculable. I was blindsided by the turn in this relationship and by the depth of my desire. I was ashamed of the emotions that controlled me—my need and how I met it in such an unacceptable way. Separating myself from Jill brought back memories of losing my mother with the same tsunami of grief and regrets. When I began to realize how my same-sex relationship would be viewed by others, especially believers, a shame seeped deep into my marrow. I went into full-time ministry to gain more acceptance, more importance, subtly thinking it would increase my worth with God and people. Not only was I wiped out emotionally and spiritually, I now felt professionally disqualified. Hearing of my same-sex relationship would send most evangelicals caterwauling into their own closets. I wondered how a relationship that seemed so good could have caused such wreckage. It would be decades before I discovered the motivation from my past that caused me to yearn for the emotional intimacy and nurture of a woman.

Successes and failures constituted my identity, so it wasn't just that I failed, but I was a failure, incapable of receiving Christ's mercy. I stayed at Medway Ranch while I was in Austin and visited my old horse friends. I realized the horse bond never really turned me loose and wondered where it might lead me in the future.

Returning to DC, I moved back in with my old housemates where I was living when I left but told no one about what happened in Colorado. I had been renting a house with two roommates, Susie, who was a wildlife biologist, and Stasi, a teacher. Both were lots of fun, and our house became the popular singles' spot to socialize.

But, I felt I had lived the words of the old hymn, "Come Thou Fount of Every Blessing," "Prone to wander, Lord, I feel it, prone to leave the God I love."

Feeling disqualified, I left staff. My soul needed to be with horses, so I sent my resume to local riding schools. Intellectually, I knew the theology of grace and forgiveness, but my heart struggled with feeling unworthy. I couldn't accept the work He did on the cross, and I couldn't crucify Him again.

A month later my Texas staff friend, was visiting DC and called, "How are you?"

"Fine," I replied.

"'Fine, the Christian F word," he said, "Mary, I have a lot of people to meet with in DC, but if you want to meet and tell me how you are really doing I'm glad to meet with you."

"Okay then, let's meet at Denny's." He was one of the few people who knew my situation, other than my bosses, and I had long since stopped sharing my heart with them.

Over a cup of coffee, as black and bottomless as my mood, I said, "I left staff because I am unworthy to serve Him, and I am shackled by a guilt I can't shake."

He considered my words and asked me a question with such kindness it momentarily pierced though my failure, depression, and spiritual devastation, "Mary, what part of the cross wasn't good enough for you? What did Christ leave lacking that you have to make up for through your remorse?"

My throat felt like chalk dust. I blinked, hoping my lashes could hold back my brimming tears. I felt the powerful truth behind his words, "I just feel totally defeated and wiped out. He called me to do a job, and I failed Him."

"Satan has you just where he wants you—off the front lines and out of the race. Are you going to stay there?"

I shrugged, "I still struggle with this issue."

"We all struggle with something, our thorn in the flesh. Temptation is not sin. Jesus was tempted. "The only difference between the saint and the sinner is that every saint has a past, and every sinner has a future," he said quoting Oscar Wilde. "Why don't you go to a Christian counselor and work through the traumas of your childhood?" he suggested.

"Yeah, maybe," I said, thinking, *when hell freezes over I'll go to a therapist. I'm not crazy.*

My shame made me sad, which translated into anger and control. *At least I can escape this conversation; we are done here,* I thought. "Hey, thanks for your time. It was great seeing you." I said, still wanting to look like I had some starch left in my soul. I stood up, paid the check, and left.

CHAPTER 16
EUROPE—THE RISE

Travel can be one of the most rewarding forms of introspection.

—Lawrence Durrell

The summer I resigned from staff, my housemate, Susie, was going to Rome, Italy for an internship with the Food Agriculture Organization. My other housemate, Stasi, and I had never been to Europe, so unemployed, depressed, and directionless, I did what any logical person would do. I took off for a month "across the pond."

To prepare for our trip, we threw a pre-Europe party, inviting our well-traveled friends to get advice on cheap places to stay. The week before, my housemates visited Fourth Presbyterian Church and met Jack, the guy in charge of visitors. He was a handsome, young, single banker who lived in DC. When Jack called to follow up on their visit, Susie told him about her travel plans and learned that he spent a semester in Denmark while studying at Vanderbilt. Thus, he made the cut for our cosmopolitan invite list—unbeknownst to me.

At our gathering, I was surprised by this party crasher, and I asked the charming stranger who he was. Despite this awkward introduction, the conversation soon flowed easily between us. As I sat cross-legged on the couch, he told me all about his adventures in Europe, "I ended up in Rome when I was supposed to meet someone in Venice. Be careful, the train cars unhitch and go in different directions at certain stations." I soaked up every second, wondering what my trip would be like.

"That is a handy bit of info, thanks," I replied smiling.

"It will cost you a visit to my church when you return," he replied, flirtatiously.

Armed with advice from our friends, we boarded a plane the next day. My father, thankful I was no longer doing the "Christian stuff," gave me a Eurorail pass that made escaping my current life that much easier. Our first stop was London. I made a beeline to the Tate Gallery to see paintings by my favorite equestrian artist, George Stubbs. The precision of his art was enthralling; he dissected horses and studied anatomy to perfect his depictions of the animals down to the smallest muscles. But, as interesting as these first paintings were, my jaw dropped when I beheld the life-sized portrait of Whistlejacket, rearing above me. The chestnut stallion's eyes bulged, ready to defeat any challenger, and gave me a fearful pause.

I continued wandering through the wing, feeling my soul fill from the banquet of imagery. Then I stopped in my tracks: two paintings of enamel on copper. The first was a gorgeous white stallion meandering carefree down a hill. In the cave at the bottom of the hill crouched an immense lion, muscles taut, ready to spring. The next painting showed the lion clinging to the terrified horse's neck, fangs ripping flesh, imparting mortal wounds. No one else was in the room, and I sat a long while, brooding over the painting. Something about it hit me. It wasn't just about sadness for the horse, I somehow saw myself in the painting. *I am just like that stupid horse, attacked by the enemy and mortally wounded. I was captured by the strength of my desire and now am shackled by shame.* "Lord, why is this so unshakable? Why does it continue to hold my jugular? Will you at least try to help me?" I cried out and sunk my head into my hands.

Tattered bits of St. Peter's words drifted into my mind, "Be alert. Your enemy prowls around like a roaring lion looking for someone to devour." "No joke, Jose," I mumbled, glowering, as I reviewed my year. *Why did I leave Medway Ranch, only to be devoured?* I heard a still, small voice say, "Yes, dear one, you are wounded, but not mortally. Resist the devil, and he will flee from you. Draw near to God, and he will come near to you." I sat silent, surrounded by the musty smell of old paintings. It was a long time since I heard God speak to me. Spiritually, I tried living my childhood motto, "When the going gets tough, the tough get going," but I wasn't tough enough to stand against the enemy's lies or my own. Richard Rohr in his book *Redemptive Suffering* says, "Suffering is the only thing that is strong enough to destabilize our imperial ego for us to begin to see who we are in God and who He is in us. Here we are indestructible."

The Lord was calling me to shed some of my false selves and to have a deeper identity in Him. I realized that to embrace God's mercy, I had to embrace my weakness—admit the things I did—and then forgive myself. Only then could I accept and feel His forgiveness.

I walked to the paintings and looked the lion in the eye and, with a heart of faith, said, "I resist you; now flee from my life." My words alerted the guard in the next room; he walked in knitting his eyebrows together and cocking his head sideways to warn me not to filch the paintings. I left the gallery, bought a sandwich from a street vendor, and sat on a bench with the pigeons. Mulling over my time with the Stubbs's painting, I recalled Lawrence Durrell's words, "Travel can be one of the most rewarding forms of introspection."

I fed the soggy portions of my sandwich to the pigeons and watched as a small sparrow bossed them around and stole the crumbs. I felt bossed around by the enemy's accusations and that Christ's forgiveness and love for me had been stolen. Sitting there in the sunlight, a warmth started to thaw something frozen inside me, like the king released from Sauron's spell by Gandalf in Tolkien's, *Fellowship of the Rings.* Tossing my trash in a waste bin, I walked to Shakespeare's Globe Theater and read the quote, ". . . then the world's mine oyster" from Shakespeare's *The Merry Wives of Windsor.*

Great, that figures; my world is a gooey glob between two shells covered with barnacles. The magnificence of the horse paintings lifted my spirits enough that my humor returned. The next three days, Stasi and I traipsed through London. Touring Westminster Cathedral, the plaque for the missionary doctor David Livingston inspired me: FOR 30 YEARS HIS LIFE WAS SPENT IN AN UNWEARIED EFFORT TO EVANGE-LIZE THE NATIVE RACES, TO EXPLORE THE UNDISCOVERED SECRETS, TO ABOLISH THE DESOLATING SLAVE TRADE, OF CENTRAL AFRICA . . .

Seeing the Poet's Corner at Westminster and reading the epitaphs of the writers buried there got me thinking about recording my adventures at Medway Ranch. Feeling the allurement of writing, I walked through the British Library. Reading handwritten works by C. S. Lewis and J. R. R. Tolkien inspired me to go to Oxford the following day to retrace their steps. Catching the tour bus, we drove past the city of spires and then followed the guide through various colleges on campus before being set free to explore on our own. As I stared at the red geraniums denoting the rooms where Lewis lived, a handsome young man in a tweed jacket asked me, "Have you been to the Lamb and the Flag, the pub where Lewis and Tolkien discussed their work?"

"No, I don't know where it is," I said.

"Follow me; I'll buy you a warm beer," he said, surprising me with his American accent. Over the next hour, he told me he was a playwright and asked if I was a writer.

"No, but just yesterday I thought about doing some writing. I managed a ranch in Texas, and I want to tell the funny stories about my experience there."

"Go for it," he said, inspiring me further.

The next day, I told my housemate on the bus ride from London to Dover, "I may become a writer."

"Good for you; I may become a spy," she said, poking eye holes in the newspaper she was reading and laughing.

We waved goodbye to the white cliffs of Dover as we ferried across the channel to France. Arriving in Calais, we eventually found the train station. Saving money for a room, we caught the sleeper train to Venice, arriving at seven in the morning. It was already steamy, and we sweated as we looked for a place to stay that night. An older man watched as we went in and out of three expensive hotels before offering us a cheap room in his house. He seemed nice enough, and we were poor enough, so we took him up on the offer. Smelling the garlic wafting in when I opened the window, and seeing women hanging laundry and singing opera in the alley, my roommate hooted, "Mama mia, this is the real deal!"

Dropping our bags, we left to explore the city. We were charmed by the narrow cobblestone streets, marble fountains, and the black-lacquered gondolas with their good-looking men togged out in black-and-white sailor outfits. Walking to St. Mark's Square, I sat in the cathedral's shadow, feeling the peace one encounters in the sacred space created from generations of believers' prayers, like the aroma of candle scent remaining after the flame is out. No doubt some ancient saint in the past prayed for a lost soul like mine. The gentle sea's rhythmic lapping against the pilings drew my eye to the sparkly water. I sat for some time gazing silently across to an island in the distance, the mending forces of His creation knitting the torn fabric of my soul, quieting my condemnatory voices. As I walked back across the square, a rug of pigeons rose up before me, startling me out of my pensive mood.

It was the last night in Venice before we left for Strasbourg, France, to meet our housemate, Susie. We splurged and ate a delicious Italian dinner. My roommate complimented the waiters, "Italians make fabulous pasta."

"That is not the only thing we make well here," he responded, slipping a free bottle of wine on our table. "Meet us here at midnight, and we will show you our nightlife."

"Tempting," I responded as the waiter left, "but I would like to live to see Paris. Let's leave the money and sneak out when he is busing another table." Having hatched a plan, I signaled to my roommate when to bolt. Unfortunately, after consuming the bottle of wine, she tucked not only her white shirttail but also the white table cloth into the top of her skirt. When she stood up, it yanked her plate onto the floor, splattering the horrified patrons next to us with red sauce and foiling our smooth getaway. After exiting the restaurant, flushed with embarrassment, we went down a few wrong streets just in case the waiters were following us. In the process, we got ourselves quite lost. When we finally arrived at what we thought was our house, the key did not fit. Wrong house. Wrong street. Finally, after about two hours, we were back in our room packing up to catch the morning train to Strasburg.

Our roommate Susie, who was on break from her internship, greeted us and gave us a tour of the city. The next day we picnicked in a park where swans swam on a lake. Spreading a slice of Brie cheese on a warm, crusty, truly French baguette, I reflected on the Stubbs paintings, nothing else made my heart beat fast like those horses. *Could vet school still be in my future? Maybe I'll work at a vet office when I return to the States and take some prerequisite classes. Perhaps I will write that book about Medway Ranch.*

A small spring was in my step two days later, when we joined the throngs in the streets of Strasburg to celebrate Bastille Day. The roads were packed for the two-hundred-year-anniversary celebration, and we jostled our way, shoulder-to-shoulder in the crowd, to the Strasburg Cathedral for the light and sound show. When we arrived, classical music played, and lights shone through the stained-glass windows in a fantastic display. Feeling canned-in like a French sardine on the street, my merriment turned to claustrophobia. I escaped through the massive stone doorway into the dimly-lit cathedral.

An old French woman, her face a web of soft wrinkles, lit candles with shaky hands. Seeing me, she nodded kindly that I could do the same. I lit the candle, breathing in the sulfur smell of the match, and stood bathed in the soft glow from dozens of ivory candles. Walking past the ornately carved statues to the front of the nearly-empty church, I sat in a walnut pew, burnished smooth from decades of wear. I breathed deeply and inhaled the lingering smell of incense. I read the bilingual brochure, "Nearly two hundred years ago, the French people stormed the Bastille. Bastille is the French word for fortress. The French people, on July 14, 1789, took the Bastille prison starting the French Revolution, freeing them from their oppressive government."

In the stillness, my gloom from the last six months resurfaced. I lived in my own Bastille, shackled to the walls of shame and unable to experience Christ's forgiveness. The questions my friend asked me, followed me like Gollum through Europe, popping out from behind rocks, leading me to the place where I could rid myself of my own "Precious," called shame.

In the quiet of the cathedral, my friend's words drifted back, "Mary, what part of the cross isn't good enough for you? What did Christ leave lacking that you have to make up for through your remorse?"

The Bastille celebration that night, with the rowdy streets of inebriated French patriots, enabled me to forget the questions and my gnawing guilt. But now in the stillness of the pew, all I saw were the confessional booths looming before me, both inviting and condemning. I was afraid, and yet I was ready. I knelt in silence, still struggling with my sin and barely able to pray, but as I looked up at the huge rose cathedral window, the light shone through it so brilliantly, it took my breath away.

The shaft of light coming through the red stained glass covered me as if it were the blood of Christ. The warmth of His love and the cleanness and completeness of His forgiveness overwhelmed me; it was tangible and irresistible. The red beam, like a laser of mercy, cut through my manacles, and the heavy emotional chains holding me captive fell onto the floor where they belonged. I wept with a mixture of joy and relief.

After some time, I stood up and breathed in a lighter, cleaner air. I licked my dry lips, threw my head back, and laughed through my tears. I felt embraced by the old French woman as a secret knowledge passed between us, and she smiled fondly at me. I danced out of the cathedral to the rich classical music of the ancient pipe organ as it lifted me higher. I fell on the true Jesus and accepted forgiveness on His terms. In his song, "Come to Jesus," Chris Rice put to lyrics my emotions that day. I was a weak and wounded sinner who came to Jesus, He took my burdens away, and now I wanted to dance with Him, fly to Him, live with Him.

Back at the hotel that night I packed my bags for the flight to Virginia the next day to begin my quest for admission to veterinary school. I was happy to leave one piece of baggage in the Strasburg Cathedral.

CHAPTER 17

JACK—MY TWO-LEGGED KNIGHT IN SHINING ARMOR

All journeys have secret destinations of which the traveler is unaware.

—Martin Buber

God's GPS is always set on the true north for our lives, and I made the next available U-turn back towards my veterinarian dream. This new direction, coupled with the joy of restorative forgiveness, gave me the courage to take the courses required to apply to veterinary school: physics, biochemistry, and both general and organic chemistry. Squeaking by with a D in freshman college math, I avoided taking physics like a cat does a bath. I thought if, at twenty-eight years old, I made an A in physics, I could withstand the rigors of vet school. I latched onto Fatima, a bright Muslim girl from Lebanon, who became my good friend and study partner. I went to her apartment and her mother, who only spoke Arabic, made us delicious Lebanese food. I loved learning their customs, and my heart broke hearing devastating stories of how they left their war-torn homeland. I admired their commitment to Islam, except during Ramadan, when Fatima would be cranky during her fast and puff twice as many cigarettes. By prayerful effort and her coaching, I made A's, thus completing one of the necessary academic requirements. But, a competitive application requires clinical and research experience, not just high grades, and Graduate Record Exam scores, so I found a job at a vet office in northern Virginia. I started as a technician, holding the pets for their exams and running the diagnostic tests. All of this confirmed my desire to be a veterinarian. But, because of my management experience from the ranch, my boss promoted me to office manager, which I hated. I wanted to work with animals, not be involved in office soap operas. The boss was a talented veterinarian but drank like a fish during work and made erratic management decisions. His alcoholic behavior brought up memories of my childhood.

At the Strasburg Cathedral, Christ's love and forgiveness streamed into my heart, and I surrendered to it. Now home, I wanted to get my emotional and spiritual life on track. I didn't want to go but felt the Spirit prodding me to see a Christian counselor. Thus, I began the painful process of debridement. Debridement is a term used in wound management when the infected tissue inhibiting healing is cut away. The scalpel is inserted below the level of the bad tissue and cuts to the healthy skin, causing it to bleed. This procedure, known as *freshing up* the edges of the wound, speeds up the healing process. Satan wounds God's children, but God allows it, so He can debride the wound and bring a deeper healing. My soul's response to my childhood trauma was a lonely sadness, masked by toughness. I had gutted it up and gritted it out on my own. As an adult, this strategy didn't work, and my brokenness was the Jesus path to growth and restoration.

Therapy ain't for sissies. Each week, before entering the counselor's office, I stood outside the door shaking and nauseated, wanting to bolt. The Lord's power kept me entering that door, week after painful week. My childhood had so many shattering moments that the therapist was hard-pressed to know where to begin with me. He circled around my mother's drinking and death and their impact on my life. My family hadn't admitted that my mother was an alcoholic. We all knew she hit the bottle hard, but to classify her as an alcoholic seemed disloyal. For families in the South, it just wasn't done. The counselor gave me Janet Woititz's book, *Adult Children of Alcoholics*. Woititz wrote with such a thorough understanding of my emotions and the confusion of living with drinking parents that it felt like she had telescoped into the den of my childhood. As I read the bullet points on the back of her book, I realized twelve of her thirteen points were true of my life. *Ninety-two percent, yeah, I made an A,* I chuckled to myself. The counselor helped me unpack her points: having to guess at what normal behavior is; judging myself without mercy; taking myself very seriously; having difficulty with intimate relationships; overreacting to changes out of my control; constantly seeking approval and affirmation; feeling that I was different than other people; being extremely loyal, even when loyalty was undeserved; and being impulsive. Understanding these points brought clarity to my life. The counselor had me write a letter to my mother, detailing what I would like to say to her. His eyes brimmed over with tears as I read it to him and he said, "It sounds like a love letter," which it was, and I felt a healing warmth in my heart.

I asked many questions about why the things that happened to me did. Finally, my counselor told me a joke about the kid who was peddling his bike down a country road one day as he passed a farmer struggling in the field. The farmer yelled out, "Hey son, can you give me a hand?" The farmer was exhausted from trying to help his cow deliver her oversized calf. "I've been pulling this calf for an hour, and I am plum tuckered out. Will you grab that leg and I'll pull this one?"

"Sure," the boy said, jumping in to help and after two good heave-ho's, the big, black calf was delivered. The farmer reached into his pocket to give the boy a dollar for helping. "No sir, you don't need to give me nothin'. Just answer me one question."

"What's that son?"

"Just how fast was that calf going when it ran into the back of that cow?" My therapist said, "Like that boy, you aren't asking the right questions. You are asking me the *whys*, but contentment often means finding peace with life's unanswerable questions and learning how the Lord will bring you healing and use your life's pain to help others. We can be broken like glass and cut others with the shards from our trauma, or we can be broken like bread and nourish others like Jesus's broken body at communion, the body of Christ, the Bread of Heaven."

I pressed into my healing, taking comfort learning that I wasn't the only one to have this type of childhood. In fact, it was so common we had our own initials—ACOA (Adult Children of Alcoholics). I saw how my feelings and responses were not necessarily linked to my current situation, but an overreaction caused by something triggered by my past.

As the vet office manager, I recognized my boss's alcoholic behavior and how the office staff covered for his drinking. I wasn't going to get sucked into my boss's addictions and the staff's co-dependency. My counselor was surprised the next week when I said, "I quit. All the craziness seemed normal to me when I started working there. I grew up with that kind of "normal," but I realized I don't have to live or work in that chaos anymore."

"Good for you. What are your plans now?" he asked with concern.

"I sent my resume to some stables. I need to get back to working with horses. I won't be able to come see you for a while until I find work." I said, half relieved at the thought.

"I can let you come for a reduced fee," he said compassionately.

Realizing he was willing to give me sessions for almost nothing, I wept. There was nothing mean enough one could do to make me cry, but kindness could. He was the first man I remember trusting. In the past, there was a price tag attached to the seemingly kind acts of men. The gifts Frank bestowed on me I paid for with my body and soul.

This man was so different. There was a Jesus-like tone to his voice and the truth in words. When I lifted my shame-laden head and our eyes met, there was a brightness behind his expression, both a sorrow and energy. I felt God, loving and powerful, drawing me and bringing me comfort, insight, and healing. Our sessions reminded me of Roberta Flack's song, "Killing Me Softly with His Song," as if he were strumming my pain with his fingers.

Before finding a job at Meadowbrook Stable in Chevy Chase, Maryland, I started writing my horse book. I loved being back with horses and riding cleared my head and helped me process my soul's healing.

My housemates took me to Fourth Presbyterian Church and we sat at Jack McDonald's table, the same young man from our pre-Europe party. Later that week, he asked me out. I accepted. We started the evening at the grand reopening of Washington, DC's Union Station. Staring up at the gold-leaf-filled reliefs in the ceiling, we trotted to the top of the cafe stairs for champagne and then went for dinner.

"We have dinner reservations at 9:00 p.m. at the Marrakesh restaurant," he said opening the car door for me. *Nice, a southern gentleman. My mother would approve.* I felt bubbly, so as he backed up I hit the inside of my door with my hand, making a banging sound like he hit the car behind him. A bold move for the first date, but I wanted to see what kind of sense of humor he had. He was mortified. I hit my door again to show him I made the sound. He laughed, passing my sense-of-humor test. He was fun, handsome, and a good conversationalist. I surprised myself by thinking, *I really like this guy.* Meanwhile we had driven to a shady part of town and parked by a huge wooden door with no name on it and no one around. *Figures, just my luck; I would like a serial killer,* I thought to myself as he walked up to the big door and knocked. A one foot by one foot window opened, and two jet-black eyes peeked through. Drug deal or mafia? I tried to decide when I heard, "Reservations?"

"Yes, Jack McDonald, for two."

The ornately carved door swung open, ushering us into the heart of the Moroccan restaurant. Savory smells of exotic food wafted into our nostrils, as we went to a small wooden table with overstuffed pillows. *No silverware or chairs, I guess that is one way to cut costs.* Dulcimer guitars played as a belly dancer surprised me with her colorful performance. I wasn't sure what we ate, but it was just as spicy as the dancers!

Taking me home that night, I thanked him for the evening, and we shook hands goodbye. My roommates were watching the movie, *The Princess Bride.* They were used to me going on dates and didn't even look up when they asked how it went. Jack was a good storyteller, had an exciting job as an international banker, and was dashing with his dark brown hair and broad shoulders.

The relationship with Jill was like an incubation in my mother's womb. Despite its heartbreak, I learned how to be in relationship—to give and receive love. Now I was ready to be in a relationship with Jack.

"I may just marry that boy!" I burst out, stepping in front of the TV. They spilled their popcorn, hit the pause button, and stared at me, mouths agape.

CHAPTER 18

THREE STRANDS

Though one may be overpowered, two can defend themselves. A cord of three strands is not quickly broken.

—Ecclesiastes 4:12

I fell in love with Jack. His marriage proposal, nine months later, included the caveat that he had a one-year job assignment in Nairobi, Kenya, where we would move six months after the wedding.

Our engagement began when he dropped me off at the Waldorf Astoria Hotel in New York City. Jack drove us to the city, and he planned to stay with a friend for the weekend. That night we went to Sardi's, the famous Broadway restaurant, where we ate a delicious dinner under the pictures of hundreds of celebrities who had dined there. After dinner, the sights and sounds of the Broadway play *Cats* mesmerized us.

 The next day, we toured the city and in the evening, we went to the elegant Sign of the Dove for dinner. After we ordered dessert, he pulled out a small black velvet box. When he opened it, I gaped at the biggest, most brilliant diamond I ever saw, flanked by two smaller blue stones. "God is the diamond in the middle and we are the two sapphires, which is how I want us to spend our lives together. A cord of three strands is not quickly broken," Jack explained. "Will you marry me?"

"I would love to," I bubbled, eyes sparkling as brightly as the diamond.

He slipped the ring on my finger, and with great excitement I "flashed the ice" to the waiter, showing off my engagement ring. Next, I did the same thing to the taxi driver, the tollbooth attendant, and to every passerby on the New York streets. I'm sure they thought at first that I was trying to mug them. I even thrust my ring up toward the Statue of Liberty and shouted gleefully, "We are engaged!" and got the same response some of the other New Yorkers gave me.

When Jack dropped me back off at the Waldorf, we called our families, and there was great jubilation. With that call, the festivities were out of my control, set into motion by tradition and family hospitality. Of course, we would be married at St. Luke's, and we chose the date. Two engagement parties brought together all the family and friends in Virginia and Illinois. There was the requisite bridal shower at John Tree Hill with the Powhatan ladies and a formal bridesmaids' luncheon at Willow Oaks Country Club. My father remarried while I was in my second year of college, and Shirley, my stepmother, an energetic, brunette realtor, made the arrangements for the bridesmaid's luncheon at Willow Oaks in Richmond. Jack's parents provided the elegant rehearsal dinner, done in style, at the Country Club of Virginia. We decided that the reception would be at Belmead, a historic mansion on the James in Powhatan, or "The Castle" as the locals called it.

I was nervous the first time I met his parents on their visit to DC, but they were welcoming and generous southern Episcopalians like my own family. His father, Jack, was vice-president of Archer Daniels Midland a large international agribusiness company. His mother, Sis, the consummate supermom, was elegantly dressed with her perfect hair and nails. She gave me a lovely blue china bowl.

We chose Hawaii for our honeymoon destination, so friends of Jack's parents gave us an engagement party in Illinois—a luau, complete with stuffed pig, Tikki torches, and matching Hawaiian outfits for Jack and me. We flew to Decatur and stayed at his parents' house, a lovely ranch-style house overlooking Lake Decatur. Jack's father, Jack McDonald, Jr., gave him the best groom advice ever while we were planning the wedding, "Whenever Mary asks your opinion on wedding matters just say, 'Yes, dear. I would have done it that way if I had thought of it myself.'"

All the planning went as smoothly as a well-oiled wheel because we didn't need to do much of it. We followed orders, smiled into each other's eyes, and went to premarital counseling. On many occasions, I felt like bolting from the wedding because of the fear lingering from my childhood wounds. Instead, I went on many a good gallop with the other riding instructor at Meadowbrook Stables where I taught lessons. It helped me take courage and trust the Lord with my future.

The morning of the wedding, the Montgomery sisters hosted a lovely brunch. Staying true to the tradition, that it is bad luck for the groom and bride to see each other before the wedding ceremony, I ate quickly, and let Jack come after me. I drove to Medway to say goodbye to my old pony Duke. Though my father had sold it, my cousins bought it, and Duke lived nearby, cared for by our neighbors, the Paul's. Somehow, I needed to get Duke's approval of this new chapter in my life. He was my refuge during the darkest times of my childhood when everything else was crumbling. He was forty-three years old, which is ancient for horses; his back was sunken in, his old eyes had deep craters above them where the muscles atrophied, and his hair had grayed. Even though he was nearly deaf and toothless, he still perked his ears forward in greeting as I approached.

I hugged his cresty neck and buried my face in the flaxen mane that dried so many of my childhood tears. Kissing his velvety, black muzzle, I drank in the deep, earthy smell of Duke's skin, the aroma that always served to ease my fears and to give me hope. The sweet, spicy loam fragrance filled me with the same peace and joy every horseman knows. I ran my hands down his shoulders and the little legs, the limbs which galloped my heart to freedom on so many rocky days. Duke was the savior of my childhood, my knight in shining armor. I told him I found a man as brave, strong, and honest as he was, and I was getting married that day. Playfully, I asked, "Old man, will you give me away?"

He nuzzled my face and neck, and then pushed me with his muzzle, perhaps remembering the many treats I gave him over the years. I took it as a sign of approval. I handed him a mashed-up apple. Breathing in his sweet, juicy breath, I daydreamed back to the fun times we had together. He gave me another bump as if telling me to get on with it and not be late for my own wedding. Moving to Kenya within the year, I thought it was the last time I might see my first pony, and I gave him a goodbye hug.

Leaving Duke, I drove to St. Luke's Parish House which my grandfather built seventy-five years earlier. My sisters and Shirley were waiting to help me get dressed. Who knew it took three women to clothe a bride in her wedding gown and veil? I felt like Downton Abbey's Lady Mary with all my attendants. Jean, Catherine, and Shirley scurried around like mice, attending to all the details of getting my hair and gown perfect. The satin dress was the same one my mother wore marrying my father in April, 1950, when the small dogwood trees lining the St. Luke's sidewalk were in their spring splendor. Now, forty years later, larger dogwoods were parading their flowers of the fall, with brilliant waxy leaves of quilted reds, golds, and orange. My friends and family sat in the walnut pews of the small church; the locals knew to get there early. Most of Jack's friends and family arrived on time to an already-full church and had to sit on folding chairs in the churchyard.

In his black tuxedo, my still-handsome father, now graying but stylish and trim, waited with me outside the church. Seeing me in the dress his bride wore on their wedding day, his eyes misted. I felt the pain in his voice, as well as the loss, regret, loneliness, and love. Did he picture his beautiful young bride walking on her father's arm down the aisle into his arms? Did he think back to the bright hope they had on that day and wonder why it had taken so many tarnished turns and ended tragically? I don't know. I do know there was a sadness in his voice as he faced the prospect of giving away their youngest child, without her mother to share the moment. We both knew only the grave could have kept her away. In his honeyed Virginia accent, he tenderly whispered in my ear, "I wish your mutha' were heah today."

"She is!" I shot back with a quick smile. It was a trite phrase I used to keep my heart from tearing apart at the thought of my mother's absence and because I was uncomfortable with Dad's uncharacteristic emotional tenderness. Mother was buried just fifty feet away. I had so many emotions swirling around—excitement, love, joy, fear—that I couldn't afford to contemplate my mother's loss. I had to maintain my composure to make it through the service.

"She is here," I whispered again, wishing the organ music would begin. I focused on the dogwood leaves to keep the tears from forming.

There were times when I missed my mother more sharply than just the dull daily pain. Sometimes the emotions caught me off guard, like when I watched the mother-daughter relationship in the movie *Steel Magnolias*. I sobbed into my popcorn box and had to wipe my nose on a buttery napkin, unprepared for the flood of emotions. At those times, I would have to pinch myself and think of something funny because my friends were uncomfortable with my unusual display of tears. At other times, I bit my lip hard, afraid I might fall into an abyss of grief and never stop crying.

I expected to miss my mother at certain times, like my high school graduation, the first lifetime event where I felt her absence profoundly. Then came college with its Parents' Day weekends and graduation, but today, my wedding day, wearing her dress, was certainly the biggest lifetime experience since her death, and I felt her loss deeply. When we were engaged, I longed to have the female link to the one who birthed me and went before me down that aisle. During the days of my gender confusion, I wished my mother were there to help me. Now I was embarking on marriage and motherhood, aggrieved in her absence.

No doubt it was the "what might have been," the good things that her alcoholism stole from us all that fueled the ache. I realized she was never able to be the mother that she wanted to be. A lump rose in my throat as I drew an image of how she would look: beautiful; beaming; proud; and strong—sitting straight on the front row with her shoulders back and her head held elegantly high. She would have an orchid corsage pinned to her chenille mother-of-the-bride dress, and of course, she would be dabbing her eyes with the white linen handkerchief Rose Watson had pressed for her. Rose would be seated at the back of the church.

I tried to remember how Rose would look, but I realized sadly that I had forgotten the shape of her smile. Just then, the first note of "Here Comes the Bride" jolted me into motion. I put my arm through my father's, and he walked me down the aisle, giving me away into more sober hands. As I turned to face the crowd, I smiled at Granny in the front row on the right side of the church where she had sat for nearly a century. It was such a joy for me and for others to have her there. I was the youngest of her grandchildren and the last to be married at St. Luke's. How many weddings, baptisms, and funerals she attended there in her white gloves, I could not count. At ninety-six, she was the last of her era; she sat slumped in her wheel-chair with her corsage and nurse, so happy to be back in her beloved church with family.

Looking behind her, I saw the afternoon sun's splendor radiating through the ancient stained-glass windows, sending colored beams of red and blue throughout the pews. The white roses filled the small church with their fragrance. The brass candlesticks, polished silver communion pieces, and starched white linens on the altar were the same as when I was christened as an infant in the marble baptismal font that stood in front of me. The scents and sights opened the storehouse of my mind and brought back a flood of both joyful and tragic memories: Christmas pageants; homecomings; the rifle sounds firing at Grandad's military funeral; and my own mother's burial.

At the same altar, where my parents and two of my siblings tied the nuptial knot, Jack and I knelt and took our vows.

But as I knelt, a streak of doubt shot through me clear to my spine. *Maybe Jack wasn't the right man for me. He was married before, but his wife left him for another man. How could I know it would work out for us?* My distrust of men and fear of commitment bubbled up again and threatened to undo me. I wanted to fly out of the church, but St. Luke's with her powerful memories, ceremony, and tradition had glued my knees to her needlepoint kneeling cushion in *Noblesse Oblige*. The ivory walls seemed to creak. Besides, my sisters would have blocked my exit, and my father would have killed me. I swallowed hard, gulping down my fears. We said our vows. It was over, and peace washed over me once again. Jack beamed as he kissed me and paraded down the aisle with me on his arm, clearly proud of his catch.

The reception was a delightful party, with an open bar and plenty of champagne. Everyone was flying high as we made our get-away and drove an hour away to Orange, Virginia, where we would spend the first night of our honeymoon at the historic Mayhurst Bed and Breakfast. Having waited for our marriage, that night we consummated it properly. I wept with joy at the goodness of God's gift of Jack to me.

I planned the wedding, but it was Jack, a closet tour guide, who planned the honeymoon. I knew he had a penchant for adventure, but I wanted to relax after the wedding so I chose Hawaii, thinking it would be a tranquil place—probably our last vacation without a near-death experience. The first evening was indeed quiet, and so were the two days on the Honolulu beach. However, these hours were only a lull before the tempest of activity! Jack began the third day with, "Pack up! We are flying out to Kauai."

Upon landing, Jack, not one to lounge around sipping fruity drinks with umbrellas in them, rented a convertible and once the top was down, off we went on an adventure.

Who knew Hawaii isn't just one island and that we wouldn't even go to just that one? Who knew one could hike in the rainforest? Who cared? I thought hiking up to the crater of an active volcano with sweat streaming off my sunburned face would be the worst of Jack's planned adventures, but that was before Jack dragged me out snorkeling in the rough waves and I drank half the Pacific Ocean. Surely, that would be the worst of it, I thought queasily, dragging my nauseated self onto the beach like a drunken dolphin.

I was wrong again because, on the heels of snorkeling, we went on a helicopter ride. Jack was so excited that I didn't want to throw a wet blanket on his exuberance by telling him I was feeling a little green around the gills. The daring Vietnam vet pilot darted the little helicopter in and out of the waterfall ravines like a mosquito being chased by a fly swatter. Despite the travel brochure's boast, "Air sickness is practically unheard of in helicopters," I managed to fill up both barf bags while Jack took four rolls of film. It was the first glimpse of our many married adventures covering twenty-two countries, four continents, and more near-death experiences than a cat should have to face. It was clear, though, that Jack and I were well matched. I needed someone as active and adventurous as me, and after all the sorrow, pain, fear, and loss, there he was—my two-legged knight in shining armor!

Following our Hawaiian honeymoon, we returned to our work in northern Virginia for six months. I taught riding lessons at Meadowbrook Stable, and Jack worked as a loan officer for the Overseas Private Investment Corporation before gearing up for our next real adventure—Kenya, East Africa.

PART III

DOING THE DREAM

CHAPTER 19

KENYA

Kenya has become a country of ten millionaires and ten million beggars.

—J. M. Kariuki

"Ahh," I yelled, jumping out of my skin when Jack walked in our bedroom unannounced. "Why don't you say something when you come up behind me?" I yelled at him, angry that he scared me.

"I just walked into the room," he said. "I'm your husband, not an ax murderer. Why are you so jumpy?" he asked, irritated that I startled him with my reaction.

We don't get a "Happily-Ever-After Pass" when we marry, but thankfully we do get a new setting to work out old issues with love for one another. In Gary Thomas's book, *Sacred Marriage*, he asks the question, "What if marriage is designed to make us holy and not happy?" He casts truth into the current myth of a romantic, idealized Hollywood marriage, which no one really has. It is in the crucible of marriage that we bring together two different elements and, with a bit of heat from the chemical reaction, our rough edges of independence and selfishness turn into harmony and a deeper union. Our first few months of marriage were remarkably blissful, but there were a few relationship wrinkles that needed ironing out before we moved to Kenya. So, we returned to our premarital counselor.

In our session, Jack relayed how I easily startled. Our counselor responded, "She has a condition common to adult children of alcoholics (ACOA), and those suffering from post-traumatic stress disorder, known as hypervigilance. Because of her past, Mary has an increased sense of awareness and exaggerated responses to detect danger in her environment. This quick response to stimuli kept her safe as a child."

Jack nodded, half understanding. The effect of having been in an alcoholic home, coupled with sexual abuse, created a guardedness and edginess in my approach to life. Having lost my mother when I was a teenager, I knew that bad things not only could happen but in my life, they did happen. Growing up, I needed to assess the situation quickly when I entered my house to see who was drinking, and if a wine bottle might be thrown, I would be ready to duck quickly. I learned to be on constant patrol mentally, and this wariness carried into my adult years and into my marriage. Humanly speaking, Kenya was the last place to which a hypervigilant person should be moving, but ignorance is bliss and the heavenly hosts had a bigger plan for my soul than allowing me to trust in my own defenses for my security.

"Another thing," Jack added, "we will be doing fine in our relationship, and Mary just picks a fight for no good reason."

"That is another trait of ACOAs," the counselor said. "Chaos was her normal, so chaos is what she is the most comfortable with. It is her fallback."

It was true. When things were going smoothly, this felt abnormal to me, so I would toss an itty-bitty grenade into the relationship just to blow things up enough to make me feel that things were normal again.

"I'll try to be more patient," Jack said, meaning it.

Despite these quirks, we got along well. We were in love. That is, we got along as well as our wounded hearts permitted us. We weren't present enough emotionally to know how distant we were from our true selves or our hearts' depths. But there was chemistry between us, we were united in Christ, and we had a common goal of moving to Kenya in six months, so we were happy together.

The first thing I needed to do for the trip was to get the vaccinations necessary to live in East Africa, and these were legion. When my mother passed away, all knowledge of my childhood vaccines went with her. Having no proof of previous inoculations, I needed thirteen vaccines to travel to Kenya. Since we were to be attached to the US Embassy in Nairobi, we were officially diplomats, so I went to the State Department health clinic. At that time, before injecting, the nurse read you the warnings about possible side effects for each vaccination, and you had to sign a release form. The nurse read the risks from the yellow fever vaccine, "A vaccine, like any medicine, could cause a serious reaction. But the risk of a vaccine causing serious harm, or death, is extremely low."

"Death?" I said aloud, my hypervigilant reactions kicking in.

"The chances are extremely low," the nurse smiled. I didn't think it was anything to be smiling about, but she continued, "Severe problems—severe allergic reaction to a vaccine component (about 1 person in 55,000); severe nervous system reaction (about 1 person in 125,000); life-threatening, severe illness with organ failure (about 1 person in 250,000). More than half the people who suffer this side effect die."

"Are you kidding me? I have a better chance of dying from these vaccines than I do of winning the lottery," I exclaimed to the nurse.

"Well then, there's no point in playing the lottery if you are going to die now, is there?" she asked, handing me the release form to sign. "No worries! I've given this to 124,999 people without a reaction," she said, laughing.

All the world's a comedian, I thought to myself as she swabbed my arm with alcohol, and jabbed the long, stainless-steel needle into my unsuspecting arm. Digging my fingernails into the red-vinyl chair arms, I glanced at my white knuckles and tried to think happy thoughts of our Kenyan adventure. Ever since my bout with spinal meningitis as a child, when I was tied to the bed for injections, I feared needles and nurses. I started feeling cold and clammy after hearing the yellow fever warnings and feeling the pain of the needle piercing through my muscle. By the time she finished with the last injection, my blood pressure had dropped. I was ready to go but when I stood up to leave, I passed out cold onto the linoleum floor.

"How are you feeling?" were the first words I heard when I came to.

"Am I having a reaction?" I asked the nurse, certain I was having the severe variety where half the people die.

"No, you had a vasovagal reaction, also known as needle anxiety or needle allergy; it happens a lot. I had a big man in here last week who was afraid of shots. I nearly didn't get him off the floor."

She handed me crackers to munch on and apple juice to sip. I felt like a child sitting there for the next hour, waiting for my blood pressure to rise enough for me to leave. Finally, the nurse patted me on the back, handed me a bottle of the chloroquine antimalarial pills, and sent me on my way, "Have fun in Africa and watch out for crazy drivers, coups, wild animal attacks, and, of course, vaccines. Take the chloroquine weekly. We had a Peace Corps worker die from cerebral malaria last month. Start the chloroquine now."

A week later at Dulles airport, we called our families to say our goodbyes. They gave us warning after warning of the dangers we could encounter on the "Dark Continent," adding to my apprehension. They thought we were taking the leave-and-cleave marriage verse too seriously, and hoped our nuptial knot would hold us safely together. However, neither of our families ever lived overseas and only knew half of the dangers we were to encounter. It was to be a year in which I was continually in a state of hypervigilance, certain that death lurked around the next corner. Our time there was the perfect antidote for my old patterns.

It was nearly fifty years after Isak Dinesen penned, *Out of Africa,* detailing her life in colonial Kenya that we flew to an independent Kenya. The new Kenya had declined from the orderly British rule into a country rife with tribalism and corruption, ruled by the dictator President Daniel Arap Moi, one of the richest men in the world. As the Kenyan politician, J. M. Kariuki, who was assassinated in 1975, said, "Kenya has become a country of ten millionaires and ten million beggars."

The Kenyan plains we flew over en route to Nairobi were still filled with vast numbers of wildlife, but poaching had drastically reduced the population. The asinine Asian trinket trade of illegal ivory left orphaned elephant calves starving in the bush, and Middle Eastern and Asian lust threatened the extinction of rhinos under the mistaken premise that their horns acted as an aphrodisiac. This was the state of affairs when we landed at the Kenyatta International Airport in September of 1990. We saw the multicolored Kenyan flag—black for the people, green for the fertile land, and red for those who died fighting for Kenya's independence from the British rule—proudly hanging outside the customs building as we entered to claim our bags. President Moi's picture also hung in every building, public and private. Determining in advance not to pay bribes, it took us eight hours to get our suitcases out of customs. The final blow was the last signature, which could only be obtained if Jack contributed to the customs officer's favorite charity. Worn thin, Jack relented and appeared at the car with ten hand-stamped customs forms and our baggage. With little emotional reserve left, we negotiated the insane traffic, potholes, and roundabouts to the guest house the bank where Jack was to work arranged for us to rent. It was a small bungalow on the outskirts of Nairobi in the area known as Westfields. The owners, the Hooks, were an American couple in their sixties who ran a restaurant in the city. They were hard-driving people who ran with the fast ex-patriot crowd.

"On the left-hand side of the road, not on the left-hand side of the sidewalk," I shouted when Jack nearly took out a pedestrian driving the car the bank loaned us.

Finally arriving at our new landlords', our nerves already frazzled from leaving our families and the recent customs fiasco, we shuddered at Mr. Hooks's warning as he walked us to our house, "Be careful at the entrance gate. The last tenants pulled up and honked the horn for the guard but instead were accosted by carjackers. The thugs jerked the mother out of her SUV, jumped in, and took off with the baby boy sleeping in the back seat. They never did find the child."

Mr. Hooks was tall and fit with a square jaw and crew cut. As he unlocked the tiny guesthouse door, we saw the large white button on the wall, inscribed with red letters, *Ultimate Hatari!*

"What does that mean?" I asked, still reeling from the car-jacking story.

"It is Swahili for ultimate danger. The police here are corrupt and don't have gas to come to your aid if you call them. The people who can afford it hire a private guard company. If there is any trouble, push that button, and they'll be here in a flash. Also, don't feed the dogs. They are trained not to eat from strangers. Thieves throw poisoned meat over the fence to kill the dogs, and then break in. The rent is due the first of the month; you can pay in dollars," he said, walking out the door and heading back to his house. He was brusque at first. I'm sure he wondered what he got himself into renting to two naïve Americans who had never lived overseas, but then he softened and took on a protective, fatherly countenance and added, "Why don't you come for dinner tonight at eight?"

"Thanks," we said in unison since there was no food in the little house.

Jack and I unpacked a few of our bags, and then went out to explore the property. It was a spacious compound with every variety of tropical flower growing lusciously in the vast gardens, a swimming pool, and Jack Russell terriers scampering after the troop of black-faced vervet monkeys bounding through the flame trees.

"A piece of paradise," Jack said.

"Yeah, except for the little things like thugs, carjackers, and corrupt customs officials," I quipped. "At least it has a high wall, and there is a guard with a bow and arrow to protect the property."

We walked back to the guest house, which was so small you couldn't swing a cat around by the tail without getting fur in your mouth, but since it was on their property we wouldn't have to hassle with hiring gardeners and guards.

Jack tried to lighten my mood, "Mary, come into the bathroom and watch which direction the toilet water spins when I flush. It's below the equator and goes in the opposite direction from in Virginia."

"Really?" I said walking into the cupboard of a bathroom.

Putting down his pineapple juice box, he pulled the long string hanging down from the water tank four feet above the toilet. "See," he said excitedly.

"Yeah, like who knows which direction Virginia toilet water spins?"

"I don't really, but I know this is going the opposite way," he said before handing me an antimalarial pill.

Feeling rascally, I said, "Let's take our pills together and see which one can make the other laugh."

Chloroquine is extremely bitter, and if you didn't swallow it quickly, it would gag a maggot.

Just then Jack saw a mosquito, and he nearly shattered the mirror trying to kill the insect, certain his new bride would die from malaria. Having dispatched with the insect, he put the pill in his mouth. I made him laugh. Gagging on the bitter pill, he took a swig from his juice box and got a mouthful of wriggling ants, which had crawled into the straw. "Welcome to paradise," I joked.

Falling into our double bed laughing, we discovered it was two twin beds pushed together. No matter, newlyweds only need a twin.

We spent a fitful first night with Jack having to dissuade me from pushing the Ultimate Hatari button at every unknown shout outside the gate.

The next day Jack went to work, and I set about turning our bungalow into a home. After lunch, I decided to take a dip in the pool but was deterred by the guard's lustful glare when I walked to the edge and dropped my towel. Walking back to my house, the purple flowers of the long-stemmed Lily of the Nile plants captivated me until I heard a ruckus behind me. The Hooks's terrier had grabbed a monkey. I watched as the primate dug his powerful teeth into the dog's back leg, ripping a six-inch gash out of his flesh. I carried him, bleeding, to Mrs. Hooks and held him in the car as we drove to her veterinarian. Still chasing my vet school dream, I intended to find a Kenyan vet to shadow. After assisting Dr. Susan in suturing the dog, I told her I was pursuing vet medicine and asked if I could work with her. She was a middle-aged Kenyan, who used her keen mind to get an education and establish her own practice in a male-dominated culture and profession. She had a strength and crustiness that many accomplished women acquire having to fight for their rightful place in society. As is so often the case, the same men who made it so hard for the women to break through the glass ceiling wonder why so many women of achievement are tough skinned and defensive. Hearing about her difficult journey, I said, "All pioneers have arrows in their backs."

She nodded and jokingly pretended to pull out an arrow, "Certainly, you can come Mondays. It is important to get practical experience. Half of the vets here can't tell the difference between a tick bite and a chumah."

It would take me weeks of working with her before I deciphered the Kenyan accent enough to understand that tumor is pronounced "chumah." Weekly, I boiled the instruments in a tea kettle to prepare them for surgery. Little did I know that quality veterinary medicine could be performed without all the bells and whistles we had at the office I managed in Virginia, and little did I know that God was preparing me to be a veterinary missionary in the years ahead.

But that was later. In the meantime, after the pup suturing, Mrs. Hooks drove us home. En route, we saw two policemen in the road with a spiked barricade blocking one lane, waving for her to stop. Swerving around the barrier, she sped past them, "I never stop. They just want money."

"Aren't you afraid they will shoot you? I saw their guns," I exclaimed, ducking in my seat.

"No. Here they respect the elderly," she said pointing to her white hair, "They don't give me trouble, and besides, they have no bullets or gas. But be careful driving at night; they leave the spikes in the road, and you can't see them until you are on top of them."

Once back in our little bungalow, I waited excitedly to tell Jack about my vet opportunity. He knew when we married that I wanted to be a vet. We were near the equator, so the sun always set at 6:30. It was nearly dark when I heard a rap on the door and looked out the bars on my windows to see the Kenyan Electric Company vehicle. The guard let two young men in uniforms enter the gate, so I assumed they were legit. I opened the door and one of them walked straight to the fuse box and pulled out the main fuse, blanketing the three of us in darkness.

The short fat man asked me, "Do you have a torch?"

Puzzled, I stared in his direction, too new to the country to know that *torch* is the Kenyan name for a flashlight.

"No, I don't have a torch, but I'll get a flashlight," I said scampering into my bedroom.

"What can be done?" the tall skinny one replied. I would come to learn this phrase was code for, "I want a bribe."

Clueless to his shenanigans, I shrugged my shoulders.

"What can be done," the other one said, implying I knew.

"You can stick the fuse back into the wall, so I have electricity!" I said.

"You are new to this house, and you must pay us to hook up your electricity," the man said calmly.

"It was already hooked up and working just fine. I am renting, and I do not know what you are talking about. I will go ask my landlord," I said, shaking and trying to slide past the men blocking the doorway.

"No, what can be done?" he asked, now with a hint of fear creeping into his voice.

"You can put the fuse back in—that's what can be done!" I said again sternly but shaking on the inside as the man stepped toward me with his hand outstretched. Bolting past him out the door, I ran through the dark to the main house. The two men jumped in their car and took off out the gate.

"Probably just a scam," Mr. Hooks said sympathetically and walked me back to the house. Finding the fuse they dropped in the grass, he stuck it back into the box, giving me light again. "They must have bribed someone to get a list of people who recently moved in to see if they can extract a few shillings from unsuspecting ex-pats. No worries," he added as he walked out the door.

When Jack arrived home, he was surprised to find the door not only locked but with a barricade of brooms and mops behind it. The happy bride he left that morning joyfully watching the monkeys was now ready to catch the night flight back to Virginia.

"We have a security briefing tomorrow at the embassy, so we can ask them about the electric company guys," he said trying to calm me.

"Security briefing? I don't want to live any place so insecure that I need a security briefing!"

The next day I rehashed the incident with the security officer who said, "If Kenyans put half as much energy into carrying out a legitimate business as they do in planning scams, this would be a very wealthy country." Then he told us of other scams that were perpetrated in the city and about the street crimes, "Sometimes a person will bump into you and then fall down, and when you go to help them up another person will run by and steal your purse. It is safer just to tuck a money belt into your pants."

I did not have the top-secret clearance that Jack had, so I was asked to leave the room so Jack could get his briefing. The only information I squeezed out of him was the location of the Palestinian Liberation Army's office, which was at that time the largest terrorist organization in the world. He pointed to it as we walked out of the embassy. "There have been some threats," was all he said.

A few blocks down the street, I felt a piercing pain in my ankle and looked down to see a nail sticking out of my joint. We went back to the embassy health clinic.

I asked the nurse, "Have you heard of any scam artists shooting people in the ankle with a dart gun and then stealing their purses?"

"No, that's a new one on me," she said, thinking I was paranoid. After giving me a tetanus booster she smiled, "You guys should get out of the city. Take a safari. The wildlife here is incredible."

"Great idea! Let's get the bank's SUV and go!" Jack lit up.

"Drive carefully. Remember, if you need a transfusion, the embassy has our own blood bank. Kenyans aren't screening for HIV, and it is rampant here. Never drive outside the city after dark. Have fun!" the nurse added smiling, trying to put a happy spin on the serious warnings.

"I want to introduce you to my office staff. It's just around the corner from the embassy, on the eleventh floor of the Barclay's bank building," Jack said, excited to show off his new bride.

"Who are those noble-looking, lighter-skinned people setting up camp on the sidewalks?" I asked Jack.

"Somalis. Their country, just north of Kenya, is having a civil war, and those are refugees fleeing before the total collapse of the government."

"What? The country right above us is having a civil war?" I asked incredulously. "How are the leaders of the other surrounding countries doing?"

"Well, Sudan is in a civil war, Uganda has fighting up north, and the Ethiopian government might fall, too. But Tanzania is stable!"

The elevator doors in the bank lobby opened, interrupting Jack. We wedged into the already-overstuffed elevator. It stank to high heaven as few people used deodorant. The elevator guard was carrying an A-K 47 machine gun. Because the maximum weight capacity was exceeded, when the elevator reached its destination, everyone had to climb up a foot to get out onto each floor level. Already claustrophobic, I pondered if they would have to get someone from the Otis elevator company from the US if the elevator got stuck to rescue us. Breaking out in a sweat and feeling nauseated, I decided that this was the last time I took the elevator. I didn't care that Jack's office was on the eleventh floor, and Nairobi was 6,000 feet above sea level—I would take the stairs.

Finally arriving at the Equator Bank floor, I met Jack's colleagues, the secretaries, and the two drivers, James and George, who would chauffeur me around Nairobi until I was competent driving on the left-hand side of the road. The office had two vehicles, a Toyota sedan and a Pajero SUV. Sometimes James was assigned to us, and I laughed inwardly when I said, "Home, James," and he hit the gas. I asked him if he ever saw a lion, which I pronounced as an American, *lie-in*. He had no idea what I was talking about. After several minutes with me growling and trying to pantomime a *lie-in*, he said, "Oh, are you referring to a *lie-on*?" It would not be the last time I failed to communicate to another English speaker in Africa.

George, who was from the Kikuyu tribe, was assigned as my regular driver, and I would learn much from him about the culture and politics in the months to come. He was tall, slender, and quiet, and had a dry sense of humor. The next day, he arrived at the Hooks's to take me on my first shopping trip to the ex-pat grocery store. I picked up a basket in which to put my groceries, and one of the shop workers hastily came and took the basket out of my hands and asked me what produce and meat I wanted. Everything was in kilograms/shilling and I had no idea how much to ask for. I ended up saying boldly that I wanted five kilos of ground beef, which turned out to be over ten pounds! It was so lean that it stuck to the pan when I tried to brown it, but we ate it for the rest of the week.

George took me to his friend Alfred's produce stand, which was on the side of the road near our house, to buy fresh fruits and vegetables. They were amazing. My refrigerator was so small I had to shop every week, so I struck up a friendship with Alfred. He always had a big, round smile and a warm greeting for me, shaking my hand with his strong, six-fingered hand. The funny thing was, his cat also had an extra digit on his toes. I told Jack and he worried he might become a polydactyl himself by eating the fruit.

"You should be more worried about ingesting amoebae by eating the fruit. Make sure you wash it in this iodine solution, or you will feel like you are vomiting from both ends," I warned.

The next day, George took me to a local beauty parlor that Mrs. Hooks had recommended. On the way to get my hair done, I asked, "George, what kind of car do you own?"

He laughed and said, "I cannot afford a car. No drivers own cars." It made me sad that he had a job driving but could never afford to own a vehicle. He parked outside while I got the popular "permanent wave" of the '80s. When I came out, he looked at my manmade curls and asked with concern, "Did you pay for that?" The women he knew only wanted to straighten their hair.

Laughing, I said, "George, there are things you don't question in women—our hair, clothes, weight, age, and our right to change our minds."

"That's why I am single," he smiled and drove me home.

By the end of his first week working at Equator Bank's Africa Growth Fund, where he encouraged big businesses to invest in East and South Africa, Jack took me on a safari. He borrowed the four-wheel drive Pajero from the bank, and we headed to the Nairobi National Park just outside the city. As we pulled into the game park, I read the sign aloud, "Caution. You are likely to meet dangerous wild animals on this trail. Please proceed quietly and with caution. You proceed at your own risk. The National Parks are not responsible for any eventuality."

"That's comforting," I said sarcastically. Jack just smiled and kept driving. He was in his element.

We saw giraffes at the Giraffe Manor, tons of Thompson's gazelle, and a small elephant herd. I sat mesmerized, watching the elephants interact in the wild. They quickly became my favorite species. Their size, uniqueness, and family bonds captured my heart.

That Sunday, we visited Nairobi Baptist Church. The pastor had visitors stand and a couple on Crusade staff, Carolyn and Larry, greeted us with their southern accents. Larry was tall with brown hair and a welcoming smile. Carolyn was more outgoing with lovely blonde hair and a bubbly personality. Both of their boys had graduated and moved away, so they were happy to have a young couple to enfold into their lives. We became fast friends and soon found comfort and community in their Bible study house group. Carolyn decorated her house like one in a *Southern Living* magazine, but with African accents. It was spacious compared to our small bungalow.

Hearing of my interest in elephants and desire to help preserve the declining population, Carolyn recommended I volunteer at the David Sheldrick Wildlife Trust. She said, "When poachers machine-gun down the mother rhinos and elephants, the infants are left to starve, but the lucky ones are taken to the David Sheldrick Wildlife Trust. It is a sanctuary in the Nairobi National Park that hand-rears the calves and later releases them into the wild. Orphaned and sick animals are taken there from all over Kenya. Daphne Sheldrick started it in 1963 after the death of her husband David Sheldrick, the anti-poaching warden of Tsavo National Park. If you would like, I'll take you to meet her."

The next week we went, and I was thrilled to have tea with Daphne Sheldrick, the international grand dame of elephant calf rescue. She explained the program to me and said, "You can keep the baby ellies and tourists corralled when they go on their daily forage into the park. When the half-starved babies arrive, they are each assigned keepers who stay with them 24–7 and become their family. Sadly, in the early years, we lost many babies until we discovered that they were lactose intolerant. Now, the Royal Air Force flies in lactose-free formula for the babies, and we can save many more than before. They cry tears and even have nightmares of their mother's slaughter, reaching out their little trunks in the middle of the night for the comfort of their keeper. You can start tomorrow if you would like, and come every Wednesday."

That night I read the brochure Daphne wrote to Jack:

> Every piece of ivory is a haunting memory of a once-proud and majestic animal, that should have lived three score and ten; who has loved and has been loved, and was once a member of a close-knit loving family

similar to our own; but who had to suffer and die in unspeakable agony to yield its tusks for trinkets and ornaments. The contributor and buyer of the ivory has left behind others that have sorrowed and mourned deeply, among them dependent young left to die of hunger and of thirst, in terror and lonely hopelessness and isolation. That is a high price to pay for ivory. Is there no humanity left in modern man? Every person who buys ivory has killed an elephant and its dependent young.

"I would love to help these noble creatures, and wouldn't this look great on my vet school application?" I asked, pausing for a breath. Jack nodded.

The next morning when I arrived at the sanctuary, five boisterous older calves greeted me, almost ready to be released into the wild to the care of Eleanor (a former orphan and now matriarch who adopts the orphans in Tsavo Park), a zebra foal, named Malika, and Ajok, the youngest elephant calf who would be my charge. Patting Ajok, I loved the feel of his wrinkled hide with its short bristles of hair, and the look of his limpid eyes set in his fresh little face. After he got to know me, whenever he needed motherly comfort, he ran to me  with his funny straight-legged amble, his soft feet silent on the path. Sucking my fingers like a pacifier, he wrapped his truck around my neck, squinting his small eyes contentedly, as a child snuggles with his blanket. I was careful to keep my hand in the center of his mouth so his large molars didn't crush my fingers. Many nights I laughingly complained to Jack of my sore neck from being loved on by a four-hundred-pound baby.

At night, the calves slept in their stalls with their guardians, as they were easy prey for lions, but during the day they were taught how to forage in the 28,000-acre Nairobi National Park adjacent to the sanctuary. The keepers led them to the edible species of plants, which their mothers normally would show them. I learned orchids were one of their favorite treats. Reflecting on the expensive orchids my mother wore every Easter, I watched astonished as the ellies gobbled the lovely flowers down like french fries. Normally, the calves stood under their mothers for shade. Orphaned now, sunburn was a constant threat to their young, tender hides. Every few days, the keepers shepherded the babies to a mud hole where they frolicked before being smeared with red clay for protection.

When taking Ajok into the park on foot, I always kept my eyes peeled for poisonous snakes like the deadly black mamba, but I only felt in danger on two occasions. The first happened when Ajok stepped on a thorn, and I pulled it out. He emitted a cry for help, imperceptible to my ears, a very low-frequency vocalization called infrasound, which travels long distances. I looked up to see the larger calves thundering through the bush to his rescue, flapping their big ears, threatening to gore me with their five-inch tusks and to mash me into the ground with their strong legs. As soon as I sprang up and dropped his foot, Ajok stopped emitting the infrasound that drew his bodyguards, and they wandered peacefully back into the bush.

The second time I feared for my life was when the keepers and I were taking a group of tourists out with the ellies into the park. While bringing up the rear, I heard crashing in the bush and felt the ground trembling under my feet. I turned and saw a one-ton black rhino with a two-foot horn charging toward me. All I could breathe out was a faint, "Jesus," knowing I was about to be tossed over the tourists' heads and into His arms. Just then the rhino slowed to a jog, brushed by me, as I leaped off the path, and walked up to his former keeper. Unbeknownst to me, the rhino was an orphan now living in the wild, and he was just paying a friendly, social call to his old friend.

In October, an orphaned rhino calf arrived. Terrified for his life, he charged everything in sight. The Gulf War in Iraq and Kuwait had broken out, so he was aptly named *Scud Missile*, after Saddam Hussein's infamous missile. Scud's keepers wore soccer shin guards for protection from the battering one-inch horn. It was weeks before he calmed down.

The next month, Jack booked two Kenya Railways tickets to Mombasa to celebrate my birthday, our anniversary, and Thanksgiving, "I thought this would be a good diversion to prevent homesickness."

"Jack, death is always a good diversion. Mombasa is primarily Muslim, and we are at war with Iraq, a Muslim country. Saddam Hussein said that this will be the mother of all wars. Is it safe to go to the coast?"

"Sure, the embassy has its warnings but not restrictions," he said relishing the risk. "I have a business meeting there," he added, thinking that would somehow make me feel the trip was safe.

"I don't like it."

"I already bought the tickets."

"Well, I guess we have to go then," I said sarcastically. George, our driver, dropped us off at 6:30 that night to catch the train because it wasn't safe to leave a car at the station. I've always loved the adventure of riding on a train, and this was the ultimate. We had a sleeper car, still complete with the British properly starched linen sheets and tea brought to our cabin. As the long train lumbered down the curving track, we could see the engine at one end and the caboose at the other. Looking out the window, we saw the plains sprinkled with antelopes.

As we walked to the dining car, Jack shouted, "Look, a rhino!" We high-fived.

We ate a scrumptious dinner in the dining car, the faded glory of the British Empire still evident on the embroidered linen napkins and silverware with the East Africa Railway monogram. After dinner, Jack and I nestled together in the cool linen sheets, feeling like British royalty before being lulled to sleep by the rhythmic clanking of the train wheels on the track. By ten in the morning, we were in Mombasa, perspiring in the humid heat of the beach hotel lobby. In the courtyard, monkeys played, and the vast view of the Indian Ocean was jade green and eye-filling. A ruddy-skinned man wearing a long, white gown and headwrap poured us chai from a beautiful copper pot. I was learning that the exotic was worth the risk.

The next day Jack went to his business meeting, and I set out alone to explore the sights. Hailing a taxi, we drove under a gigantic pair of metal elephant tusks hanging over the city entrance. I was impressed with the Arab-style architecture and the ornately carved wooden doors. Seeing a mosque and knowing little about Islam, I stepped in. The first thing I learned was women are not allowed in the mosque, as I was escorted out by a very nice man who tried to convert me.

"Jesus actually was God, and Mohammed was not," I insisted. My dogmatic stance helped me to feel tightly in control. It would take me years to loosen religious Mary's grip and realize that emphatic statements, instead of descriptive ones, push people away.

"You are brainwashed," he said, stomping off.

My taxi driver who observed the conversation, laughed when I got in the cab, flustered and red-faced from the encounter, and he said, "That was the mother of all arguments."

The conversation was unsettling, and I was disappointed at myself for getting so angry and sad for the man to be in such darkness, and for the Muslim women who couldn't even enter the mosque. I began to feel threatened, walking around by myself in the Muslim city, so I went back to the hotel. When Jack finished his work, we went with guides in their dugout canoes to snorkel. The water was warm, salty, and relaxing until I saw a group of deadly leopard sea snakes swimming toward me, and I nearly walked on water back to the canoe.

Before we knew it, our time was over, and we boarded the train back to Nairobi. It would be the last trip we took on the train. Because of poor maintenance, trains started to derail, and I did not want to risk flipping over in one of those old cars.

George picked us up at the station. On the drive home, I was horrified when I saw the government bulldozed all the produce stands on the side of the road where I shopped, "What is going on? Where is our friend, Alfred?" I asked George.

"Gone. When the government thugs bulldozed the kiosks, Alfred raised his two fingers in the air, signifying he believed in a two-party system. They beat him and carried him away. President Moi is a different tribe than Alfred and the other vendors, and he wanted them gone. He has a way of eliminating the competition from other tribes, and his opponents are never heard from again," George replied sadly.

Jack said, "Moi is cracking down on the local opposition and even foreign governments who oppose him. Today, he kicked the Norwegians out of the country, and their staff is in a panic trying to find homes for their pets before they must leave tomorrow. The United States may be next as our salty Ambassador Hempstone stands up for democracy against Moi's one-party system. Last week, Moi cracked down and arrested twelve opposition leaders and stationed riot policemen with tear gas on the streets to keep people from attending an opposition rally."

That night I was feeling vulnerable and afraid of more riots or a coup, and I wasn't happy Jack was leaving me the next day to go to Botswana. We said our prayers together and went to bed with heavy hearts.

After Jack left, I drove to my friend Beth's house. She was my prayer partner from church and she invited me over to play tennis and for dinner since both of our husbands were out of the country. Beth was a brunette in her late thirties and a speech therapist at the international school. Her husband was the Marine colonel in charge of security for the embassy, and they had embassy housing.

The two of us were lobbing the tennis ball back and forth when suddenly a black kite swooped down and picked up our only ball. These twenty-four-inch winged, brown raptors are opportunistic and usually eat carrion, but today he thought a tennis ball might be tasty. "That's it!" I yelled. "I'm already worried about coups, terrorist bombings, civil war, refugees, street crimes, getting kicked out of the country, and now an aerial attack."

Beth just smiled, packed up our gear, and headed to her car. "Sounds like you could use a glass of wine," she said driving us to her house. We were halfway through dinner when the embassy alarm sounded.

"What does that siren mean?" I asked frightened.

"There is a security threat. We need to go up the stairs into the safe haven immediately," she said, taking my hand and trotting up the stairs to an area I had never seen. Closing the steel door behind us and then bolting the thick wooden door as well, we sat in the room the embassy designed for protection from intruders.

"What do you think it is?" I asked Beth.

"I couldn't tell from the siren, but it could be a coup, terrorists, or a mob," she said.

"Oh, is that all? No worries then," I said sarcastically.

"What have they trained you to do to protect us?" I wanted to see how safe I should feel with her.

"They say to stay up here until someone rescues us or the threat is over. But if we were driving, they taught me how to slam on brakes, and pull the emergency brake to do a J-turn to get away."

"That's not exactly handy up here," I quipped.

Beth screamed and jumped onto the single bed in the room.

"What is wrong?" I asked startled. She pointed to the floor where a 6-inch-long roach was crawling across the tiles. I had to laugh at the irony of it, "We could be killed right now, and you are worried about a bug?"

"I hate roaches."

I stomped down hard and killed the creature. It was huge, and it felt like stepping on a crunchy mouse. Just then, the siren sounded again, signaling the coast was clear.

"I want to drive home before it gets dark," I said leaving my half-finished dinner on the table. Still jittery, I drove home and impatiently honked the horn for the guard to open our gate. He slowly meandered to the gate, stuck the key in the lock, and swung the heavy metal doors open for me to enter. He was wearing a ski mask and down jacket; it was the rainy season and colder than the rest of the year but still only in the 50s. I unlocked the metal door to my little house, went in, and piled all the mops, brooms, and chairs I could find in front of the door to create my own safe haven. I climbed into my bed, pulled the covers over my head, and wept.

There are four emotional stages in cross-cultural living. The first is the honeymoon stage when you arrive, excited about the new country. The second stage is when you slide into irritability, negativity, and culture shock. You adjust and are happier in the third stage. Finally, in the fourth stage, you adapt and become bicultural. I was in culture shock; the honeymoon stage was over.

I was still crying into my pillow fifteen minutes later when the electricity went out. I looked out to see if the street lamp was on—nope. That meant there was a blackout in the city, and not that some thief had cut my wire. Inconsistent power supply was normal. I sat in the dark on my bed, not wanting to waste valuable battery power unless I had to do so. I missed Jack and was homesick for my friends and family. My dear grandmother, Jean Quintard, passed away the February before we left, but I was so busy preparing for the move that I didn't have time to grieve her loss. Fear, along with my homesickness and grief cascaded into a flood of tears. My grandmother's death brought back grief from my mother's loss as well. Having neither of them my first year of marriage was especially difficult with the added strain of adjusting to a foreign culture.

I was on mental alert in the States, but living with the clear and present danger in Kenya was like putting Miracle Grow on my hypervigilance. However, the part of me which strove to create my own safe haven was being dismantled.

Judith Haugen writes in *Transformed into Fire* that our false self's foundation is built upon shifting externals rather than upon God, which creates a frightening sense of instability because the false self constantly craves security from its environment.

God was loosening my grip on this false self. In the fetal position, I sobbed convulsively into my pillow when I saw a bright light on the ceiling. I sat up; the electricity was still off, so I didn't know what it was, but it was brilliant, brighter than any light I had ever seen and flooded me with warmth and peace. I felt the Lord's safe arms comforting me and I heard, "Rest in me."

The political instability, gnawing needs, and ever-threatening violence set my nerves on edge but through it, I began to trust the Lord for my security and not in my ability to protect myself.

Our year in Kenya was ending, and I left a month before Jack did. Still wanting to pursue my dream of veterinary school, I returned to take organic chemistry. Little did I know it was a class I would not finish.

CHAPTER 20

A, B, Cs

ACCEPTED, BABIES, CHANTILLY

I kissed the runway when I landed at Dulles airport. The welcoming asphalt was warm, gritty, and smelled of tar. After a year of feeling vulnerable, now back on Virginia soil, I felt relieved. Still wanting to pursue veterinary school, I signed up for organic chemistry at George Mason University.

In Kenya, Jack and I talked about having a family, but at thirty-one with my biological clock winding down, we decided to get pregnant sooner rather than later. When Jack returned, we bought a small, split-level house with white aluminum siding and brown shutters in Chantilly, Virginia. It wasn't fancy, but the closest affordable place to DC because Jack's office was in the District.

The very next month, I was expecting! The thought of parenting gave me enough to fear without taking organic chemistry, and I worried the fumes in the lab would harm a developing baby. So, I withdrew from the course. Without the benefit of my mother's guidance when I was growing up, it had never been my dream to be a homemaker. I knew as much about children as I did about the life cycle of a fruit bat. We were both the youngest in our families, and Jack was equally clueless. When we took the birthing classes our Ob/Gyn, Dr. Solano, offered, I was perplexed as to why all the expectant mothers were so excited. Was I the only one who knew this class taught us how to deal with the worst pain we would experience in our lives? Dr. Solano said jokingly, "The problem with the world today is that there are too many women in labor who are not taking drugs and too many women not in labor who are taking drugs."

"No worries here. I am not a fan of pain. You can start the epidural right now," I thought after hearing about the delivery process. *Save that natural delivery stuff for nature.*

While I was in Kenya, I was devastated when I received word that my good friend from college, Pat, who I was with on the horse judging team at Tech, died tragically from complications of childbirth.

I was nervous, as always, at our next pregnancy check-up. But at the doctor's office, we were delighted to see Diane and Phil, some of our old friends, who were also expecting a baby. Before going to Kenya, we were in a Bible study group together. They were master pranksters, and we still owed them a prank. To take my mind off my nervousness, I talked Jack into helping me pull a trick on them. Filching the doctor's office stationary, Jack typed a letter notifying them that they were having triplets and offering them a "multiple-birth support group." That night, after secretly delivering the letter, we called to tell them it was a joke and all had a good laugh.

Since Jack and I knew nothing about birthing babies, we memorized the book, *What to Expect When You Are Expecting* by Heidi Murkoff and Sharon Mazel. Like so many young couples who have either lost their parents through death, work, divorce, or geography, birthing classes and books were our surrogate guides. Jack packed everything on the husband's list of what to take to the hospital, so when I went into labor, he was prepared with his cooler of snacks, a CD player, a stack of books, and his pillow. When my water broke,

Jack took me to the hospital. He parked the car, and in front of us was the expected typical scene: the husband helping his pregnant wife out of the car and into a wheelchair before a nurse tenderly pushes the pregnant mother to the maternity ward. We did not play that script. When we pulled up, Jack had so many accoutrements, the nurse put all his essentials in the wheelchair and held the door for him as I waddled along behind, carrying my small overnight bag by myself.

In her book, *Motherless Daughters,* Hope Edelman writes, "As a daughter experiences such female rites of passage as menstruation and loss of virginity, and later, childbirth, and menopause, she's aware that her mother has experienced them first. She needs the support of someone who understands the intricacies of the female body when she feels alone inside of hers."

Fortunately, I had my dear, older sisters, Catherine and Jean, who had seven children between the two of them. Both helped me decorate the nursery, mainly by paging me, and mortified, accompanying me to the baby section of Walmart, and throwing in the shopping cart whatever I hadn't received at my baby shower.

"A nipple brush, really? Looks like it will hurt. I'm not using that!" I said pulling it out of the cart.

"That is for cleaning the bottle nipple, stupid," they said doubling up laughing while they put it back in the cart. Both of my sisters were "on call," waiting for Jack's message that I was in labor to make the drive from Richmond.

After twenty hours of labor, my doctor gave me Pitocin to speed the process. When the pain kicked in, Jack lasted three minutes as my pain coach. "You are fired! Find someone to give me an epidural. I don't care if it's the hospital janitor!" I gasped loudly, catching my breath between contractions.

"It's a girl," Dr. Solano announced, and quickly prayed a blessing over her. I thought, *how wonderful to have the first words you hear be a blessing*, and I cried with joy, relief, and pain. Jack cut the umbilical cord and counted ten fingers and ten toes. He called my sisters when delivery was imminent and they arrived minutes after delivery. The nurse said, "Your sisters are in the lobby, but they can't come up yet."

"There are not enough security guards in this hospital to keep my sisters out of here," I said with a smile, just minutes before they burst through the door with a big container of animal crackers and flowers from Dad and Shirley. The nurse frowned and whisked the newborn out of the room to the nursery. After a quick hug for me, my sisters followed Jack down the hall to see the new baby. I was left alone in the room unable to stand up, still numb from the epidural and exhausted. *What am I, chopped liver? For nine months, I've been the center of attention, and now the baby has arrived. The new has come, and the old is gone. I guess that is the way parenting should be,* I thought, adjusting my ego to its lowered status, joyful that my seven-pound-eight-ounce daughter stole the show.

Southerners are more traditional than original; hence our beautiful, brown-haired, brown-eyed daughter was named after me, Mary Ashby McDonald. This was a decision we regretted every time we flew, filed insurance forms, and used social media.

Having no affection for babies before, the depth of emotion washing over me when I held my daughter overwhelmed me. I fell in love, hook, line, and sinker with the heart-skipping, euphoric feeling of a first crush. However, nursing made my toes curl with pain, but soon it became a tender bonding time between us. The next day, the nurse came in and told me Ashby had a nearly perfect Apgar score and that she could go home. Home? I thought, terrified, *what on earth am I going to do with a baby?* Afraid of breaking the newborn, I asked the nurse to put her into the going-away outfit. I had no idea how to dress a baby. The first week at home I felt helpless and out of my league, fearful I would do something wrong and hurt the tender child in my care.

The second week, Jack's parents came to see their only grandchild. Jack, in his socked feet, proudly paraded down the steps with baby Ashby in his arms, slipped five steps from the bottom, and landed with a stair in his back. The baby popped out of his arms. We stared horrified as she was airborne, hit the floor, and slid into the opposite wall. Immediately calling the pediatrician, he assured me that babies were much tougher than they looked, "Just wake her up every several hours to make sure she doesn't have a concussion, and she'll be fine."

She was. Jack's accident lowered the baby-care bar for me, and now I began to relax and enjoy our sweet child. She ate everything I put in front of her, took two naps a day, and slept through the night. Thinking we had this parenting thing down, seventeen months later, our son Jack McDonald, IV arrived, and we quickly learned we did not have this parenting thing down.

"Looks like it is going to be a redhead," was the first surprise I heard from the delivery doctor. *How on God's green earth could Jack and I, both brunettes, have a redhead?* I wondered to myself. I later learned Jack's mother and grandmother had red hair when they were younger. The next surprise was that he didn't sleep like his sister did. He woke up every two hours for the first six months. We soon called this beautiful, bouncing boy "Jumping Jack," and I loved him with all my heart, but with two in diapers, vet school was officially out of the picture.

We joined a prolific young church. I threw seven baby showers in one year. My former college friend, Melissa, and I started Moms and Tots, a support group for new mothers who were clueless. The group included women from Nigeria, Hungary, Ghana, Denmark, Brazil, and about five other Americans of the plain white-bread variety. The Ghanaian mother taught us how to tie the cloth and carry our babies on our backs. I learned the Nigerian custom of giving a new mother a chicken when she delivered and gave a stuffed one to my friend. The cross-cultural lessons would serve me well on the mission field in the years to come.

We were all culturally dislocated in some form or fashion, having no family in town to help us navigate this exciting new stage of our lives. We discussed and prayed over post-partum depression, adoption, colic, miscarriages, and difficulties in marriage. We watched each other's kids, so we could have date nights with our husbands, cooked for each other when we delivered babies and supported each other during the good and bad times. We were aunties to each other's kids, applauding their first words and steps. Through the Moms and Tots group, we learned to serve and love one another, and through this deep fellowship, we found true community.

Not only did I learn from the other women how to be a mother, but also how to be a woman and wife. Things I had disdained as weak in my tomboy past, I came to appreciate. Each of the moms taught different classes: scrapbooking, flag making, calligraphy, flower arranging, cooking, and so on. We had Christmas cookie exchanges, Vacation Bible clubs, and Resurrection egg hunts. We went on outings to the National Zoo, White House Easter Egg Roll, and to see Peter Pan fly at the National Theater. As is true with many support groups, it was a time of healing and growth for me and many in the group.

With no grandmothers around, books became our experts. Armed with Susan Yates's book, *A House of Love,* we tried to get siblings to love one another or at least stop hitting each other in the head with wooden blocks. Jim Trelease's *Read Aloud Handbook,* was a treasure chest, arming us with book lists, which we took to the library.

It was a thrilling and exhausting time rearing two toddlers, but by God's grace, Jack and I learned to parent, pray, and cry together.

The previous year, one of the mothers in the group who was from Denmark had met Veronika in the park and invited her to our meeting. She and her daughter Juliana, who was Ashby's age, were soon part of the tribe. Growing up under Russian communism, she was indoctrinated with atheism. But, enfolded by the love of Christ through the other moms, she softened to the gospel message. Sitting on the beige sofa in my living room, she bowed her head, asked Christ to forgive her and to come into her heart, thus beginning her personal walk with the Lord. Together all the women in the group mentored her in her newfound faith.

A year later, before the Moms and Tots meeting, I got a call from Veronika, "I think Juliana has an ear infection. I am taking her to the doctor, and I won't be at the meeting."

"Sure. Call me when you get back and tell me what the doctor says," I said hanging up the phone. After returning from the meeting I listened to her message, "Julianna has a brain tumor. We are at Children's Hospital in DC. They are doing surgery tomorrow."

"Pray for Juliana," I said, stunned as I called the group and started the prayer chain going, and then drove with another member to Children's Hospital.

"Family only. Are you family?" the nurse asked us. Like so many suffering from cultural dislocation, her closest family support group was 5,000 miles away, and like many immigrants, she was like an orphan in this new country.

Struggling between honesty and compassion I said, "Yes." I justified myself in that we were sisters in Christ.

Noting my tentative answer, the nurse asked, "How do you spell the last name, Bohuczky?"

"B-O-H-U-C-S-Z maybe Z-K-Y" I stumbled. "She has no family here; we are sisters in Christ," I pleaded. The nurse looked in both directions and waved us in. We hugged, prayed, and wept with Veronika and her husband, Steve.

Juliana couldn't speak or walk after the surgery. A week later, I took Ashby and Jack to see her. Jack came bouncing in with a balloon and, serving it to Juliana, it hit her shaven head. I stood mortified until Juliana gave her first giggle since the surgery. The kids laughed, and the parents wept. Over the next months of cancer treatments, feeding tubes, and grueling therapy, she bravely learned to eat, walk, and talk again. The Moms and Tots group cheered her on and supported the parents. After all, we were her tribe. She would be in remission for the next several years.

I continued writing my manuscript about the horse business, and finally, the day came to submit it to publishers. Jack made an elaborate celebration out of going to the post office, praying, and taking me to tea. He presented me with a lovely gold necklace, saying, "You deserve this even if it never gets published. You have worked hard." I cried.

After months of rejections, I called the acquisitions editor at the only publisher I had not heard from, Deborah Burns at Storey Publishing in Pownal, Vermont. She apologized profusely, telling me that they had misplaced my manuscript, but she found it and promised to read it that week. God was faithful; she called and said they wanted to publish it and would I take a flat fee? Having no idea what I was doing, I went to the library and checked out a book on negotiating the writer's contract. Following the book's advice, I asked for an advance and 6 percent royalties. They agreed. Now, with the book, *Starting and Running Your Own Horse Business,* having over 85,000 books in print, I am glad that I did.

In the fall of 1994, I began to feel restless. We went on a family getaway to Graves Mountain Lodge. Being in the countryside and seeing the horses and cows grazing against the glorious fall colors, I felt the vet-school pull again. I had put my dream on His altar when I had my children, but now I felt the Lord leading me to go to vet school. Tenderly, I broached the subject with Jack. After some thinking and praying about it, he said, "Well, Mary, if you can get accepted, I will leave my job and move to Blacksburg."

I was thrilled at his support, even though I think he was fairly certain I couldn't get in and so felt safe making that promise. I felt such a flood of joy and peace, I knew the Lord was behind it all. Over the next four years, every semester, I would finish one more of the prerequisites, study for the Graduate Record Exam, and get some research experience at the Equine Medical Center only thirty minutes away. Two months after submitting my application, I was invited for an interview at the Virginia-Maryland Regional College of Veterinary Medicine in Blacksburg, Virginia. There were two interviews: hot and cold. In the cold interview, they asked why I wanted to go to vet school and made sure I had done everything on my application. In the hot interview, they asked situational questions like, "If you were in vet school and a classmate was struggling and asked for your help, would you help them study even if it meant that you sacrificed your own score?"

"Yes," I replied, "maybe down the road, they would hire me." They smiled at my response, so I was feeling confident. Then one of the professors, who lived in Kenya, asked me if I met Dr. Richard Leakey while there. I said "yes" and told him I thought it was wonderful to have a Kenyan helping with conservation efforts.

"He isn't exactly a Kenyan," the professor said sarcastically.

"He is a white Kenyan," I corrected him.

Regretting arguing during an interview and certain I lost my seat in vet school, I berated myself on the drive home. I prayed, "Your will, Father, not mine," and with that surrender, my shoulders relaxed, my self-depreciation fled, and peace surrounded me. Two months later, I received my acceptance letter. Calling Jack, I was blubbering with joy so hard he couldn't understand me and thought one of the children had died.

With Jack starting kindergarten and Ashby beginning second grade, the three of us would enter school in Blacksburg full-time. The kids weren't thrilled to be moving and leaving their friends, but a house with a pool on a wooded mountain lot was enough enticement to make them happy. Husband Jack was willing to give up his career but by grace kept his job in Washington at the Inter-American Development Bank by telecommuting. I was ecstatic to be "doing my dream" of becoming a veterinarian. However, I soon learned that it was just as difficult to stay in vet school as it was to get in.

CHAPTER 21

VET SCHOOL—THE PIG SKELETON EXPERIENCE

It is only through labor and painful effort, by grim energy and resolute courage, that we move on to better things.

—Theodore Roosevelt

My hopes finally crystalized as I took my seat in the freshman lecture hall at the Virginia-Maryland Regional College of Veterinary Medicine. The anatomy professor, clad in his long, white coat, wheeled a cart with a pig skeleton to the front of the classroom. Staring at the porcine frame, joy, relief, and excitement welled up in my chest. Tears rolled down my cheeks, leaving wet drops on my notebook. The twenty-two-year-old student beside me, glanced out of the corner of her eye, wondering how this nut got into vet school, but she had not waited four decades to fulfill her dream, and I was not ashamed to bask in my pig skeleton experience.

"Congratulations, class of 2003," the balding professor said, peering over his gold-rimmed spectacles, "You are some of the brightest students in the country, but let me warn you, doctorate work is difficult. The other night I was at a cocktail party when a therapist from Virginia Tech's counseling center confronted me and asked, 'Do you know that 90 percent of your students require counseling at some point during their four years of veterinary school? What do you do to those students?'"

The professor went on to say, "This is a professional school. The curriculum is intense. Get counseling if you need it."

Over the summer, he had sent a list of anatomy terms for the students to memorize. In the remaining forty-five minutes of the lecture, he covered all the terms that took me three months to learn, and he wondered why we needed counseling. Several years later, the school put a counseling office on the second floor, so when they drove us to the end of our ropes, there was someone in the building to hold the other end.

It wasn't that classes were intrinsically difficult. Rather, it was the total volume of material to memorize. A popular student coffee mug with cow, dog, chicken, antelope, and elephant tracks encircling the ceramic surface read, "Real doctors treat more than one species."

Reading the semester's schedule of exams and class assignments threw me into "syllabus shock"; the school required twenty-one credit hours, but coupled with electives, most students took even more. The first year of core classes included Anatomy I, Histology, Physiology I, Medical Biochemistry, Immunology, Ethology, Large Animal Husbandry, Anatomy II, Neurobiology, Physiology II, Pathology I, Parasitology, Epidemiology, and Fundamentals of Nutrition, but unfortunately, not a Basket Weaving class in the line-up. The professor's philosophy was, "the more crap we throw on the barn door, the more will stick."

I soon realized most of the students were up for the challenge, asking one fellow student, "What was your major in college?"

"Math," she said dryly, as a math major might.

"Oh, you must have made a perfect score on the math section of the GREs," I said joking, and thinking only God could do that.

"Yeah," she said, in a like-what-moron-doesn't kind of way.

When most of these vet students in college were becoming summa cum laude in undergrad, I was struggling with organic chemistry and praying *Come soon, Lordy*. Many of these perfectionists would make their first B's ever while in vet school, necessitating counseling and antidepressants. For some, these were the gateway drugs to lifelong addiction struggles. At forty years old, with two kids and a husband who traveled to Washington every other week, I was happy with B's.

The administration said if you failed a class or made three Ds, you were out of the program. You would be given a second chance, but you had to take the entire year over. Thus, the students joked, "A students go into Academia, C's hire the B's, and no telling what the D's could have done if they had just been able to stay in school."

But the pressures weren't just academic for me. Through the Moms and Tots group, I had become more comfortable in my skin being a wife and mother. I was also confident that God had called me to vet school, but children, husband, household duties, and studies all pulled at the fiber of my being. However, the sheer joy of finally being in vet school carried me through the first year.

Those who haven't gone through the intensity of a professional school don't understand the tremendous pressure during exam week. I apologized to Jack, "I am sorry I have to go and study so much and that I am so cranky."

Jack responded, "Yeah, it's tough not being with you much during finals, but during finals, it is also tough being with you."

I was grateful when I became good friends with my neighbor, Mary. We prayed together often. Walking together up the mountain where we lived, I told her, "I have a new motto in life: I can do all things poorly." My performance mentality had loosened enough for me to be able to laugh at about it. I shared some of the freshman quotes with her, "C = degree! C = DVM. They say you go from wanting A's, to worrying about getting Cs, to praying that you will pass, to wondering if the Marines still need a few good men!"

Some students had a photographic memory, like my anatomy lab partner. The professor would show us a muscle, and he knew it. I carefully highlighted each page one color and a second time in a different color until there were more words highlighted on the page than not, and still, he did better. At the beginning of the second semester, he returned his textbook, having never removed the plastic wrap.

Thousands applied to only nineteen vet schools in the country, and the entering classes were small, making it the most difficult of all of the professional schools to which to be admitted. Many went on to other careers first, but some returned to do their dream as I did. One student, a human-medicine anesthesiologist, always yearned to work on animals, so she applied to vet school. After graduating, she was happily practicing as a vet, but still moonlighting as an anesthesiologist in the local ER to pay off her vet-school loans. One morning, she spayed Mrs. Jenkin's cat in the vet clinic. That night Mrs. Jenkins needed emergency surgery, and the vet was the anesthesiologist on call. Just as the doctor was putting her under, the woman looked into her face and said incredulously, "Wait, didn't you spay my cat this morning?"

The anesthesiologist just smiled and said, "Breathe deeply!"

All the vet professors had advanced degrees, master's degrees and PhDs. As one epidemiology professor put it, "Ph.D. stands for, Piled High and Deep. We get so specialized that we know more and more about less and less. My daughter told me her cat was sick; I told her she needed to take it to a vet."

After listening to these cerebral professors for eight hours a day, I conducted an informal survey and determined a correlation: the more letters behind their name, the less their sense of humor.

Some did have a sense of humor, like the one who told us the story of the importance of observation in diagnosing diseases, "A professor was instructing students how to perform physical exams. 'I want you to observe closely everything I do as I examine this dog, and then I want you to do it yourself.' He listened to the heart and lungs, took its temperature, and stuck his index finger in the dog's rectum to do a fecal exam. He then licked his finger. 'Your turn,' he told the horrified student. The student obeyed the professor and copied the physical exam procedure, just as he had observed, even licking his finger after sticking it in the dog's behind. The professor congratulated him saying, 'That was very good, your powers of observation are keen, except I used my index finger to perform the fecal exam and licked my ring finger. More things are misdiagnosed by not seeing than by not knowing, so be observant.'"

Not a detail person, I knew I needed to work on being thorough. Before entering vet school, my MD friend said, "Mary, I think you have ADD. Let me test you." The results were in, "You passed; here is a prescription to help you focus. You don't get any points in Heaven for being drug-free," she warned me.

But I wanted to be in control and get through vet school on my own power. After all, God called me. Surely, He would help me. I soldiered through my studies each night when the kids went to bed, turning the furnace off because its little noises were enough to break me out of my study zone. I ran on coffee and five hours of sleep, but after raising babies, this wasn't an entirely new phenomenon to me. One student commented on the amount of time she spent studying, "I can make it on five hours of sleep a night, but four is really pushing it."

"No joke," I replied, old enough to be her mother.

The courses became even more difficult because English was not the first language of some of the professors. After dragging my kids to an evening study session, my nine-year-old daughter asked in all seriousness, "Mommy, what language was your teacher speaking?"

"I wonder that every lecture, dear," I replied wryly.

Our professors were difficult to understand at times, but no one could question their commitment to the profession. Take, for example, our parasitology professor who put in his own ear a cat's ear mite to determine if they were specific to cats or could thrive in a human ear as well.

Balancing parenting and studies was a constant challenge. There were doctor's appointments, carpooling, soccer, gymnastics, Boys Brigade, and Pioneer Girls. Fortunately, their teachers were wonderfully understanding, and the atmosphere in the Christian school was so loving that our children thrived. Every night we read the Bible, said our prayers, and snuggled up to read their favorite books aloud, even acting out *The Chronicles of Narnia* and *The Lord of the Rings*.

After a full day of classes, many nights I would go back to the vet clinic for a post-surgery check and take the kids with me. We made a game out of finding the funniest pet's name in the clinic. One night after reading the card on the kennel, Jack said, "Look, Mommy, that dog's name is Bites."

"Yeah, don't pet that one, son," I said, hurrying him away from the pit bull cage.

We also had a ferret, two Jack Russell terriers, a cat, and a pony to care for. The stress of balancing everything often left me impatient with the kids and barking out orders when they were slow getting ready for school. One morning little Jack asked, "Mommy, were you bossy when you were little?"

"Yes," I snapped, "Now hurry up and get in the car! We are late for school, and I have a big exam at eight."

Sleep deprived and test-stressed, my constant prayer was to be more loving and kind. My time with the Lord was paltry, and my relationship with Him had become stale and ungrateful. I fell into the same mire of comparison that traps most professional students whose performance defines their identity: criticizing professors, grumbling over grades, and grousing about the workload. How I felt and who I was began to be determined increasingly by how well I did on the last exam or surgery. My identity was taking the form of DVM more than a child of God.

Always on the lookout for fun things to do with the kids, when Jane Goodall came to Virginia Tech, we went to hear her. She walked out on stage and said hello in Swahili, "*Jambo*," and then continued greeting us in several other languages before howling like an ape at the top of her lungs making everyone's hair stand on end, wondering if she had lived in the jungle too long.

"That is how I would greet you if I were a chimp," she said catching her breath.

Fascinated by her amazing work in Africa and hints of spirituality during her lecture, I bought her book, *Reason for Hope, A Spiritual Journey*. I was impressed by her early love of Jesus Christ and her personal relationship with Him. Throughout the book, she made many references to Scripture and to God but seemed to drift from believing that Christ alone was sufficient and added the parts she liked from all religions into a spiritual smorgasbord from which she chose what she believed. Instead of her book giving me a "reason for hope," I began to doubt my own faith. I missed the certainty in my faith which was now riddled with doubts. I even wondered at times if Christ was the only way to God. All truth is from God, I reasoned. Are all gods just as valid? Does Buddha = Christ = Mohammad? My apologetics came back to me. If all religions lead to God, then why did Christ have to die on the cross? Jesus is the only one who had eyewitnesses who saw Him resurrected from the grave and the only religious figure who is still alive today. But is any of it true? A dark shadow of doubt enveloped my soul.

The second month of school, I dragged my tired and discouraged soul into the Christian Veterinary Fellowship meeting and slumped down. The faculty advisor, who saw many bedraggled freshmen, consoled us, saying,

"Vet school is a pressure cooker. You must run with the pack. You don't have to be at the very front, but you can't lag behind, either. If you need to talk, my office is downstairs. I'm having a BBQ at my place Friday night. Next month, there is a Christian Veterinary Mission conference called "Real Life/Real Impact" in Atlanta."

I learned that Christian Veterinary Mission is a group of vets whose mission is to send veterinarians to the poorest countries in the world to help with animal healthcare, food production, and to share the love of Christ through veterinary medicine. I told Jack about the conference, and in November the four of us attended. The weekend proved pivotal to our future. One of the vets on their staff spoke to Jack about working overseas.

Jack said, "I can see how Mary could use her vet knowledge helping in the rural villages, but I am a banker and not sure what I could do."

"In Bolivia, we are looking for a vet and a banker. The banker is needed to help the micro-finance program there," was the response he received.

Driving home, Jack told me about the need in South America, "It fits our family profile so well that lightning might strike us if we don't check Bolivia out. Remember, Isaiah 58:10, spending ourselves on behalf of the hungry, *is* our life verse."

"I just want to make it through vet school, but if you plan the trip, I'll go." I was exhausted and couldn't force another decision in my overcrowded mind.

Before I knew it, the first-semester cumulative final exams were coming down the pike. Trying to narrow my study scope, I asked the histology professor what was on the final. Smirking, he replied, "Let me tell you a story. In the English Department, a professor strolls into class and says, 'Good morning, class.' A student, in shorts, with a ponytail, leaning his chair against the back wall, nods, 'Mornin.'

"In the Business school, a professor saunters into class, 'Good morning, students.' The students in their three-piece suits with their perfectly sharpened No. 2 pencils say, 'Good morning, Professor.'

"In the vet school, a professor strides in and says, 'Good morning, class,' and all the students immediately looked down and frantically scribbled, 'Good morning, class.' That is what is going to be on the final," he said and walked away.

The meaning was all too clear. We were responsible for every word he spoke in class. Overwhelmed, I went to the CVF group and shared my fears of failing. The wise professor who attended the meeting said, "Mary, have you seen the class pictures of the students who graduated that are hanging on the wall in the Commons cafeteria area? They made it through, and God will give you success as well. He did not bring you this far for nothing. Before you know it, people will be calling you doctor, and your picture will be hanging on the wall with the rest of them. Go to the hospital and see some real cases to remind you of why you are here."

I took his advice and went to see sick horses being treated. *Yes, that's why I am here—to become a doctor,* I thought, standing up straighter. That is motivation for all this hard work and pain. I walked through the Commons, glanced at the pictures of the students, and smiled, feeling God's reassuring peace.

Seeing a discouraged classmate with his head in his hands, I said, "Hey there, look at the wall. One day your picture will be hanging there, and people will call you doctor."

"Thanks, I needed to hear that," he said. I laughed as he read to me from a sheet entitled, "You Know You Are a Vet Student When." In it were gems, such as you look deep into your lover's eyes and pull out a pen light; you study at stop lights; you get a blood test and they diagnose caffeninemia; someone asks your name and you think it is a trick question; and you walk away from dishwashing with your hands in the air."

The time quickly came for the second-semester finals. Jack and the kids hid Post-it notes around my desk, "You *can do it*!" "A+ 100," and most importantly, "We love you, Mommy." Their love, His strength, and the excitement of being in vet school gave me the perseverance to make it through the first grueling year. Physically, mentally, and spiritually exhausted, I was relieved to be off for the summer. We relaxed by the pool, rode the pony, and spent a week at the beach. Jack booked flights to Bolivia. I took the kids to get vaccines and antimalarial pills, and off we went on a trip that would change our lives.

CHAPTER 22
MISSION TRIP TO BOLIVIA

*Every person must make a decision about the words that Christ spoke,
"I am the way, the truth and the life. No one comes to the Father, but
through me.*

—C. S. Lewis

"They make cocaine from coca leaves, so don't take a drug test next week," Jack said as the flight attendant served us coca tea to help with the altitude sickness. It was August of 2000, the summer following my first year of vet school. We flew from Miami to La Paz, Bolivia.

"You could grow anaerobic cultures up here," I sighed to Jack as we touched down on the highest runaway in the world, at over 13,000 feet. Oxygen masks were ready for unfortunate passengers who stood up too quickly and passed out.

Thirty minutes later, the sun rose, bathing the jagged snow-crested Andean peaks in liquid gold as we flew to the tropical lowlands of Santa Cruz. Phil Bender, the World Concern Latin America Director, picked us up, but our luggage remained in Miami. Leaving the airport, a rhea (South American ostrich) strutted across the road, "Toto, we aren't in Kansas anymore!" I exclaimed, as we narrowly missed the pterodactyl.

No one smiled except my husband, Jack. He always smiles when we are in a Third World country with no luggage, no sleep, and strange animals that can kill you within thirty feet.

The beauty of the country was as breathtaking as the poverty. Five-foot-tall poinsettia trees, brilliant orange bougainvillea vines, and tall elegant palm trees welcomed us into the city. At every stoplight, kids hawked sodas or jumped on the hood to wash the windshield, hoping to earn a boliviano, about a penny. At his office, Phil put the "Club" locking device on the steering wheel, and paid a man to watch his old Land Cruiser, "We've had three vehicles stolen."

Upstairs in the meeting room, Phil briefed us on the country and the work they were doing. "Bolivia is the poorest country in South America. The per capita income is $995 annually. President Hugo Banzer staged a coup and was a dictator in the '70s but then was democratically elected last year." In the next six years, there would be five presidents before the election of Evo Morales who, once elected, changed the constitution so he could stay.

The staff introduced themselves. Ashby and Jack couldn't understand a word anyone was saying and disliked everyone kissing their cheeks in greeting.

"*Yo soy gallina verde,* I am a green chicken!" Little Jack introduced himself with the only Spanish phrase he knew.

Everyone laughed, and the secretary served Coke and Tampico along with *salteñas*, a fabulous concoction of meat, potatoes, gravy, and hard-boiled eggs in a soft dough blanket. The trick is to eat them without spilling a drop of gravy, which every Bolivian worth his salt can do. With gravy spots dotting our only clothes, we toured the office. The expedition led us to a door with "*Misión Veterinaria Cristiana*" painted on it.

"This is where the Christian Veterinary Mission vet's office was," Phil said staring hopefully at me. "Here is CAMS, (*Capacitación, Arrorrós, Microcrédito, y Solidaridad*) the micro-finance office," he explained to Jack.

Observing our bleary-eyed kids, Phil drove us to the Mission Guest House to catch a nap, but the sight of the coconut and mango trees revived the kids. They ran to the back yard where they discovered a gray boulder with four scaly legs. As we ran our fingers over the four-foot-long domed shell with its decorative square patches, the old tortoise kept chewing the soft, white pulp of a Cherimoya fruit. Our steps became as torpid as the turtle's, and we climbed into the unpretentious beds of the guest house.

That night we had dinner with Phil and his wife Fannie, who lent us clothes for the week. We met Lourdes, the new World Concern Bolivia Director, who had taken over from the former director, a veterinarian named Dr. Susan Stewart. Dr. Susan and her husband, Mark, also a veterinarian, had been in Bolivia for years and catapulted the development work there before Mark died tragically. Susan had trained Lourdes and came back to Bolivia that week to evaluate the programs. They planned for me to go with them to an animal health-care workshop the next day.

Leaving the city in the morning, the asphalt streets turned to partially paved roads, then to potholes connected by dots of pavement, and eventually just to dirt. Dust from sugar cane trucks swallowed us up as they passed.

White plastic bags, caught in the wire fences beside the road, blew in the wind, lending a festive look to the area. The only clothes not on their backs dried on the fence, too. Besides thatched roof huts, women weeded around the starchy tubers of yucca and papaya plants. I learned boiled yucca tasted like an old sock, but it was quite tasty fried, and that the soft salmon-colored papaya had an aftertaste of cat pee.

Driving along, I peppered Susan, a development guru, with questions. I wanted to glean all I could from her experience and to impress her with my interest. We arrived in early afternoon to the training site, which was ten miles past the middle of nowhere. It was a lone shelter carved out of the rainforest hills, made of wooden planks on three sides, a thatched roof, and no door. The training was in progress, so we slipped in and sat on hard wooden benches. It was hot, and the sun rays beamed through the openings between the planks, burning like lasers across my back. I feigned interest for several hours, thinking it was in Spanish, but later learned it was the local indigenous language, *Quechua*. I fought a gastro-intestinal demon with Pepto-Bismol. I surmised from the pictures that the lecture was on cattle parasites, then snake bites. It looked like most snakes were venomous, and if these didn't kill you, others would squeeze you to death. Surveying the room, I noticed the burlap bag in the corner move. Halfway through the lecture, a woman picked up the bag and a machete and went out of eyesight and earshot. Another woman walked out, started a fire, and shelled green peanuts. The first woman returned and put a freshly plucked chicken in a pot of water, which she placed on the flames.

Unable to communicate in Quechua, I sat in lonely silence, absorbed in my thoughts. It was a long, grueling year. I wondered if the painful effort and grim energy was worth it. I had fracked the depths of my being and was exhausted. This was the first time in nine months that I just sat, with nothing to study and no family responsi-bilities clambering for my attention. I tried to let out a deep sigh, but there was heaviness in my chest, so it was a shallow puff. Staring into the green-blanketed hills, I asked the Lord, "Why have you brought me to this remote mountain in the poorest nation in South America?"

My doubts cast long shadows over my soul, keeping me from God's love. I thought of C. S. Lewis's words in *Mere Christianity,* "Every person must make a decision about the words that Christ spoke. 'I am the way, the truth and the life. No one comes to the Father, but through me.'"

Clapping ended my tormented cogitations. Everyone was walking outside, "Time for a *refrigerio*, a snack," Susan said.

Rising stiffly from my primitive seat, I stepped into the sunshine and was handed a bread roll and a clear liquid drink that tasted like Mr. Clean detergent. "*Limón,*" someone says, but it didn't taste like any lemonade I'd ever had before.

"*Gracias,*" I replied, hoping the Pepto-Bismol would guard my stomach from further insult. Everyone smiled at me, and I smiled at everyone. Unable to communicate, I felt like the village idiot. After a few swigs of the tepid brew, I ran for a private bush. Black diarrhea spewed. The overdose of Pepto-Bismol had turned my stool black.

The training had already started when I returned, and everyone laughed when I walked in. Susan explained, "Latecomers have to sing to the group."

I sang off-key, in bad Spanish, "Jesus Loves Me This I Know."

Sitting down, I asked the Lord the deep question in my soul, "Do you really love me, Jesus?" It started to rain, and large drops pelted the sun-scorched ground sending up little puffs of red dust. "Lord, you promise to satisfy my scorched soul. Will you rain on me?" I felt no refreshment. To be sure, I felt a thinness in my soul. I also felt a darkness, an oppression. These were the same feelings I had sensed in the jungles of Bali, Indonesia, on a mission trip I took after college. I recalled what one of the World Concern staff told me, "The Bolivians offer blood sacrifices to appease Pacha Mama, the goddess of the earth, usually a llama fetus, but sometimes they offer a human sacrifice to her."

This is not a good place to be unsure of my spiritual state, I thought as I tried to cast off my doubts.

I wrestled with the great trilemma, "Lunatic, Liar, or Lord," or "Mad, Bad, or God" of which George MacDonald and C. S. Lewis wrote. Was Jesus a lunatic who really believed He was God, but He wasn't? Surely other signs of mental illness would have surfaced and turned the crowds and his disciples away. They wouldn't have been martyred for a lunatic. Was Jesus a liar and just said these things and they weren't true? But Jesus did so many good things and had so many followers even after His death; it seems implausible that He lied about it all. What liar would take the cross? Or was He in fact Lord, God in flesh? When I embraced Christ in college I was so solid in my faith. But over the past year, I decided to be more open-minded, and embrace all forms of spirituality, but instead of feeling free, I felt jiggly, like spiritual Jell-O.

A vicuna bug, which transmits Chagas disease, fell from the ceiling onto my leg and broke my theological wrangling. They hide in the thatched roof, and then fall on your face, biting and defecating there. When you scratch the bite wound, the protozoan gets into your blood, and years later destroys elasticity in muscle cells, mainly heart and intestines. Crushing the bug under my boot, I recalled Susan's words, "Seventy percent of the villagers die from Chagas disease in their forties. Last year, our best trainer succumbed. We'll pitch our tent inside the shelter, so we won't get bitten."

The rain slowed to a sprinkle, and the room stirred into action. The trainees were going to practice what they learned and gathered up the syringes, vaccines, and dewormer. We sloshed down a narrow trail to where cows grazed on their tethers. First, the trainers demonstrated, followed by the rest of us, deworming and vaccinating the jumpy beasts. I realized what an improvement this would make to the community's livelihood.

A decrepit, old farmer walked up to me; Susan translated his plea, "We work hard, but we are still poor. We want a better life for our children. Please come here to Bolivia and help us."

I smiled and shrugged my shoulders in a *maybe* gesture. The rest of the afternoon, I couldn't shake the old farmer's words from my heart.

Bedraggled and soaked to the skin, the alluring smell of green peanut soup drew us back to the shelter that evening. Knocking back my poncho hood and wiping my wet bangs from my mud-streaked face, I bowed my head as we prayed. I had never tasted a more delicious soup. Helping the villagers filled me with joy, and I breathed a deep sigh of contentment.

Devoid of city-light pollution, the pitch blackness was crisply branded with white stars as Susan and I crawled into our pup tent. I asked her about her family and how she dealt with her husband's death, thinking she would give some super spiritual answer.

"It ruined my life," was all she said.

"Oh," I said, having no idea how to respond, "well, goodnight then." Unable to sleep, my mind reeled at the unfairness of the tragic death, the end of their ministry, and a ruined life. Where was His protection, especially to His most favored servants, missionaries? Why didn't He fulfill His promise, "that all things work together for the good of those who love Him?" Where was the "ashes to glory" he would make from this tragedy? I dozed in a fitful sleep on ground as hard as my heart, doubting God's goodness. But God's plot had not fully played out. Three years later, Susan would marry a medical doctor and together they would serve in Asia.

At sunrise, howler monkeys woke me. As I slathered on 98 percent DEET to ward off dengue and malaria mosquitos, I recalled telling my husband that, at forty, I wasn't camping anymore. *God has a sense of humor,* I thought, as I crawled out of the tent, nimble as a double amputee.

I smelled no coffee. I accepted a hot cup of *Api*, a purple oatmeal brew. Its warmth melted the frost in my marrow but did little to soothe my caffeine headache. Once the group assembled, the leader read a Bible story. When finished, they bowed their heads and prayed. Peeking through, my not-quite-shut eyes, I stared at their heads. *How did they get their parts so straight? How were they so neat and clean without running water? Why so happy? God's love was shining through their poverty. I'm as sloppy as a soup sandwich, and my faithless heart feels as dirty as my jeans.*

At *refrigerio*, not recognizing the snack, I prayed the missionary prayer, "Lord, I'm willing to put it down, if you are willing to keep it down."

Susan asked, "How's it going?"

"My spiritual life feels like dry toast," I said, tearing up.

"Let's take a walk," she said. We sloshed down the sodden road, my mood as thick as the mud. A growling dog, hackles raised, rushed toward us. *I'm glad I had my rabies vaccine because I am about to get the snot bitten out of me,* I thought.

"Just bend down like you are picking up a rock, the dogs are used to having rocks thrown at them. If you pretend to pick one up, they take off," Susan demonstrated, and the dog turned tail and ran. "Tell me more about how you are feeling."

"Spiritually I feel like the wheel is still turning, but the hamster is dead."

She smiled and spoke to me from a deep place in her soul, sharing with me her own doubt journey, "You have to be honest and face the doubts. You have to go into it before you can get out of it."

"Yeah," was all I could muster. I realized I was afraid to tell God I doubted Him. Did I fear He couldn't handle it, or that I would lose what little faith I still held if I ventured onto this doubt journey?

"Meditate, saying a mantra about God's love twenty minutes, twice a day, and get a spiritual director," Susan suggested.

I sat outside the shelter the rest of the afternoon, basking in the rain-forest-filtered sunlight and telling God I didn't know what I believed. Vet school taught that only what could be proved by the scientific method was true. Investigating other world religions, I found no loving relationship. "Where the heck else can I go, Lord? Atheism, Buddha, Pacha Mama? I know you have the words of eternal life." Finally, by faith, I said, "Lord, I fall back on you, thank you, Jesus."

Yielding to Him, I sensed something softening and relaxing in me. Accepting His truth, I felt the Lover of my soul's strong and tender embrace, more real than anything I could ever see or prove. I would need this strength and a softened heart to face the months ahead.

CHAPTER 23

A PERSPECTIVE CHANGE

Give your life to something larger than yourself and pleasure—to the largest thing you can: To God, to relieve suffering, to contributing to knowledge, to adding to literature, to something else. Happiness lies this way, and beats pleasure hollow.

—Annie Dillard

Never do anything that someone else can and will do, when there is so much of importance to be done which others cannot or will not do.

—Dawson Trotman

The second year of vet school we moved from the "Dungeon"—the basement classroom, where no one could hear our screams—to the first-floor classroom where we could get quicker coffee refills. Most students were in counseling by then, so the administration, thinking the "elopement risk" of us escaping was low, put us on the ground level.

Many students say the second year is the most difficult because of all the "ologies": theriogenology; pathology; radiology; pharmacology; bacteriology; and mycology. For me, the experience was less intense than the first year. I learned to study better, and more importantly, I found a wonderful nanny. Ana was my classmate's fiancée. Matt met her in Guatemala when he was in the Peace Corps. She loved my kids and cooked and cared for them like her own, teaching them some Spanish. Despite having her help, I was back in the pressure cooker. By the first day of classes, I was already two weeks behind.

After studying hard all semester, I was looking forward to some breathing room over Christmas break, when I started feeling feverish. The next thing I knew I had a 104-degree temperature and went to the hospital with the flu. I missed the reviews and final exams. I had never skipped a class because I feared failing, and now I missed the most important weeks of the semester. After four days of high fever, I felt the physical presence of Jesus's finger touch my cheek, and the fever broke.

The administration said I had to take my finals before the second semester or I would have to repeat the entire year. Furthermore, the professors would not accommodate me with lab reviews. The rest of my cohorts studied the bacteria slides and radiographs, but I was at a considerable disadvantage.

The first exam I made up was pharmacology, a brutal marathon of drug calculations and minutia. Still dehydrated and feverish, it took me four grueling hours. Any one of the professors could have shown concern, but only the two pathology professors did. They called to check on me and spoke words of mercy, "Mary, you have worked hard in this class and have an A–; you don't have to take the final if you want that grade." This unexpected kindness, so rare in vet school, was such an expression of Christ's love that I cried when he spoke his words of grace. Both professors were followers of Jesus, and their compassion reminded me of Christ's mercy in my life, giving me so much kindness that I didn't deserve.

One by one, I took the finals. Returning exhausted but triumphant the next week to start the second semester, I learned more than the "ologies" that semester. I realized on a deeper level that it was God's power and not my own that was responsible for getting me through vet school.

The second semester flew by, and I finished my finals without any bouts of influenza. My sisters, Cat and Jean, came up to celebrate. We were enjoying the sunshine and eating strawberry shortcake by the pool, when I presented Jean with a bumper sticker, "Life just hasn't been the same since that house fell on my sister."

Laughing, she plopped the bowl of whipped cream on my head, and a battle ensued until we were all slathered in white. Hearing our laughter, the kids jumped out of the pool, stunned that adults were having a food fight. God was redeeming the ashes of our childhood, and I felt blessed to make some happy memories with my sisters.

In between year two and three, more travel opportunities were on our horizon. Jack worked for the Inter-American Development Bank, and they sent him to Costa Rica for Spanish lessons. This presented us with the opportunity for all four of us to begin learning a foreign language.

Summer ended too soon, but this was the last year of lectures and we had more hands-on training. I became the president of my Christian Veterinary Fellowship (CVF) chapter and planned to host the Real Life/Real Impact conference at Virginia Tech.

As the conference approached, our need to raise funds became apparent. Hill's dog food company donated dog food to the clubs for them to sell to raise money for their activities. I went to the professor in charge of the disbursement of the funds. "Sorry, but you are a Christian club; we don't want to give you any money," was the stiff reply.

Even though we were a legitimate club under the Student Chapter of American Veterinary Medical Association and recognized by the vet school, we were denied. When I told our CVF group the results of my conversation, one student said, "The first week of vet school we went to a diversity talk. If we were any other orientation than Christian, we would not be denied. How is it they can discriminate against a Christian club?"

"I don't know," I said, "Let's just pray for the professor to come to know the Lord." Little did we know that God would answer those prayers, and the very next year I helped that same professor become a Christ follower.

God faithfully brought in the funds, and students from four other vet schools attended the Real Life/Real Impact conference we organized in Blacksburg. The CVM founder, Dr. Dorminy, and his wife came and motivated the students to use their education to be the hands of Christ in developing countries by helping the poor better care for their livestock.

In addition to organizing the conference and taking classes, we learned to perform surgeries. I was glad to be out of the lecture hall, but the dog, cat, and horse sterilizations were intimidating. Putting an animal under anesthesia is risky. Keeping everything sterile, making precise incisions, and knowing the beloved pet's life is in your hands is stressful.

I finished the third year and headed into my final year with only a week break. The last year involved rotating around areas of practice for seventeen different three-week blocks, some in the vet school and others in private practice. After our initial trip to Bolivia, Jack and I both felt that the Lord was leading us to be missionaries there, but we needed to determine the feasibility of living with children in South America's poorest country. The vet school allowed a trip to Bolivia as a rotation.

I briefed the kids before landing, "Don't pet the dogs. There is a rabies outbreak. Bolivians don't require seatbelts, but I do, so strap in."

Bill, the new Christian Veterinary Mission vet, and his wife, Heidi pulled up in their red Toyota pickup with their children sitting in the truck bed. After welcoming us, Bill pointed to the truck and said, "Kids and suitcases in the back."

I made a face like a pug eating wasps, but our son Jack was so excited that my husband said, "They'll be fine," and motioned them in.

"The kids keep people from stealing your luggage," Bill said.

Bill was a small-animal vet from Wisconsin, with kind, blue eyes that matched his lovely wife Heidi's. When we arrived at their house in Barrio California, she was quick to make us feel at home as she showed us to our rooms. Heidi used her artistic gifting to decorate their home with local artwork and furniture.

Running out to play in their backyard, the kids were delighted to see a blue-and-gold macaw and to climb into the red hammock. "Our main objective here is to determine the suitability of Bolivia as a long-term mission location for us. Checking out the school for the kids is a priority," I told Heidi as the four adults sipped Tamarind juice.

"Tomorrow I will give you the missionary kids's school tour. I teach art there," Heidi said enthusiastically. The next day we drove down a muddy road and stopped in front of a white stucco wall that read, "Eagles . . . those who wait on the Lord will mount up like eagles . . . Santa Cruz Christian Learning Center." The guard unlocked the gate and let us in. SCCLC had a lovely soccer field and gym, and the overall facilities were nicer than the children's Christian school in Blacksburg.

"It is very safe," Heidi said. "Our kids love it here. They have sports, drama, and art, and the academics prepare the students well for college, plus these are missionary kids, some third generation, so you don't have to deal with a lot of the junk that's in the public schools back home. This is a great place to raise your kids, especially in the teenage years."

I sensed a peace in my heart as we met some of the teachers. It seemed like a good fit for our children. After the school tour, Heidi hailed a cab, "Let's go to Talita Cumi, the children's home where I am helping." The cab, an ancient Camry had a huge hole on the right side of the dashboard, a Teddy bear perched where the steering wheel once sat. Heidi said, "These are *switchovers*. They import the old ones from Japan, where the steering wheel is on the right side of the dash. Here, they switch the steering wheel to the left side but leave the instrument panel on the right and just stick a stuffed animal in the hole. They don't need a speedometer; traffic laws here are just suggestions."

We drove fifteen minutes, passing a limping horse pulling a cartful of bananas and a donkey carrying two mattresses on his back, before pulling up to a locked gate. Heidi fished a key out of her bra and opened the gate. I watched my kids's eyebrows raise as she said triumphantly, "I've had my purse snatched on the street several times, but no one has taken my wallet since I started keeping it here."

As we stepped through the thin tin opening, I noticed that there wasn't a blade of grass in the sparse yard. The red dirt had been compressed from the many little feet running around the compound, kicking a nearly flat soccer ball. Our son, Jack, joined the soccer game, and Ashby was fascinated by the pet toucan who wandered around the buildings. A quick tour showed the leaking roof and outdoor plumbing with no hot water. We walked to a dilapidated swing set, and a lovely little girl motioned for me to push her. "We are trying to raise funds to buy a better facility," Heidi said as she told me some of the children's heartbreaking stories. "Over fifty percent of the girls in Bolivia are sexually abused, usually by drunk fathers or uncles raping them repeatedly. Other children are abandoned on the streets and left to fend for themselves as early as eight or nine. The authorities bring the lucky ones here. We try to show them the love of Christ by giving them food, clothes, shelter, and hugs. '*Talita cumi*' is what Jesus said to the little girl when He raised her from dead. It means rise. We want to help these kids rise up from the pain of their childhood."

As I pushed the orphan on a rusty swing, sorrow rose from a crack within me and tears trickled down my face. Her innocence, like mine, was stolen by men's lust. After that day, Jack and I helped raise money for their new children's home. Little did I know that three years later, I would be blessed by those same children. It happened when we moved to Bolivia, and I was suturing up a horse. He kicked me badly in the knee, and I was holed up at home on crutches, feeling sorry for myself on my birthday. I heard the guard open the gate, and I hobbled to the door to see the Talita Cumi kids bringing a birthday cake. They beamed, so excited to surprise and bless me. They sang *Feliz Cumpleaños*, and their joy and mischievousness poured all over me. Despite their poverty and brokenness, they would touch my heart and encourage me deeply that day.

After visiting Talita Cumi, we left the kids with Heidi. Jack went to the World Concern office to learn about their microenterprise work, giving small loans to the poor to start their own businesses.

Bill and I drove in his green Land Rover Defender to the village of Las Gamas, half a day away. We met Dr. Sam Galphin, a dairy vet from North Carolina, and two vet students from Iowa State. We spent the week testing cattle for tuberculosis and brucellosis. The Bolivian government asked us to test because of the high incidence of these diseases among the people. The officials surmised drinking unpasteurized milk from infected cattle was the cause. Dr. Galphin had the gift of encouragement and a quick smile. We sat in a circle with the village elders. The women said, "*Chicha,*" handing me a cup of the corn-based drink. I had read that *chicha* is prepared by women spitting corn kernels into a vat of water and leaving them to ferment.

The high alcohol content sends most visitors to the hospital with projectile vomiting. I stared at my cup like it might bite.

It was a hot day, and Bill chugged two glasses. *How's he driving us back to the city?* I wondered.

"It's not the alcoholic kind. They boil water and add corn, pineapple, cinnamon, and sugar. It's safe to drink," he said.

I shared mine with two young girls sitting beside me. They stuck to me like glue the rest of the day, carrying my syringes and notebook as we went from hut to hut. The girls loved animals, and I wished that they could go to vet school. But the village schools only went to the fourth grade, so admission to the vet school in the city was impossible. Besides, the boys, not the girls, are the first to have their school fees paid. The girls stay home, carry water, and care for the livestock until they get pregnant, and then they take care of their own family. It was doubtful that I endeared them to the profession, as I lifted manure-covered tails, drew blood, and nearly got my head kicked off. I tried to tell them how Jesus loves them and encouraged them to go to church, but there wasn't one in the village. The Catholic priest came twice a year to give communion, but most of the year they lived in dread of Pacha Mama, the goddess of the earth. For centuries in the Andes, their ancestors had aborted llama fetuses with poisonous herbs and burned the fetuses to appease Pacha Mama. In fear, they wasted their precious resources to sacrifice to a god that neither knew nor loved them.

That night, we ran the blood tests. Adding antibody to the cow's blood on the brucellosis test cards, we watched tiny clumps form—20 percent of the cows were positive! When we checked the cow's tuberculosis reaction sites two days later, 10 percent were positive. The main cow that supplied milk to the school had brucellosis. We removed her from the herd. My gut turned when I realized that these precious girls had little hope for a better future. Physically, these diseases, as well as malaria, dengue, and Chagas lay in wait to infect them. With no opportunity for them academically or professionally, they would be subsistence farmers. Spiritually, they wouldn't know God's love and power to endure their hardships but only Pacha Mama's fear. It saddened me greatly, but I realized I could help them and others like them. I knew I couldn't change the whole world, but I could change their world.

I remembered the starfish story. The two men walking along the beach after a storm saw hundreds of starfish washed up on the sand. One man reached down, picked up a starfish and gently placed it back into the sea. His friend said, "Look at all of them; you are not making any difference." Again, the man picked up another starfish and put it into the life-giving water, replying, "It made a difference to that one."

Our last weekend in Bolivia, our family took a retreat to pray and think over our future. The Janeckes suggested we go to village of Samaipata, from a Quechua word *samay* meaning "to rest" and *pata* that means "elevated place." We stayed at a resort which had five little cabins and a small restaurant. Samaipata is in the foothills of the Andes and is cooler than Santa Cruz, so the first night we built a fire in the little outdoor fireplace, and the four of us snuggled up close and looked at the amazing stars until we found the Southern Cross.

The next day we visited the pre-Inca ruin of El Fuerte de Samaipata, a temple built by Arawak people, carved on an enormous rock where they made human sacrifices to their gods. That night back at the cabin, Trudi, the woman who owned the restaurant, prepared dinner and showed us her gift shop. I bought a calligraphy plaque she had made that says:

Where your treasure is, your heart is.

The next morning, I rose with the mist as it lifted off the Andes and meditated on the words on the plaque, letting the words wash over my heart. What was my treasure?

The truth of those words seared through my materialism and showed me how much I treasured my possessions—my house with a pool, all the "silver" and "gold" of my life. I repented and told the Lord I only wanted Him and would give everything up to serve Him if that was what He asked me to do. I thought of the story of how the rainforest natives in Brazil catch the greedy monkeys. The hunters carve a hole in a tree just large enough for the monkey's open paw. Then the hunters put in some bauble, a shiny item that attracts the monkey. The monkey sticks his hand into the hole and snatches it, but his closefisted paw, filled with the treasure, is now too big to remove from the hole. The avaricious monkey, unwilling to let go of his prize, is easily captured and eaten. I recalled the old saying, "it isn't what you hold, but what holds you."

In prayer, I opened my tightfisted hands and gave my possessions—the security of two professional incomes, our house, our reputation, and the children—into God's hands. I recalled a painting that a friend of mine, Barbara, had given me. It was of a white, wicker basket full of brown eggs. Scrawled on the red calico cloth encircling the basket were the words, "I put all of my eggs in one basket, and I gave the basket to God."

I opened my Bible and read Luke 18:28–30, wondering if the words would be true in my life.

> Peter said, "Behold, we have left our own homes and followed You." And He said to them, "Truly I say to you, there is no one who has left house or wife or brothers or parents or children, for the sake of the

kingdom of God, who will not receive many times as
much at this time and in the age to come, eternal life."

Jack came out, and I repeated the verses to him. We held hands and
asked the Lord for direction.

On the flight home, I began worrying and wrote in my journal,
"Lord, as I finish my senior year, help me to be more concerned about
the fate of my heart than the fate of my future."

The next week, I began the production management rotation. We
went on an "emergency" farm call where the owner just learned that
pregnant mares that eat fescue grass may not produce milk. It was just
a routine pregnancy check, but if you have enough money and are a
demanding horse owner, then everything's an emergency. Leaving the
farm, the professor shook his head, "I would like to say to her, 'Hey
honey, your crazy is showing. You might want to tuck that back in.'"

The male professor then proceeded to direct the conversation to
the male student with us, "Ben, you will do fine, but I don't know
about what Mary will do because she wants to spend time with her
kids. To be a horse vet you must work seventy to eighty hours a week
for five years. Only after that will you have arrived as a horse vet.
That's the way the cookie crumbles."

Hearing my professor's comment, I felt like a horse kicked me in
the gut. *What a male chauvinist,* I thought, but then I realized, *he was
right.* Despite wanting to be a horse vet all my life, I wasn't willing
to sacrifice my kids for the profession. *If I'm not going to be a horse
vet, then what am I going to do with my life?* I pondered. And, "If you
spend yourself on behalf of the hungry and satisfy the needs of the
poor . . ." wafted through my mind. I pictured the Bolivian girls who
followed me around when we tested the cattle. I recalled the desperate
look in the old Quechua man's eyes. His words, "We are poor, but we
work hard, and we want better for our children," were big in my ears.

I didn't want to spend seventy to eighty hours a week becoming a horse vet and sacrifice my family. I wanted to help break the cycle of poverty in developing countries, not to be a puppet controlled by the golden strings of horse owners. I sat in silence back to the vet school, reeling in the clarity of my own realization.

Blacksburg was overserved with large-animal vets, and the developing world was underserved. I recalled the quote from the missionary, Jim Elliot, that I had written in my journal. I thought of what we would leave behind, perhaps forever, "He is no fool who gives what he cannot keep to gain that which he cannot lose."

Then I ruminated on Dawson Trotman's quote, "Never do anything that someone else can and will do, when there is so much of importance to be done which others cannot or will not do."

Jack and I spent the next six months wrestling with the decision. In our times of silence and meditating, our souls prevailed upon our minds what we were to do. God cares for the poor, and we should, too. But, I still had sixteen more blocks to pass and the National Boards to take before I would be a veterinarian. Graduating proved more difficult than I imagined.

CHAPTER 24

THE BARRAGE

Our cause is never more in danger than when a human, no longer desiring, but still intending, to do our Enemy's will, looks around upon a universe from which every trace of Him seems to have vanished, and asks why he has been forsaken, and still obeys.

—C. S. Lewis

A successful man is one who can lay a firm foundation with the bricks others have thrown at him.

—David Brinkley

Upon my return from Bolivia, I faced my final set of rotations at the vet school. The professors held rounds, a teaching tool and ritual of medical education, where students present the case and treatment plan. Some of the clinicians took a warped ego-boost from making the students look like morons. Their questions went from gross anatomy to mitochondria in a matter of seconds, causing sleep-deprived students' throats to tighten and stomachs to churn.

My first rotation back from Bolivia was in large-animal medicine, and Dr. Washington, the bovine specialist, grilled me with questions on the drive to the farm. He asked in his slow, country drawl, "If you received two calls, a vaginal prolapse and a uterine prolapse, which call would you go to first?"

"Vaginal," I guessed, thinking I had a fifty-fifty chance of being correct.

"Wrong; a uterine prolapse is always an emergency!" he yelled with a "gotcha" grin. Do you know how to use the Buhner needle?"

"No, sir, I don't."

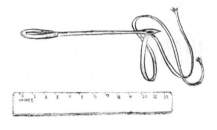

Driving around the curvy mountain road, he pulled out a piece of paper and, using the steering wheel as a clipboard, he illustrated the Buhner stitch placed to keep the uterus in. Gravel, and my heart, flew off the mountain around the curves. I kept my eyes on the road. I thought one of us should. First, he showed where to insert the ten-inch-long, quarter-inch-wide stainless-steel needle at the bottom of the lips of the vulva. "You push it out about one inch above the top of the vulva and one inch below the anus." In practice, when my epidural didn't provide complete anesthesia, I learned that cows appreciate some Lidocaine to numb the spot where you thrust the big needle in and drag a foot of umbilical tape through. But the doc was old school and didn't believe in much pain management for cows. Obviously, he never birthed a child himself!

"After pulling the tape out the top, you leave a few inches hanging down at the bottom of the vulva. Next, you stick the unthreaded needle in again on the other side of the bottom and thread it out at the top, through the same hole as the first one came out. You pull the needle with the tape dragging behind it out the bottom," he continued. "Then you pull the ends tight, and it closes the lips of the vulva like a purse string, so there can't be any more prolapses. Just leave enough room for urine to come out."

I nodded, trying to follow.

"There is a big, uterine artery, big as this," he stuck out his pinky finger for effect. "If it ruptures from the uterus flopping around outside the body, the cow will bleed out. But don't feel rained on, about 50 percent of prolapse uterus cases don't make it." He then spoke the phrase that terrifies all vet students, "It's a Board question!"

To wake up a class, professors would nonchalantly say, "This is always on the Boards." It had its desired effect. The National Veterinary Board Examination covers all four years of vet school education, and if you don't pass, you don't practice.

"Okay, thanks. I'm ready for the Boards," I said, quaking at how unprepared I felt to take them the next week.

Seven days later, I knew I failed. I was so brain-dead after an intense six hours of questions, I got lost on the way home. I pulled over and cried. The questions were so long and complicated, and everything I knew was in the question itself, *Wait, I wanted to provide that information.* I felt I wasted not only the last six months studying for the Boards, but my last four years, not to mention Jack's career. Through my hot tears, I yelled at God, "Lord, why did you bring me this far only to let me fail and never practice?"

I called Jack, "I failed."

"You probably did better than you think," he said encouragingly.

"Well, I've done everything I can. The Lord will have to change my answers before it's graded," I sniffled.

Four weeks later, with trembling hands I opened the envelope and found I passed. I did a jig of joy in the street and whooped loudly, scaring the deer out of the woods beside me.

It was the spring of my senior year, and by passing the Boards, I felt that I jumped the last big hurdle. There were only five blocks left before I graduated—at least that is what I thought.

Despite Dr. Washington's interrogations, working out in the field with cattle, goats, and an occasional pig or alpaca thrilled my heart and confirmed my call to the profession. I passed the rotation with flying colors. The next block was equine medicine, based in the vet hospital. I was ecstatic to finally be working on the species I loved the most.

"I was born to work with horses," I told Jack, and began to build my self-image around the fact that I would soon be a doctor. Next came the small-animal clinical rotations, which would shake this new identity to its core.

Jack and I sought counsel through our church's leadership to determine if we should be long-term missionaries. Receiving positive affirmation, individually we sought God. Over the next month, He warmed our hearts and crystallized our call to the spiritually and physically poor. After praying, "Where you lead, we will follow," we applied to go on staff with Christian Veterinary Mission and the Society of Anglican Missionaries and Senders. That is when the barrage began.

A *barrage* is artillery fired to keep enemy forces from moving; a heavy, prolonged attack. Was the barrage laid down by the spiritual forces of darkness to keep us from moving to Bolivia? Perhaps, but at any rate, it was a time of disappointment and tragedy.

As soon as we offered our lives for the Lord's service, the tragedies started. My friend Veronika from Chantilly called, "Juliana's brain cancer has returned and is inoperable." We went to see her, and let Ashby see her ten-year-old dying friend one last time. Twelve months later, Veronika called me, "Mary, I want to thank you. Juliana just died in my arms, and we never would have made it through all of this if you had not shown us the way to Christ."

The barrage continued. Devastated at the sadness of Juliana's news, I limped my way through the small-animal medicine block before my last rotation, the small-animal surgery block. The large-animal tech warned me, "Watch out for the head clinician, he has the God complex of a surgeon, and he hasn't failed anyone all year."

The block combined my lack of experience in small-animal surgery and computers, with a humorless head clinician looking for someone to fail. He brought to the surface my past wounds, my feelings of being powerless and voiceless. When I answered a question in rounds correctly, but with humor, he barked at me and asked someone else for the correct answer. Since I was older and didn't show him the veneration he expected, I was soon on his hit list. At the halfway point during rotations, professors give out student reviews. The one intern I worked closely with gave me passing marks; the clinician did not. Shocked, I greatly improved my performance, studying up before rounds and surgery, and volunteering correct answers. A week later, I asked the intern if I improved and if I was going to pass the block. She said, "Certainly!"

Then came the last day of the rotation, and when I saw the intern in the hall she teared up. "Did I not pass?" I asked her, stunned. She just walked away in tears and shook her head no.

Unimaginable! How could I not pass? I thought to myself and paged the head clinician. Surely this misunderstanding needed to be reversed before it became set in stone. His decision had never been questioned before, and he seethed with anger. Confronting his authority, I asked, "How could you fail me on a block where you didn't even observe me?"

No response.

"Didn't my performance improve after my midway review?"

No reply.

"Would it matter if you knew I already have a job in Bolivia helping the rural poor with their livestock?" I pleaded, knowing if I failed this block I would not graduate the next week with my classmates.

"This isn't a debate," he snarled, his lips curled up in an "I win, you lose," power smirk. Then he got up and left the room. It was the year before he retired, and he wanted to maintain his powerful, god-man image.

Stepping from the small-animal hospital, I gulped the freezing air, hoping the pain would keep me from falling apart and being seen by any classmates. Once I made it to the parking lot, I sat shaking in my car, my head spinning. Somewhere deep inside me a cord of remembrance strummed. Hadn't I made a vow during my childhood neglect and abuse never to be voiceless or powerless again? I began to shake, deep-seated feelings of betrayal and shame washed through my body, my knuckles blanched white as I squeezed the steering wheel with all my might in silent disbelief. *How did I fail?* I bolted past these feelings of sadness, to denial, and then quickly to my old standby: fury. I went from self-contempt to male contempt in a nanosecond. I found my tough-girl side and thought such murderous thoughts that, as Anne Lamott says, "If I said them out loud it would make Jesus want to drink gin straight out of the cat bowl."

God had failed me, too. I prayed I would pass the block. Had I not just decided to serve Him in missions? My knuckles bloodied as I pounded my fists against the wheel and cried out to God in a white-hot rage. My father and siblings were all coming to celebrate, but I wasn't graduating. What would I tell them? What would I say to Jack and the kids? I sat abandoned in the gutter of my pain like a disfigured orphan. The comradery my class forged through four tough years would be broken. While all my classmates were celebrating, graduating, and leaving town, I would repeat the block. I had never failed at anything major in my life, and it was the most humiliating thing that ever happened to me. As a parent might deal wounds to a child's fragile ego, the old clinician wounded me. My self-image was so wrapped up in being a doctor, it wasn't just that I failed, but that I *was* a failure, a gray cloak I would wear for years to come. All the joy of becoming a DVM was gone.

I graduated with my class and received the same envelope as the other students, except there was no diploma in mine. It was an empty tomb, like my empty heart. I felt shame walking across the stage, shaking hands with the dean and receiving an empty envelope.

The next week I retook the block with the new senior students. Three weeks later, I was finished. On the last day, the new head clinician said, "Great job. Thanks for helping the students and having such a good attitude." I struggled for air as I listened to my passing review, my face flush with emotion. I tried to stop the tears brimming in my eyes by sticking my pen in my lip, but they trickled down my face and plopped on the table in petite circles with serrated edges. I began vet school with tears of joy at the pig skeleton experience, now I ended my time with tears of relief. That was it. I packed up my belongings, took off my blue student coat for the last time, and headed to the parking lot.

The Lord in his wisdom allows certain things in our lives for our suffering. It puts us on a new path of growth, a deeper dependency on Him. This is followed by a perspective change that brings healing and maturity.

The suffering showed me who I was in Him, truly His beloved, apart from my performance. Only He, not dreams dashed or fulfilled, could give me joy.

I took my Doctor of Veterinary Medicine degree happily even if it came with slightly tarnished joy, but the barrage continued. Jack's father died suddenly. Then, six weeks later, while flying back from our training in Seattle, Washington, with Christian Veterinary Mission, I received the news that my stepmother Shirley passed away.

C. S. Lewis in his book *The Screwtape Letters* writes of the older demon telling the younger:

> Our cause is never more in danger than when a human, no longer desiring, but still intending, to do our Enemy's will, looks around upon a universe from which every trace of Him seems to have vanished, and asks why he has been forsaken, and still obeys.

We knew we were called, but it was with heavy hearts we began the support-raising journey, asking individuals and churches to donate money to pay our expenses and pray for us while we were on the field.

That summer with the kids was relaxing and lazy after the incessant demands of the clinics. We attended Mission Training International in Colorado to prepare for our eventual move to Bolivia, and my soul reset after the stress of the four previous years.

I wanted to get vet experience so I wouldn't go to Bolivia and kill the village cow, so I accepted a job working for Amboseli Veterinary Clinic.

CHAPTER 25

MY DREAM JOB

When God closes a door, He opens a window, but it's hell in the hallway.

—Anonymous

The summer ended far too soon. Before I knew it, the kids were back at school, and I was starting my new job as a large-animal vet. As I drove down Brush Mountain from my house to the vet office, I recalled the previous fall, driving to the vet school, wondering where I would work. I noticed how the maple leaves changed from their playful summer green to the more serious shades of orange, brown, and red, signaling for me my last fall semester. I watched the falling maple seeds twirl like helicopters before me, the wind catching them and sending them sailing over the side of the mountain. The seasonal shift reminded me of the change I would soon be making from the academic into the professional world and my need to find a job. My heart felt like one of those seeds, floating, light and free, excited to be finally finishing school. At the same time, I too was in free fall off the mountain, uncertain where I would land. I called the two large-animal practices in the area. The one wasn't hiring, and the other wouldn't even return my calls. Frustrated, I breathed a prayer of desperation, "Lord, it seems all the doors are closed. Please find me something." I recalled the expression, "When God closes a door He opens a window, but it's hell in the hallway."

Pulling into the vet school parking lot that morning, my eyes lit up when I saw the Amboseli Veterinary Clinic truck. This was the practice that hadn't returned my calls. One of their vets, Dr. Katharine Healer, was dropping off a sample for pathology. I saw her in her khaki pants wearing a blue polo shirt with the AVC emblem on it. She was tall, tan, and fit. Snagging her in the hallway, I said with such enthusiasm she couldn't turn me down, "I want to work for you guys. Let me buy you a cup of coffee!"

"Okay," she said, a bit taken aback, but liking my cheekiness.

Sitting in the Commons, we discovered our mutual passion for horses. Both of us went to vet school later in life. Seeing her salt-and-pepper colored hair, I guessed she was slightly older than I was. After our coffee together, she arranged a rotation for me at their practice that spring and later persuaded the owner, Dr. Amboseli, to hire me the following September.

Now, a year later, I walked into my new office. Dr. Healer had ordered a name plate for me, and I beamed as I read my name on the door, Mary McDonald, DVM! I sat down at my desk, absorbing the moment: the smell of alcohol and bleach; the sound of the centrifuge spinning; the sight of all the veterinary drugs lining the shelves; and my own vet office. I breathed it in. I opened the box of business cards on my desk, read my name listed as an associate vet, and ran my finger over the raised black print. After a lifetime of wanting to be a vet, I was finally doing my dream!

"Here are your keys. There's your truck." My new boss's deep voice and southwest Virginia accent jarred me out of my basking and caused me to drop the pair of forceps I was holding. He pointed out the

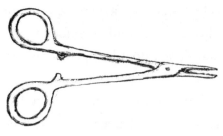

window to a dark blue GMC pickup with a white vet box on the back.

Tickled pink, I fairly skipped across the parking lot and ran my fingers down the white fiberglass box covering the truck bed. Thrilled, I lifted the side door, my fingers quivering as if I were opening the hood of Maserati. I always wanted a blue vet truck. I pulled out the sliding steel drawers and peered in. All the drawers in the compartment were empty. The symphony playing in my heart came to an abrupt halt. I would be responsible for stocking my own truck. Looking inside, I saw a heater for keeping the drugs from freezing in the winter and a refrigerator to keep the vaccines and antibiotics cool. I was excited to see the hot and cold water tanks so I wouldn't have to haul water from the client's house. I eyed the power inverter and electrical panel, where I could charge my ophthalmoscope and run the power float for filing a horse's teeth. I looked at Dr. Amboseli as I reached to open the back door on the truck, "Go ahead; it is your truck," he smiled, catching my excitement. Glancing in the back seat, I saw the radiograph machine, surgery box, ultrasound machine, fluid bags, and bulky bandages. A couple of jugs of anti-freeze/coolant resided there as well. I soon learned why. It didn't matter to me that the old truck had more ailments than most of our patients. I was elated to have my first mobile office. My exam room would be the owner's barn, and the surgery suite an open field!

The plan was for me to ride with both vets in the practice the first month before they turned me out on my own. I needed to learn practice policies like billing clients, vaccine protocols, farm locations, and how not to kill things. The first week I rode with Dr. Healer and the second week with the boss man, Dr. Amboseli. Not that anyone ever deifies their first boss in a long-awaited career, but he was a Greek god, big enough to go bear hunting with a switch. He had bronzed, powerful arms and colossal hands. His jet-black hair curled above a prominent forehead. Like Zeus, he became the presiding deity of my professional universe.

He had a great sense of humor, the gift of gab, and was an excellent vet and mentor. As we traveled from call to call, he told me his philosophy on the vet practice, life, and politics. "If a cow wants to die, there is nothing you can do to save it, and if it wants to live, there is nothing you can do to kill it," he said in summary.

That was reassuring for a vet right out of school.

"Ten percent of your clients will love you for no good reason and won't want any other vet on their farm; another ten percent of the clients will hate you for no good reason and won't want you on their farm. Don't take it personally; that's just the way it is."

The first day as I rode with him to his appointments, he told me how they did things in "real practice," where clients had limited resources, versus how things were done in the ivory tower of vet school. In southwest Virginia, most of the large-animal fees were pocketbook-driven. "If an old cow is only worth $300, the farmer isn't going to spend $400 on a C-section," he told me.

It took me only a few months to find that to be true. When I told a farmer, "Your old cow needs a C-section."

"She ain't worth that, Doc," he said and shot her in the head.

Dr. Amboseli, pointed to the business center of the truck—his calculator and receipt book—and said, "Give them the bill and get a check before you leave the farm. If they don't pay, I'll take it out of your paycheck. Stick to the price sheet; don't undersell your education by giving away services for free. If the client is a jerk and you don't like working for him, charge until you like it. But don't way overcharge because then they come and complain to me. Remember, pigs get fat, and hogs get eaten. Speaking of pigs, we no longer service pigs. The last boar I castrated helped me to decide that. It is difficult to get a vein in a boar so I use pentobarbital, the euthanasia solution, and inject it into the testicles. It slows them down long enough for you to castrate, but you must cut them off before too much of solution gets into their bloodstream and kills them. I had finished the surgery and told the owner not to let his dog eat the testicles. LeRoy, the client perked up, 'Oh Doc, don't you like mountain oysters?'

"'Those testicles have a euthanasia solution in them; they could kill you if you eat them.'

The next week I saw LeRoy's wife at the Food Lion and asked how the hog was doing. She replied laughing, 'The boar's fine, but old LeRoy nearly got his butt fired. After you left, he got liquored up and ate them hog balls. Damn fool went and slept three whole days. Prit near got hisself fired!' After the wife told me that story, I radioed into the office and told the secretary we no longer service pigs," Dr. Amboseli said without regret.

Pointing to the CB radio mounted to the dust and old receipts on the dash, he said, "Oftentimes the cell phone doesn't have signal, so you use the radio. It is cheaper, but be quick and don't tie up air space. When you radio into the office, hold down this button and say 503 to 500." He taught me the proper radio lingo, "over and out," and "10–4."

Handing me the directions log, he explained, "You need to learn these back roads. Everybody has known everybody else around here for generations, so the farmers never give directions and can't get you to their farms."

Their directions were like shadow-graphs, surrounded by the farmer's bright hope.

"Make sure you have a full tank of gas. You aren't going to find any open gas stations around here at night," Amboseli said.

I learned that if the directions included the word *hollow*, and they pronounced it "holler," and they were men home during the day, they might be drunk and unemployed, and I wasn't going to get paid. Also, after learning of a vet being raped on a farm call, I would be edgy in those hollers.

When we arrived at Dr. Amboseli's first appointment at the Dodge horse farm, I marveled at the organization of his vet box. When the client went to catch his horses, Dr. Amboseli gave me the vet-box tour. It divided up into three main compartments: one on each side of the truck, and an opening in the back where the tailgate would have been. The compartment on the driver's side had a deep storage area, where the refrigerator lived. Inside the fridge were three clear, plastic bags. The largest held the horse vaccines, another bag for the cattle, and a smaller bag was for goats. A bottle of procaine penicillin was tucked under the vaccines because it needed to stay cool as well. Above this compartment was a shelf where the different cattle, horse, and goat/sheep dewormers sat. When Amboseli opened the back, I saw two large compartments illuminated by a dome light. "Make sure you turn this light off or your battery won't start in the morning," he warned. "In the winter, you have to plug the truck into the electrical outlet at your house so the heater can keep the water lines from freezing and the medicines from being ruined."

I nodded trying to take it all in. On the left side, at the bottom of the compartment, were boxes for hoof care, teeth floating, and reproductive equipment. Opening the hoof box, I got green stains on my hands from the Coppertox medicine. The box contained hoof nippers, rasps, hoof knives, hoof testers, some 4 x 4-inch gauze, iodine, wooden blocks, and duct tape. Seeing my puzzled look, he said, "That's for wrapping up an injured foot. Those wooden blocks and the adhesive glue are for treating abscesses in dairy cows' hooves. It elevates the opposite claw and keeps the injured claw from contacting the ground. The cow walks like a drunken girl who lost a shoe on prom night; by the time the block falls off she's fine."

I noticed a tenderness in his tone as he spoke about the dairy cows and surmised that they were his favorite species. I was learning that each of the vets in the practice had certain areas of expertise and that he was just as passionate about cattle as Dr. Healer and I were about horses.

Getting out the teeth-floating box, he showed me the mouth speculum to keep the horse jaws open, floats, drench gun, and a wolf-tooth remover. "Horse's teeth grow continuously throughout their lifetime; we will file the sharp points and hooks off." I pulled out the long stainless-steel handle of the float, accidentally cutting my finger on the sharp file. Soon my arm would be in a horse's mouth, past my elbow, rasping teeth.

In addition to the float box, the compartment held the reproductive and colic supplies, a ten-foot plastic nasogastric tube, mineral oil, and electrolyte packets for treating GI disturbances. Horses have a one-way system and don't vomit, so their belly aches are emergencies.

Pulling up one milliliter of sedation into a syringe, Amboseli gave me a lecture about the drugs used to sedate and euthanize, "You have to write down every milliliter of the controlled substances you use on this pad. The state veterinary inspector comes by and makes sure your notations match the office records. If they don't, you can get fined, lose your license, or go to jail. Keep this box locked, and keep your vet box locked."

I nodded as he found the vein and sedated the horse, so we could float its teeth. Waiting for the tranquilizer to take effect, I studied the rest of his supplies, so I could stock my own truck. For poison cases, there was a packet of black, activated charcoal to treat animals that ingested something toxic. For cows, maybe it would be green onions or acorns. Goats have an affinity for poisonous azalea bushes. There were bottles of calcium to help down cows—those unable to stand, and other potions to raise cows from the dead. Beside these was the reproduction box.

"If I am working on a dystocia," Dr. Amboseli said, using the medical term for a difficult birth, "I pull out this box with Lidocaine for epidurals, chains for pulling the calf out, and gigli wire for fetotomies, when the dead calf is too big and you have to cut it into pieces to get it out. Make sure you always use lots of lube. They slide out easier."

He pointed to blades for episiotomies, umbilical tape, a Buhner needle, and a prolapse pin. In the lower right-hand compartment sat a box of white, latex, exam gloves, a box of arm-length green plastic palpation sleeves, lube, rubber boots, and an extra pair of coveralls.

Above this compartment, he pulled out a sliding fiberglass drawer divided into four-inch squares that held different-sized needles and syringes, a couple of 4 x 2-inch magnets, a weight tape, and a thermometer. His stethoscope lay on top. The rest of the spaces were filled with 100-milliliter or 50-milliliter glass bottles. He gave me a quick overview of the vitamins, antibiotics, antifungals, NSAIDS, and the steroid dexamethasone. He said, "Never let an animal die without the benefit of steroids."

Little did I know that within a month, I would treat a mare that had been in labor for hours, and by the time I got there, the only thing to do was pull the dead foal and watch the mare die. Her head was stretched out on the ground, her breathing labored, and eyes closed. I gave her ten milliliters of dexamethasone in the vein, and she got on her feet like nobody's business.

"The last and most important part of any dystocia equipment is the calf jack," Dr. Amboseli said. "It goes in this steel tube."

The calf jack is a ten-foot-long steel pole which attaches to a metal bar across the cow's rear end. At the other end is a hand winch that cranks to pull out the stuck calf. The bar across the cow's backside pushes the cow forward while the winch is pulling the calf out the back, so hopefully, the cow doesn't fall on top of you.

Besides the jack were five-gallon, stainless-steel buckets and two smaller stainless-steel containers with tops. I lifted the lids. One was Betadine solution and the other isopropyl alcohol for wound cleaning and surgery prep. The alcohol from the lid seeped into my cut finger, and the pain and poignant smell brought tears to my eyes.

Dr. Amboseli moved around to the right side of the truck where another compartment held the necropsy knife. Necropsy is the veterinary term for autopsy. We are called out to verify if cattle were killed by lightning strikes for insurance claims, or to determine the cause of other suspicious deaths, or to test for contagious diseases.

After we finished floating the horse's teeth, the horse owner went to get a check. Dr. Amboseli moved to the area behind the passenger seat. "Here is my dart gun; you won't carry one on your truck. I dart animals that are too crazy to be caught. But there are two things in my life I don't lend out: my wife and my dart gun."

Pulling out of the farm, he told me, "The last vet who drove your truck didn't shut the hood hard enough, it flew off when he was driving 75 mph down Highway 81. He left with a hard top and came back with a convertible. Make sure you slam the hood down after you check the antifreeze. It leaks. Also, your truck's dome light didn't work, so I put in a special switch."

He was a master jerry-rigger and installed a light in the cab, but it only worked when you opened the driver's side door. At night, I had to open the door while driving down the dark mountain roads to read the directions to the farms.

"Always keep your truck clean. It looks more professional," he said. "Also, wear the white exam gloves when practical. We are doctors and need to look it and charge for it."

Every week, during a lull in cases, I would take my wonderful ambulatory office to the carwash, pull off the magnetic signs and spray her clean with the wand, soap, and rinse. I laid the signs on the hood to let the heat from the engine dry them as I proudly hand dried the rest of the truck.

"We try to keep everything in the same place on the vet trucks, so if one vet's truck breaks down, they can borrow the truck of whoever is off-duty," he said as he answered a page. "We need to head to Ironto. A horse got into the grain bin."

A minute later, there was another page, "Your father's gone to the emergency room." As I dropped my boss off at the office, he smiled and said to me, "Looks like it's trial by fire for you. Head to Ironto, never leave a colic case without nasogastric tubing and palpating. You will do fine," he added, sending me solo my second week. Thinking he was more like his brother Hades, the Greek god of the underworld, than Zeus, I sped to the colic call solo.

His father, the horse, and I all survived that day. Consequently, Dr. Amboseli thought me ready to see clients on my own. Being the newest vet, I got the oldest truck, with 275,000 miles. Most of the gravy had been driven out of her. I stocked my truck the next day. The secretary handed me my directions log and a list of my appointments. Trotting out after me, she taped my vet license inside the Porta-vet door.

"She's all yours now. Good luck," she said.

I smiled bursting with joy, pride, and a touch of sheer terror. Trying to look confident, I sped out of the drive thinking to myself, *that's why they call it going into practice.*

CHAPTER 26

STRANGE HAPPENINGS

Desiring little, there is nothing that can really be taken from us. When we spend our lives attempting to acquire what we do not need and seldom use, we waste our strength on things that neither stretch our souls nor satisfy our hearts.

—Joan Chittister

The year flew by, and before we knew it, we were packing and preparing to move to South America. It was my last month at Amboseli Veterinary Clinic when Mr. Mitchell called Beulah, the secretary, "Sompins' wrong with the hinder part of my cow. Can you fetch me a doc out here?"

Beulah asked, "Has she calved yet?"

"No."

"Well, if she hasn't calved yet, it can't be her uterus because the uterus can't come out if the calf is still inside the cow. Is there a lot hanging out or a little?

"About the size of a big grapefruit," he said, signaling to Beulah it was a vaginal prolapse.

Relieved it wasn't the large uterus, I grabbed a prolapse pin and headed toward his farm. The red plastic pin, about six inches long, with two plastic discs, holds the vagina against the body wall, preventing it from prolapsing again but still allows the calf to come out.

Pulling up to the farm, I saw the farmer standing patiently by his rusty hog-wire fence. As I approached, he looked down and scuffed his boot toe across the dusty driveway, "Your secretary sure don't mind asking about the hinder parts of a cow, do she?" he blushed.

"Can you get her in the head catch?" I asked, knowing catching a thousand pounds of beef as it crashes into steel pipes, springs, and levers takes precision. The gate must be opened wide enough that the cow thinks she is heading to freedom. Just as her head goes through you pull the lever and the gate closes, catching her head on one side and her shoulders on the other. As in most of life, timing is everything. If you are slow, she runs through and escapes; too fast, you don't catch her head, and she backs out.

Lifting my hand in the air, I showed him where I caught my knuckle working the last farmer's head catch. "You skunt it good," he said, "I'll work it."

"Fine by me," I said climbing into the corral. But, every time I got close, the cow came after me, her vagina puffing out like a red helium balloon. Finally, the farmer wooed her in with grain and deftly pulled the lever. Once caught, I gave her an epidural and replaced her vagina. To keep it there, I thrust the prolapse pin through the vaginal wall but hit something hard. I repositioned, scraping along the bony surface until with great force, I punctured out through the cowhide. After securing the disc I said, "Mission accomplished; set her free."

As he pulled down the heavy metal bar to open the gates, I jacked her tail up and off she went. Her look told me she would like to kill me.

"Wait two weeks after she calves, or she might prolapse again. Then, call me and I'll come take the pin out," I said.

"Thanks, Doc," he said slowly, repeating my instructions. "I learned in school to repeat directions, so I would get them right. The kids used to say I was dumber than dirt. Kids can be mean. Adults, too, I reckon. Momma used to say I wasn't exactly broke out with good looks, and Daddy said I was clumsy enough to break an anvil."

I stared at him, absorbing the painfulness of his words. He was a kind, gentle man, even if he was a bit slow. Now, middle-aged, he still recalled childhood insults. "You did a good job with that head catch," I said, trying to inject an encouraging word into his life. His eyes, droopy but clear, knew the sorrow of rejection. But there was a sparkle there I couldn't place, a contentment. Something had soothed the critical words and given him peace.

"The Lord helps me do things right every now and again," he said.

"Do you know the Lord?" I asked. He lit up like a Christmas tree, as though speaking of his first flame.

"Yep, I love the Lord, and He loves me."

He went on to speak of Him as of an old friend, but with the freshness of a recent rendezvous. As I listened, the sun was warm on my back, and the mountains reflected the glory of their Maker. I felt as though I was standing on holy ground, privileged to bask in the emotional glow of his intimacy with the Lord. He spoke of the "never-interrupted voice of love," as Henri Nouwen's says, in *The Return of the Prodigal Son:*

> I have heard that voice. It has spoken to me in the past and continues to speak to me now. It is the never-interrupted voice of love speaking from eternity and giving life and love whenever it is heard. When I hear that voice, I know I am home with God and have nothing to fear.

Sharing my God journey with him, we connected on a spiritual plane removed from the time and place of prolapsed vaginas and schoolyard bullies. "I'm leaving next month to be a missionary veterinarian in Bolivia. People think I'm crazy, leaving here and going to help the poor. But, as the saying goes, "To love what you do and know that it makes a difference; what could be more fun?"

"Amen," he said and there was peacefulness in the air as we waved goodbye.

A week later, I was giving a down cow a bottle of calcium and letting it drain slowly from the bottle when I got his page, "Matt Mitchell strange happenings." I lifted the bottle higher to drain faster, so I could get to the "strange happenings call." What on earth was it? Was the cow levitating? The Mitchell farm was in Willis, close enough to the Floyd Zone that anything could be possible.

Just then, the cow's eyes rolled back in their sockets, her head dropped sideways, and she slumped onto her side. "Whoa!" I jerked out the line to prevent any more calcium going to her heart too fast, prayed, and waited. Seconds later, with a flash of whites, the eyeballs returned from their journey, and she staggered to her feet. I packed up my truck and called Mr. Mitchell, "What's the strange happening?"

"Water broke, bag on the ground, no labor, no calf," he exclaimed.

"I'm on my way." I couldn't figure this one out. *Did the calf somehow get stuck on the prolapse pin? That seems impossible.* Parking by the hog-wire fence, I climbed into the pen to check the cow. It isn't always nice to be remembered; she charged. Dashing through the tall grass, I nearly stepped on what was hidden behind the weeds—a beautiful Black Angus calf. "Nice bull-calf, Mr. Mitchell," I congratulated him, not wanting him to feel embarrassed for not seeing the baby himself.

"I'm sure glad you came out, I would have never found him."

"It was worth it just to see what a good calf you have produced."

"I ain't done nothing, no ways. God always be the miracle-doer," he said with a certainty that would have made Madeline Murray O'Hara believe. "I'm just blessed," he added with a smile as big as the seventy-pound calf. "I'm not rich like some, but success ain't a name of God and don't make you happy. I raises cattle and teaches Sunday school. I loves it, and it helps folks."

"Yeah, the United States, in all our success, has the highest per-centage of people taking anti-depressants of any country in the world," I sighed.

His life struggles had driven him deep in His relationship with Christ, and the result was a gratefulness and contentment I had not seen in the lives of my more-successful clients, who never knew when enough was enough.

I thought of Joan Chittister's words in *Aspects of the Heart*, "Desiring little, there is nothing that can really be taken from us.

When we spend our lives attempting to acquire what we do not need and seldom use, we waste our strength on things that neither stretch our souls nor satisfy our hearts."

Looking into his soulful eyes, I smiled and said, "You are an example of the verse that talks about godliness with contentment is great gain. So many strive to gain everything in this world, but lose their souls."

Unaccustomed to compliments, he patted me on the arm, "See you on the flipside," and with a broken-toothed grin, waved me out the drive.

"Flipside?" I asked.

"You know, Heaven," he beamed as if he were already there.

POSTSCRIPT

S o began my career as a large-animal veterinarian. In the years ahead, as a missionary vet, I would go on to learn many lessons from the people and animals in Bolivia and Uganda, just as I learned from the Appalachian farmer, Mr. Mitchell.

In addition to examples like Mr. Mitchell, I have been so fortunate on my journey to have wonderful friends and mentors, who have helped me find my true north when I couldn't even find my compass. My hope for you is that you will find the same and become mentors to others, "spending yourselves on behalf of the hungry" because the well-kept secret is that in helping others, we find our joy.

Each of us is on a different road, some more paved, others more potholed. But, the same God knows each of our journeys; in fact, He is our journey-maker. He calls to us through the gentle neigh of a pony, the purr of a cat, and through the beauty of His creation. If you are at the end of your rope, may my book be a knot for you to hold on to, giving you courage, knowing someone else made it through the dark times, reminding you that you have not journeyed this far because you are made of "sugar candy," and showing you that you have access to someone who loves you and is strong enough to pull you out of the quicksand, just like He did me.

I pray that you will feel His gentle touch upon your face, hear Him whisper words of comfort, love, healing, and strength, and one day with me see Him face-to-face.

Thank you for letting me share this phase of my journey with you. Our journeys continue; they are unique and each uniquely makes a difference in this world. May you find your magnet and may it pull out the hardware and give you starch in your soul, allowing you to live with your heart fully alive.

Psalm 27:13–14

I am still confident of this:
I will see the goodness of the Lord in the land of the living.
Wait for the Lord;
Be strong and take heart
And wait for the Lord.

—MAM

BIBLIOGRAPHY

Part I

Chapter 2

Tolkien, J. R. R., "On Fairy-Stories." In *Essays Presented to Charles Williams, by Dorothy Leigh Sayers*, 38. United Kingdom: Oxford University Press, 1947.

Chapter 3

Lamott, Anne. *Stitches: A Handbook on Meaning, Hope and Repair*, 67–68. New York: Riverhead Books, 1994.

Chapter 4

Eliot, George. *Daniel Deronda*. Volumes 1–2, 48. New York: Harper & Brothers, 1876.

Chapter 5

O'Connor, Flannery. http://theamericanreader.com/6-september-1955-flannery-oconnor/accessed August 8, 2017.

Rogers, Will. Ranch and Farm World.com 2006. http://www.ranchandfarmworld.com/ResourceDocuments/RFW_Simple_Sayings_1.pdf, accessed May 11, 2017.

Eldredge, John. *Waking the Dead*. Tennessee: Thomas Nelson, 2001.

Moore, Beth. *Breaking Free*. Tennessee: Life Way Press, Living Proof Ministries, Inc., 1999.

Nouwen, Henry. Wounded Healers. United Kingdom: Darton, Longman & Todd 1994 (first published 1979)

Allender, Dan. *The Wounded Heart: Hope for Adult Victims of Childhood Sexual Abuse*. Colorado: NavPress, 1995.

Part II

Chapter 8

Marx, Groucho. "Word Show–An Experience in the Possibilities of Language." *Los Angeles Times*. 1974.

Chesterton, G. K. *Tremendous Trifles*, 130. New York: Dodd, Mead & Company, 1910.

Rogers, Richard. "You've Got to Be Carefully Taught." *South Pacific*. 1949.

Markham, Beryl. *West with the Night*. United Kingdom: Macmillan, 1942.

Lamott, Anne. *Bird by Bird,* New York: Anchor Books, 1995.

Churchill, Winston. "Speech to the Canadian Parliament." Speech given to the Canadian Parliament prior to World War II, Ottawa, Canada, December 30, 1941.

Chapter 9

Pease, Charles Stanley. *History of Conway (Massachusetts) 1767 – 1917, 3.* Massachusetts: Springfield Printing and Binding Company,1917

Saint Augustine of Hippo. *The Confessions of Saint Augustine: Book III*, 37–38. New York: Oxford University Press, 1998.

Unknown Author, Running Bear website, http://www.runningbear. com/main/horse-quotes.html, accessed May 11, 2017.

Churchill, Winston S. Goodreads.com, Goodreads, Inc. 2017.

http://www.goodreads.com/quotes/22166-there-is-something-about-the-outside-of-a-horse-that, accessed May 11, 2017.

Chapter 10

Angelou, Maya. *I know Why the Caged Bird Sings*, 119. New York: Random House, 1969. Disraeli, Benjamin. IZQuotes.com, IZ Quotes. 2017.

http://izquotes.com/quote/296131, accessed May 11, 2017.

Leacock, Stephen. "Reflections on Riding." In *Literary Lapses*, 127. Montreal: Gazette Printing Company, 1910.

Patel, Maya. IZQuotes.com, IZ Quotes. 2017.

http://izquotes.com/quote/296147, accessed May 11, 2017.

Vaughan-Thomas, Lewis John Wynford. "Sabine and the Oryx" In *Riding in Africa*, by Ian Williams, 46. New York: iUniverse, Inc., 2005.

Chapter 11

IZQuotes.com, IZ Quotes. 2017. http://izquotes.com/quote /296163, accessed May 11, 2017.

Allender, Dan. *The Wounded Heart: Hope for Adult Victims of Childhood Sexual Abuse*. Colorado: NavPress, 1995.

C. S. Lewis. *The Weight of Glory*, 3. New York: The MacMillan Company, 1949.

Amy Grant and Tom Hemby. "Ask Me." In Heart in motion. 1991. Produced by Brown Bannister, Michael Omartian and Keith Thomas.

Chapter 12

Elizabeth Elliot. *Secure in the Everlasting Arms*, 91. Michigan: Revell, 2002.

The 1928 Book of Common Prayer. United Kingdom: Oxford University Press, 1993.

Salinger, J.D. *The Catcher in the Rye*, 94. Massachuetts: Little, Brown and Company, 1951.

Adapted from the Navigators. *The Bridge to Life*. Colorado Springs: Navpress, 2006.

Fortunatus, Venantius. "Welcome, Happy Morning!" In *Enchiridion*. Translated by John Ellerton (1868). Luebeck. 1545.

"Jesus Christ Is Risen Today." In *Lyra Davidica*. 1708.

Webber, Andrew Lloyd. Jesus Christ Superstar. Produced by Tim Rice. 1971.

Underwood, Carrie. "Something in the Water." Written by Carrie Underwood, Chris DeStefano and Brett James. Produced by Mark Bright. 2014.

Travis, Randy. "Pray for the Fish." In Rise and Shine. Produced by Kyle Lehning. 2002.

Ten Boom, Corrie. *Tramp for the Lord*. New York: Penguin Random House, 1974.

Rohr, Richard. *Things Hidden: Scripture as Spirituality*. Ohio: Franciscan Media, 2008.

Giovanni, Nikki. In *A decade along, Virginia Tech still seeks to 'prevail' over memory of mass killings*. By Matt Chittum. The Roanoke Times. April 9, 2017.

Chapter 13

Steinbeck, John. *Travels with Charley in Search of America*, part 4. New York: Viking Press, 1962.

Bush, George. Acceptance Speech at the 2004 Republication National Convention. September 2, 2004.

Adapted from *Have You Made the Wonderful Discovery of the Spirit-Filled Life?* by Dr. Bill Bright, co-founder of Campus Crusade for Christ. Cru. 2015.

Allender, Dan. *To Be Told: Know Your Story, Shape Your Future*, 76. Colorado Springs: Crown Publishing Group, 2009.

Chapter 14

Taylor, Henry. "Riding Lesson." In *An Afternoon of Pocket Billiards*. Utah: University of Utah Press, 2002.

https://www.rodneyohebsion.com/proverbs.html, accessed August 8. 2017

Chapter 15

Kennedy, John F. BrainyQuote.com, Xplore Inc., 2017. https://www.brainyquote.com/quotes/quotes/j/johnfkenn143149.html, accessed May 11, 2017.

Barry, Marion. Article in USA Today, page 2A. March 24, 1989.

Churchill, Winston. Quote Investigator.com, WordPress. 2017. http://quoteinvestigator.com/2014/07/08/but-grace/, accessed May 11, 2017.

Lewis, C. S. *The Problem of Pain*. United Kingdom: HarperOne, 1940.

Robinson, Robert. "Come Thou Fount of Every Blessing." Melody by John Wyeth Nettleton, 1757.

Wilde, Oscar. *A Woman of No Importance: A Play By Oscar Wilde*, United Kingdom: Methun and Company, 1908.

Chapter 16

Durrell, Lawrence. *Bitter Lemons*, 15. United Kingdom: Faber & Faber, 1957.

Rohr, Richard. "Transformative Suffering." *Richard Rohr's Daily Meditation*, St. John the Divine Anglican Church. April 9, 2014.

Rice, Chris. "Untitled Hymn (Come To Jesus)." *Run The Earth Watch The Sky*. Arranged by John Wasson/Andrea Handley. 2003.

Chapter 17

Buber, Martin. BrainyQuote.com, Xplore Inc., 2017. https://www.brainyquote.com/quotes/quotes/m/martinbube133855.html, accessed May 11, 2017.

Woititz, Janet. *Adult Children of Alcoholics*. Deerfield Beach: Health Communications, Inc. 1990.

Flack, Roberta. "Killing Me Softly with His Song" Composed by Charles Fox with lyrics by Norman Gimble. Written in collaboration with Lori Lieberman, 1971, Atlantic Records.

Part III

Chapter 19

Kariuki, J. M. "In Kenya's Grim Squalor Seethes beside Opulence and Corruption." *The Cutting Edge News*. June 29, 2009.

Thomas, Gary. *Sacred Marriage*. Michigan: Zondervan, 2015.

Daphne Sheldrick, Dame. *CITES Rejects Tanzanian Proposal to Sell Ivory*. Nairobi: The David Sheldrick Wildlife Trust. 2010.

Hougen, Judith. *Transformed into Fire*. Michigan: Kregel Publications, 2002.

Chapter 20

Edelman, Hope. *Motherless Daughters*. 191. Massachusetts; Addison-Wesley Publishing Company, 1994.

Chapter 21

Roosevelt, Theodore. *Public Papers of Theodore Roosevelt, Governor, 1899-1900, Volume 1*. New York; Brandon Printing Company, 1899.

Chapter 22

Lewis, C.S., *Mere Christianity*. New York; Harper Collins, 1952.

Chapter 23

Dillard, Annie. "Notes for Young Writers." In Oblations blogpost. May 19, 2007.

Enns, P. Paul. *Everything Happens for a Reason?: God's Purposes in a World Gone Bad,* Illinois; Moody Publishers, 2012.

Chapter 24

Lewis, C. S., *The Screwtape Letters*, 40. New York: The MacMillan Company, 1943.

Brinkley, David. BrainyQuote.com, Xplore Inc., 2017. https://www.brainyquote.com/quotes/quotes/d/davidbrink130590.html, accessed May 11, 2017.

Lamont, Anne. *Small Victories Spotting Improbable Moments of Grace*, 47. New York: Riverhead Books a member of Penguin Group, 2014.

Chapter 26

Chittister, Joan. *Aspects of the Heart: The Many Paths of a Good Life*, 94. Connecticut: Twenty-Third Publications, 2012.

Nouwen, Henri. *The Return of the Prodigal Son: A Story of Homecoming*, 39. New York: Image Books, 1994.

CPSIA information can be obtained
at www.ICGtesting.com
Printed in the USA
BVHW04s2359150418
513268BV00005B/2/P